<u>Misophonia</u>
The Art of Jesse Draxler

Copyright © 2018 Jesse Draxler

All rights reserved. No part of this
publication may be reproduced, stored
in a retrieval system, or transmitted in
any form or by any means, electronic,
mechanical, photocopying, recording, or
otherwise, without written permission
of the publisher.

ISBN: 978-0-9996099-0-3

Published by Sacred Bones Books
Layout by David Correll, Sacred Bones Design

First Edition

1 2 3 4 5 6 7 8 9 10

All requests and correspondence can be
addressed to

Sacred Bones Books
144 N. 7th Street #413
Brooklyn, NY 11249

SBB-006

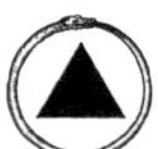

Foreword

The introduction to my most formidable one-on-one basketball foe, came, surprisingly to me, via Instagram.

I gotta admit, when I think of Jesse Draxler, right now, this instant, I don't think about the stuff in this book, the reasons why you're picking it up. You've got a different relationship with that name, but while I've got the chance, I'm gonna give you a little insight into my relationship with it. What comes into my mind when I hear it? Elbows. Potentially lethal elbows for which I do not have any kind of answer whatsoever. I have been hit by wooden guitars in the face at least a hundred times and never have I been as close to being knocked out as I've been by a fairly recent elbow to the temple.

Wait, I'm supposed to be talking about Jesse's art, right? What it all means to me, how I know him, why you should care? I don't know. I've never written one of these before. All I know for sure is: don't stand in the paint when this guy's comin' in without expecting to take some real shots. That's all I'm saying. I'm putting it out to the world. Be grateful that this isn't a pop-up book because if it was there'd be some really nasty fouls coming out of it. Honestly though I need to figure out a solution because the running win/loss tally is starting to get a little lopsided, and not in my favor. There's a bit of a height disadvantage over here as is and I may need to start throwing kicks soon.

Okay. Getting serious now.

It seems silly to me, almost too modern, to say that I discovered one of my favorite artists, someone whose work carries so much emotional weight, via such a fast paced and recent format as Instagram, a format geared towards attention deficit disposability.

What a strange place to find someone whose artwork exists outside of a trend or pop culture timestamp, and is often done on larger than average canvases, conveying emotions and themes that you would think should be far too enormous and universal to be done justice by the constraints of a tiny smartphone screen. Yet somehow it all still comes through, and that is the doorway through which I came. One look at the rapid growth of his following shows that I'm nowhere near alone.

A few years ago I was shown Jesse's art by a bandmate. I was instantly struck. The more I saw, the more I related to the anxiety, the guilt, the existential dread, the terror, the anger, the uncertainty, the distortion. The feeling that so many can surely relate to of waking up against your will as an alien in a strange world. It all resonated deeply. I reached out to him to ask about doing an album layout for a record we were working on. I expected nothing. I certainly didn't know that I was going to end up finding a now close friend who would inspire and motivate me as an artist in a way that very few people in my personal life have. Someone who would view so many things so similarly, someone whose output comes at an absolutely dizzying, nearly impossible pace, a pace that can only come when someone has an almost manic obsession with getting the absolute best, and the innermost truth, out of one's self and condition. Furiously digging into the core to bring something somehow all at once stylized, refined, raw, abstract and enigmatic, guarded and vulnerable, yet glaringly and unavoidably honest, forthright, and brazen, to the surface.

It was a relationship that came along for me at exactly the right time, the kind that, as an artist, reinforced everything that I related to, and helped me to tighten up my own path, to work harder to try and meet and recommit to my own potential and artistic journey. The kind that gives you something to be accountable to, or measure up to, in your own work, in your own output. For me to be able to understand and feel someone's work emotionally, and also be pushed by them individually, as a friend and an artist and a worker; to grow in all of those areas from just one relationship, while still also remaining an objective fan the whole time, is an exceptionally rare thing, and a testament to the creator of the contents of this book.

It's been amazing to be a witness, in just a few years, to the amount and caliber of people showing up to watch, or commission, or buy Jesse's work, and to see his focus only growing sharper, his output becoming even more relentless. It was an honor to be asked to write this.

Greg Puciato

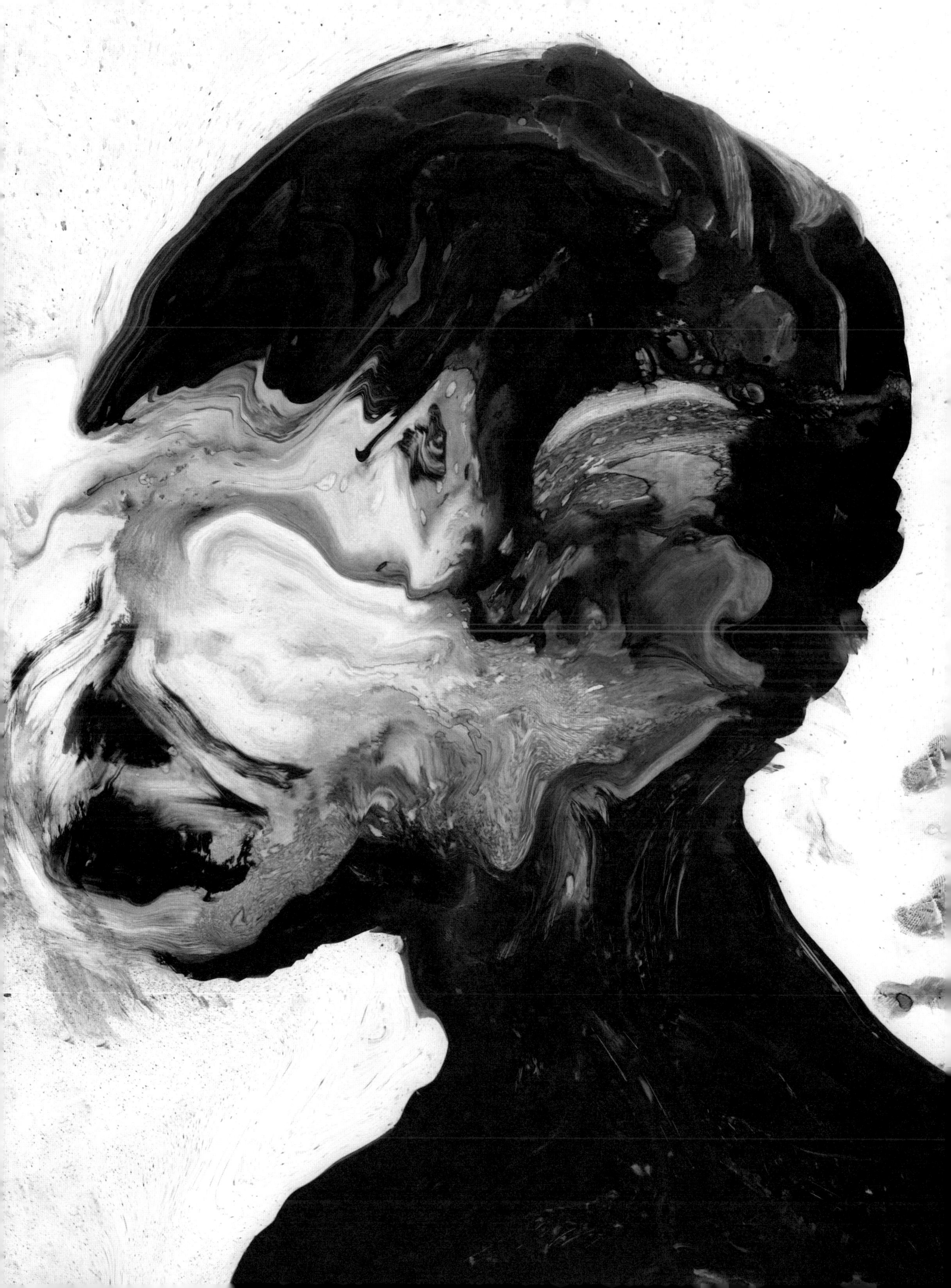

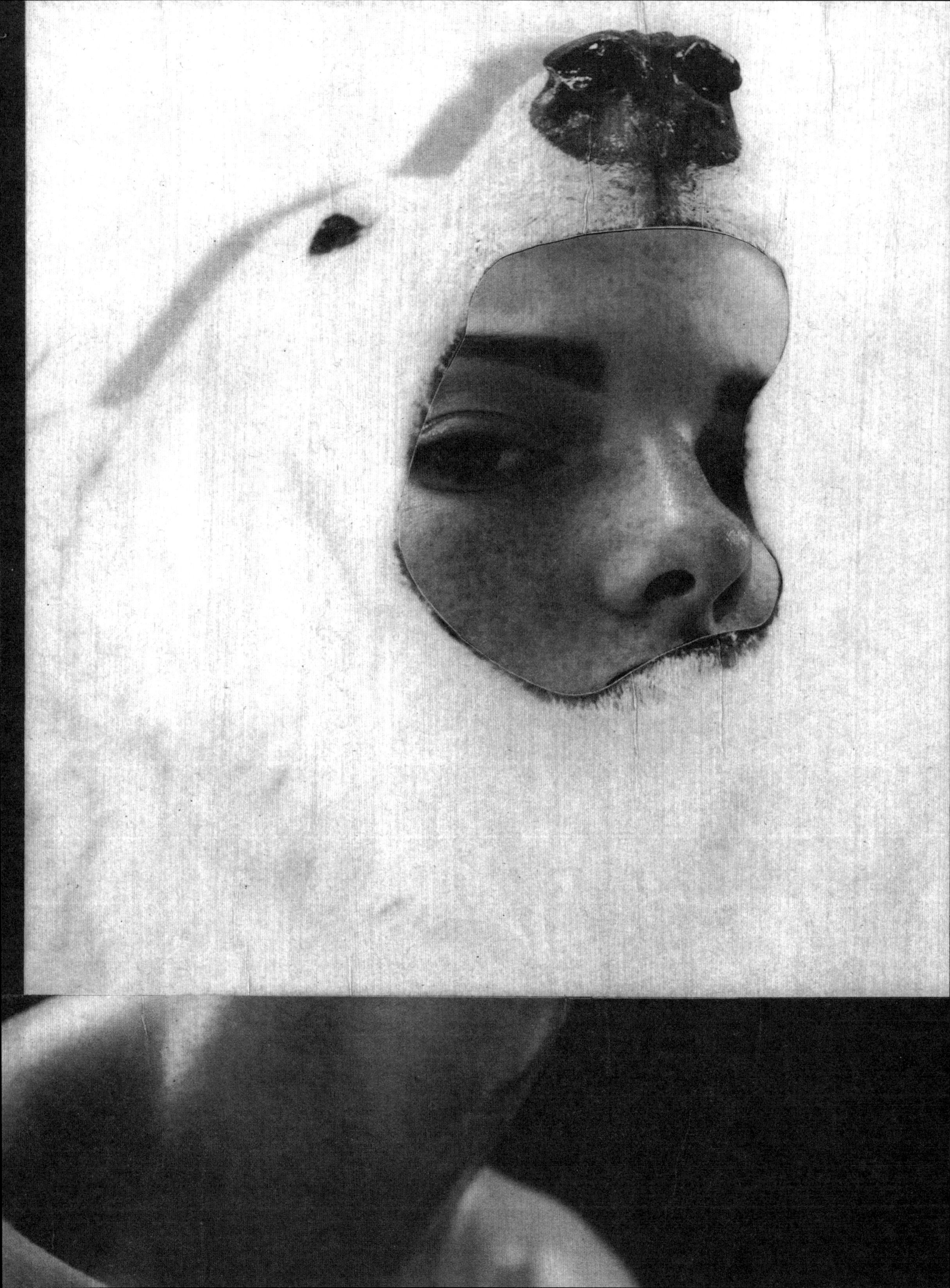

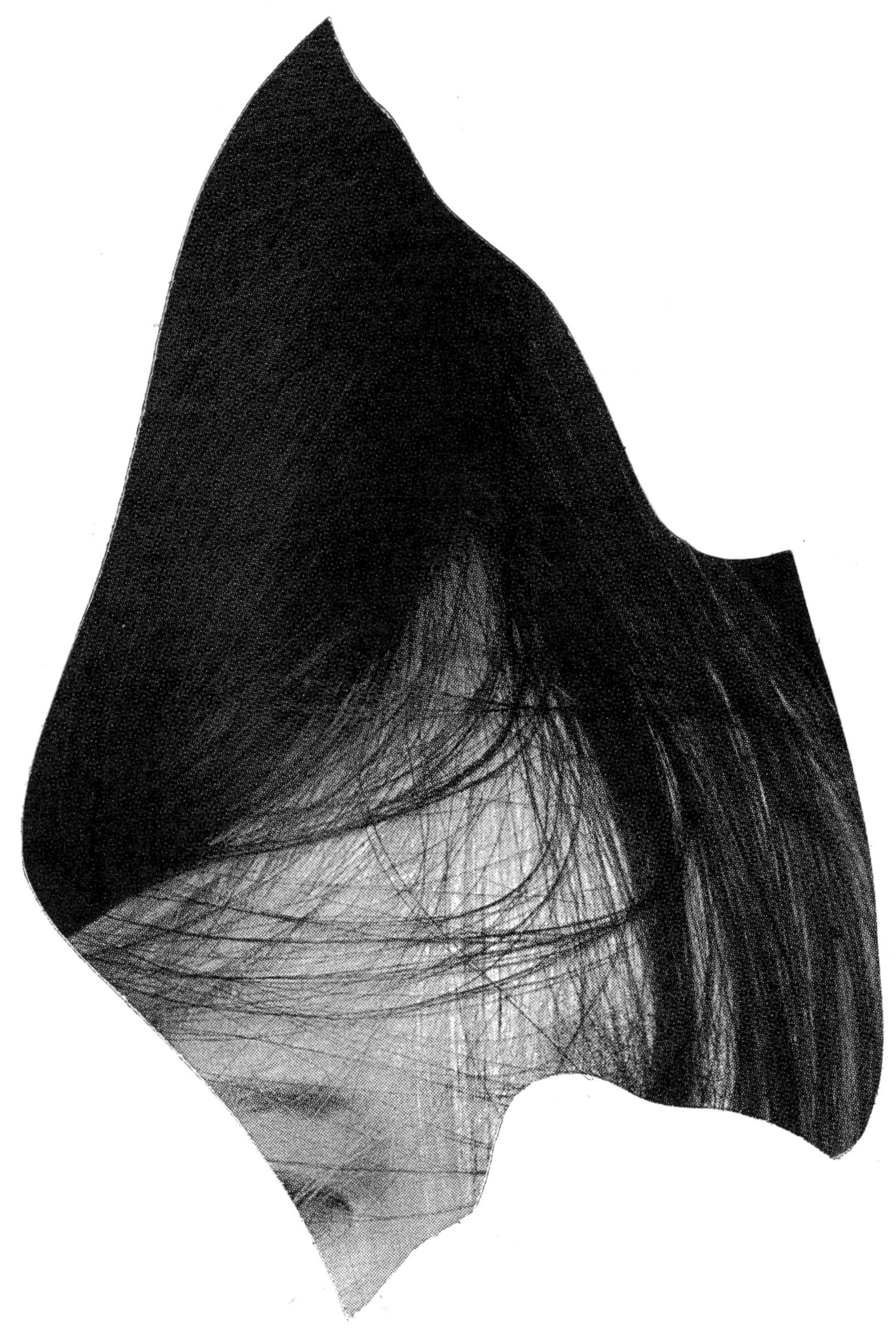

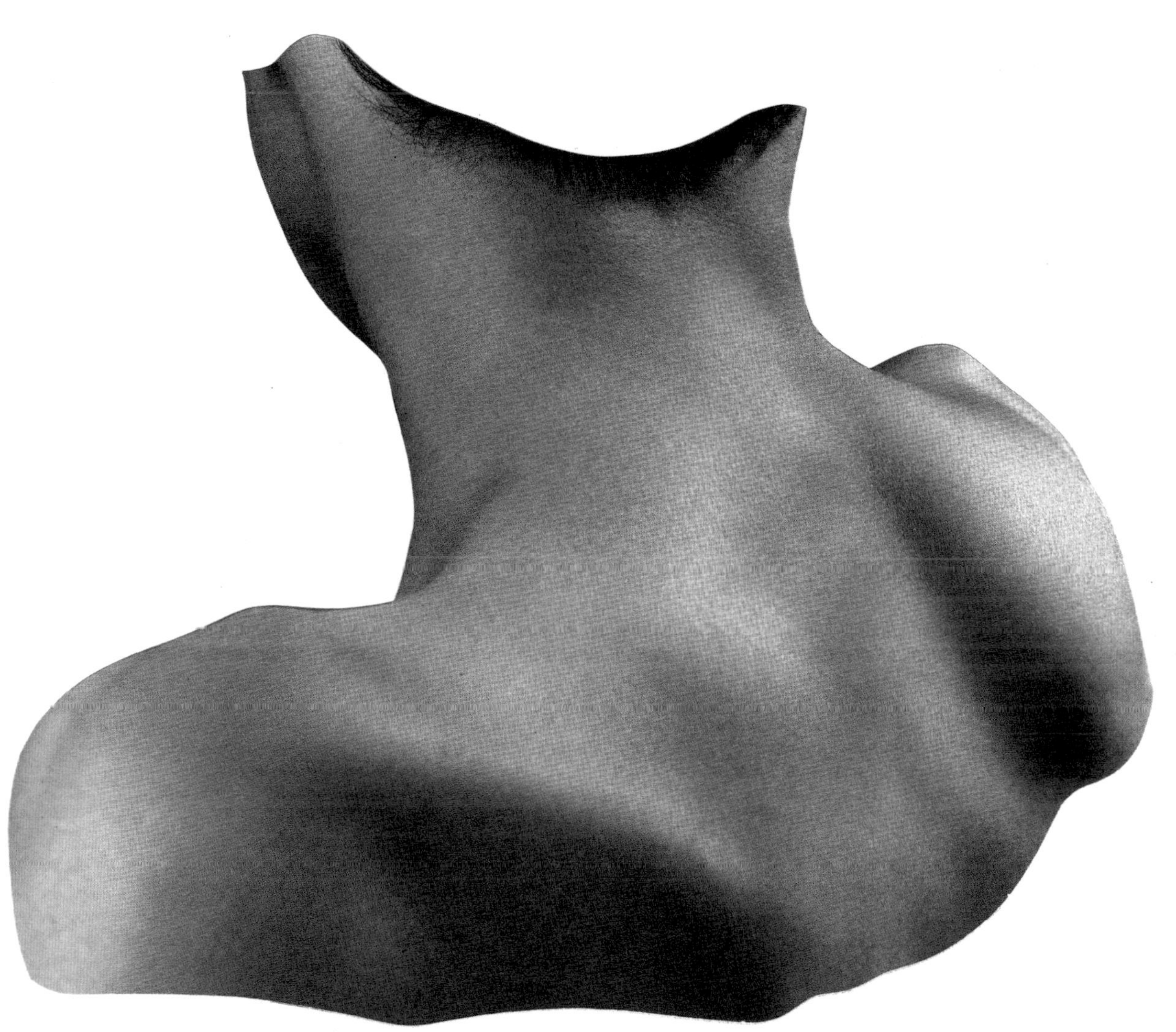

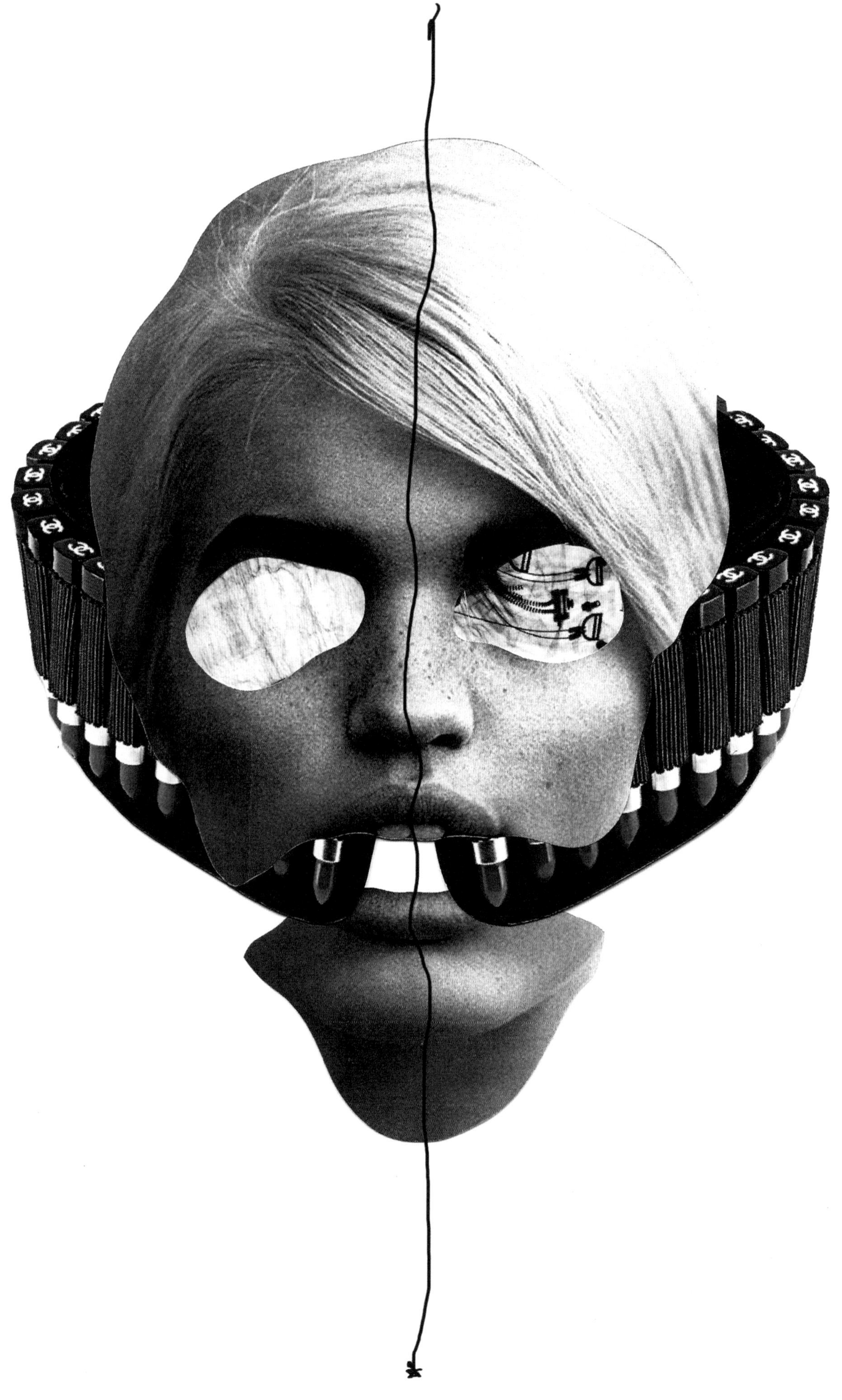

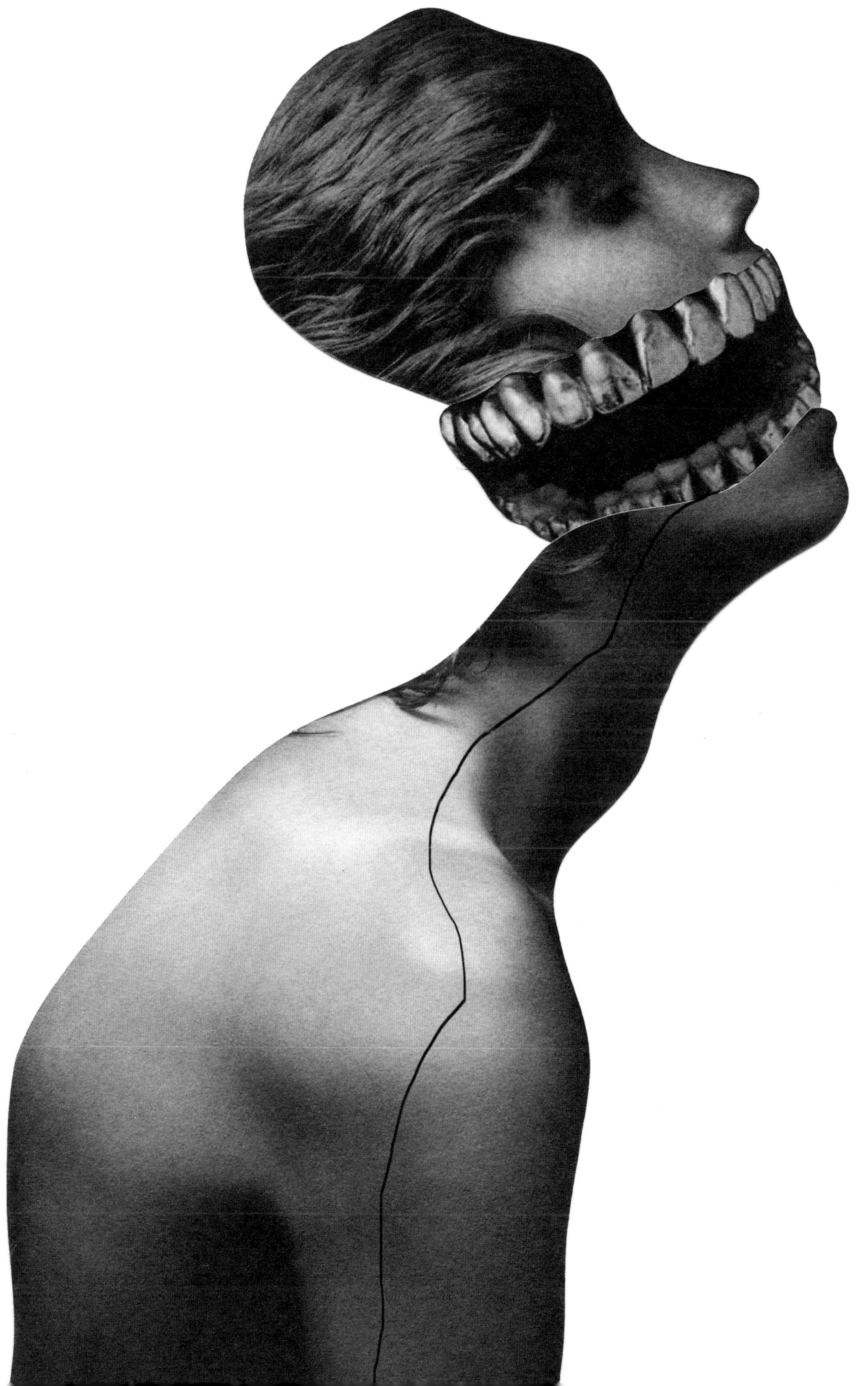

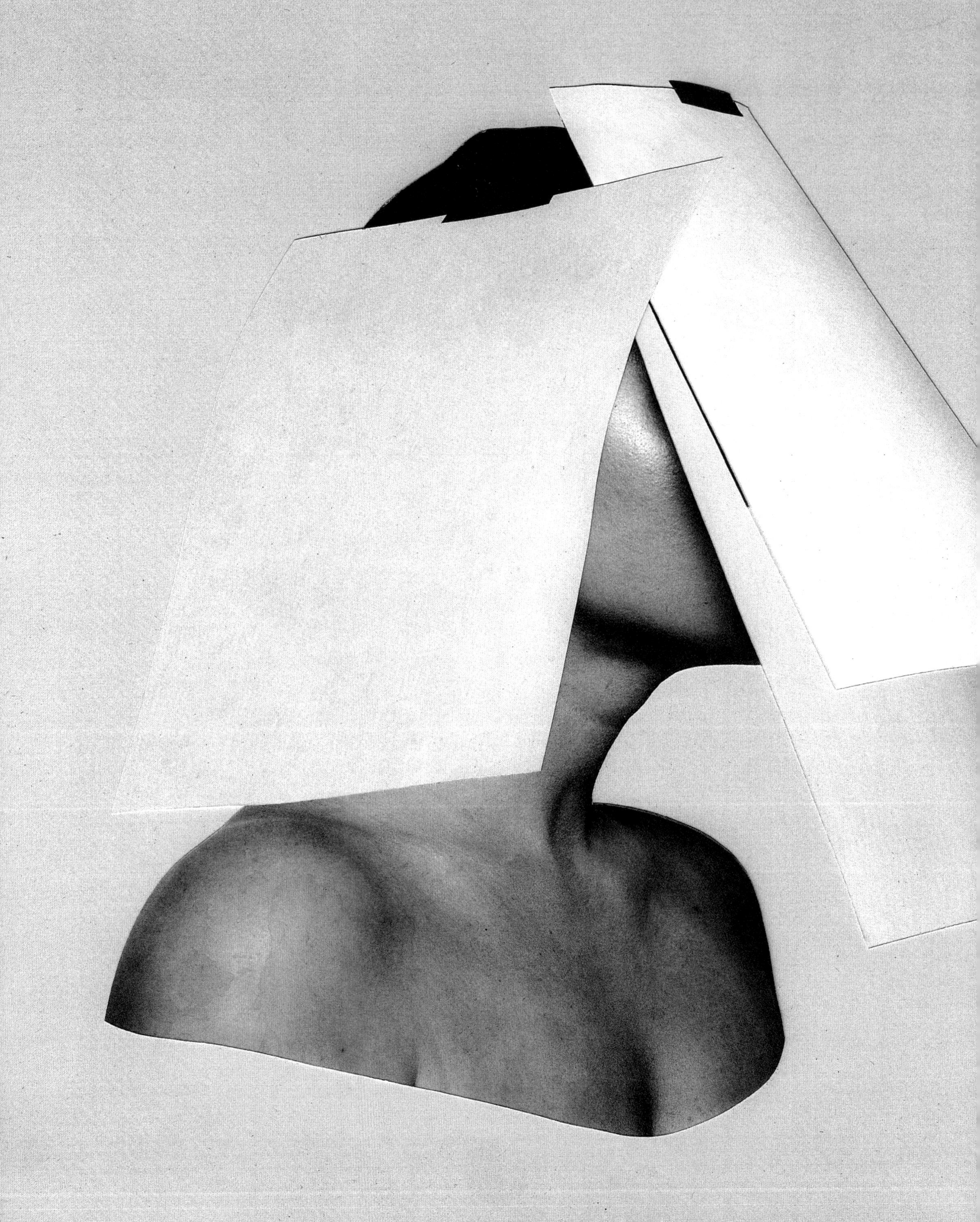

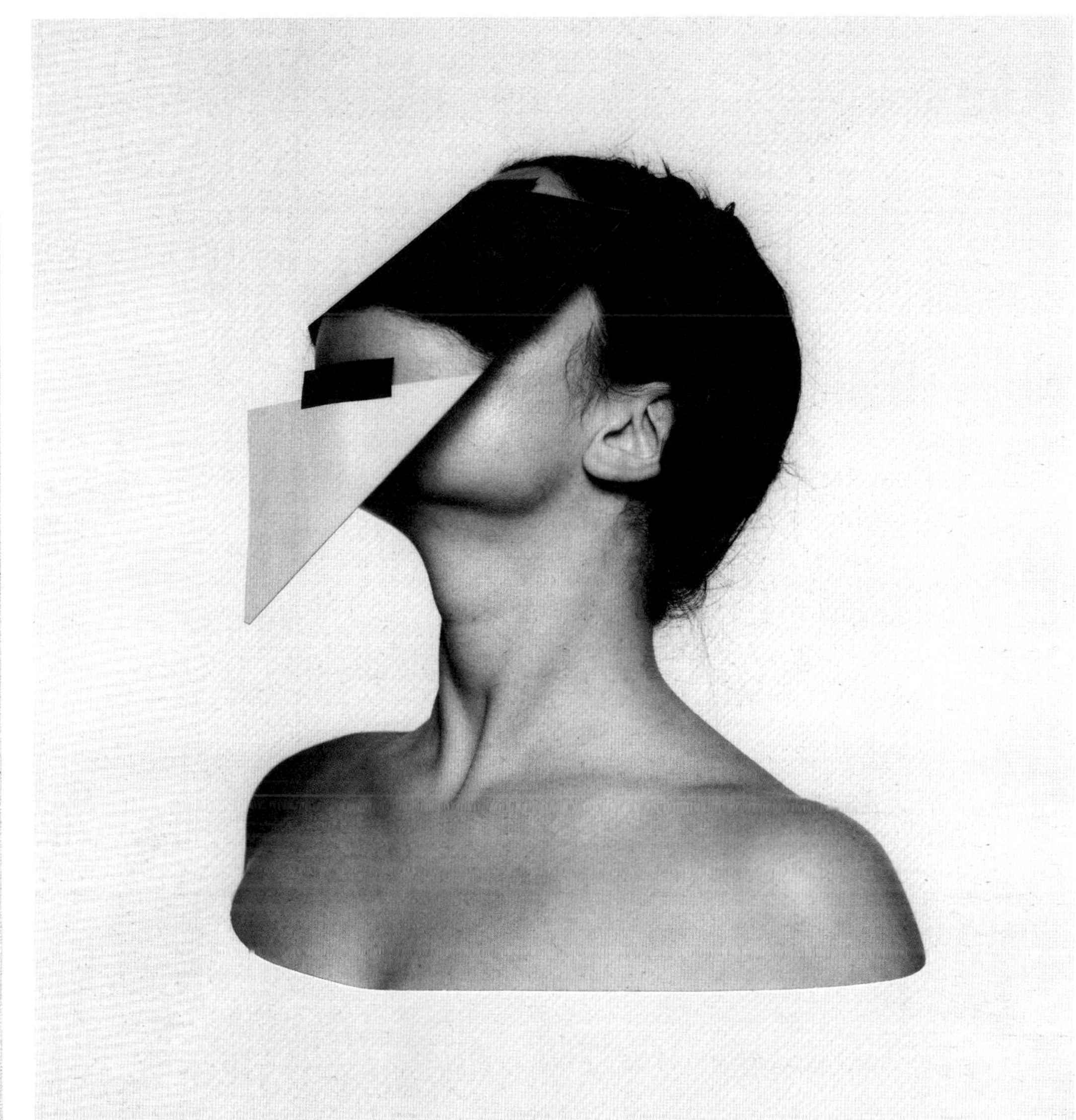

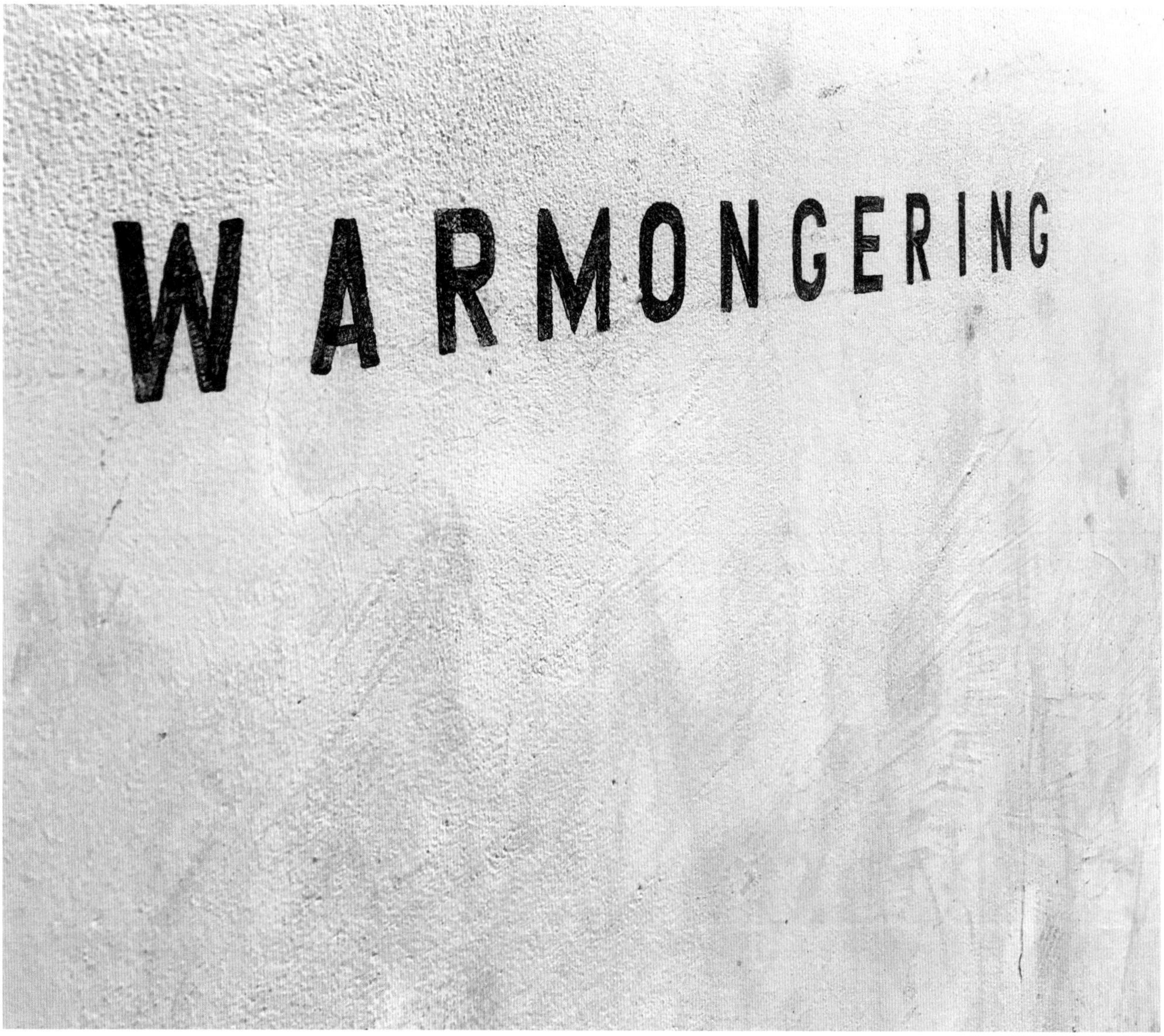

WARMONGERING

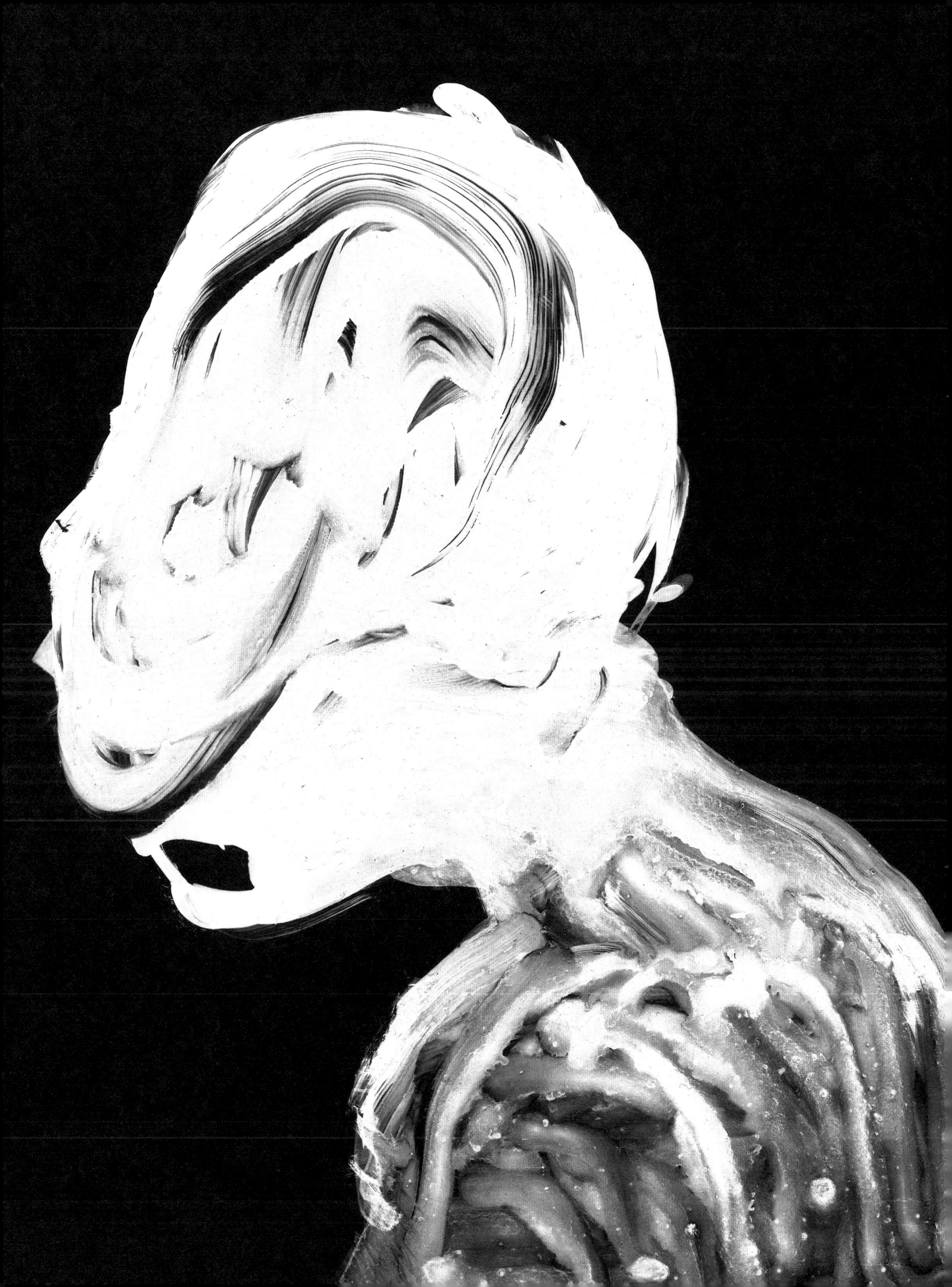

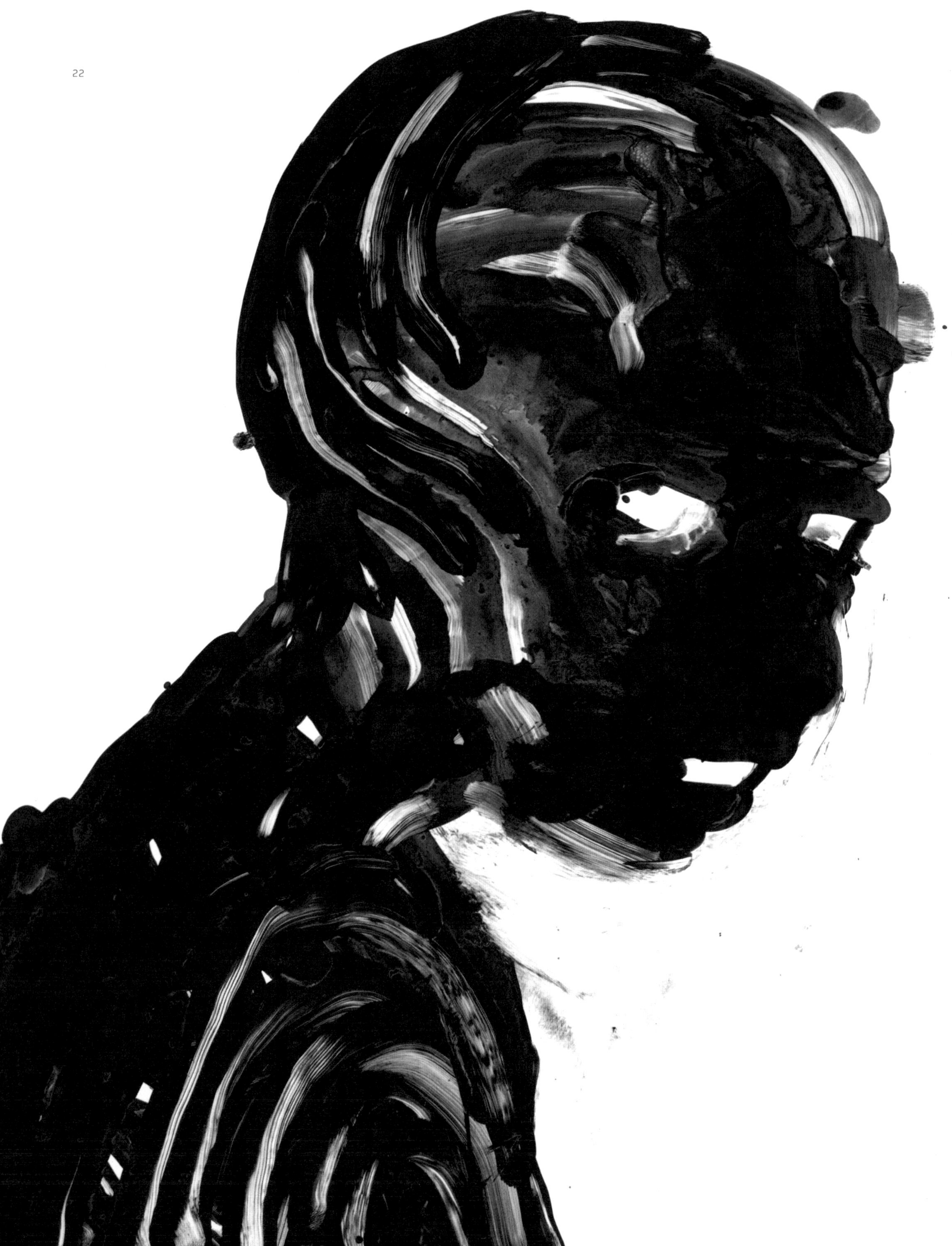

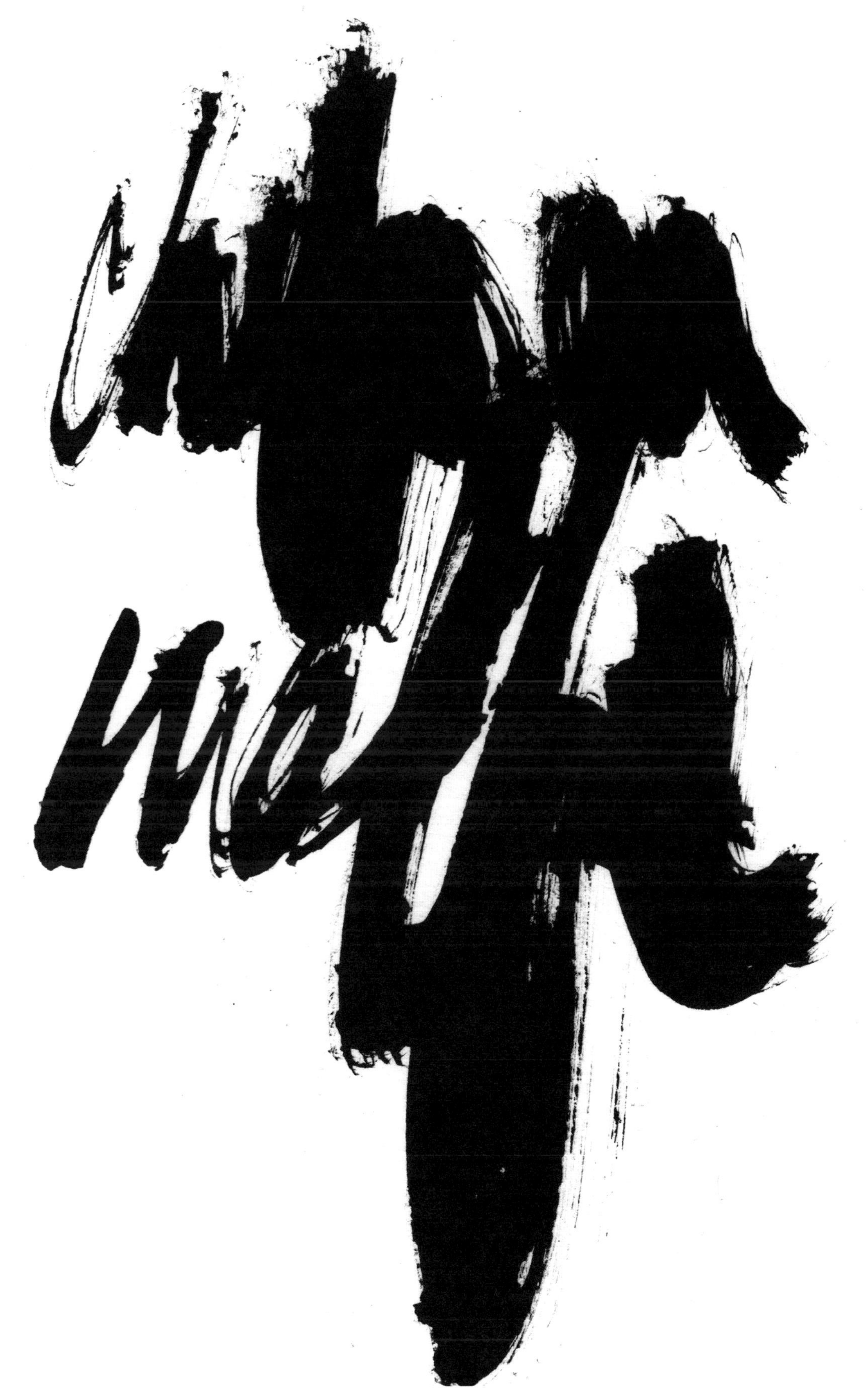

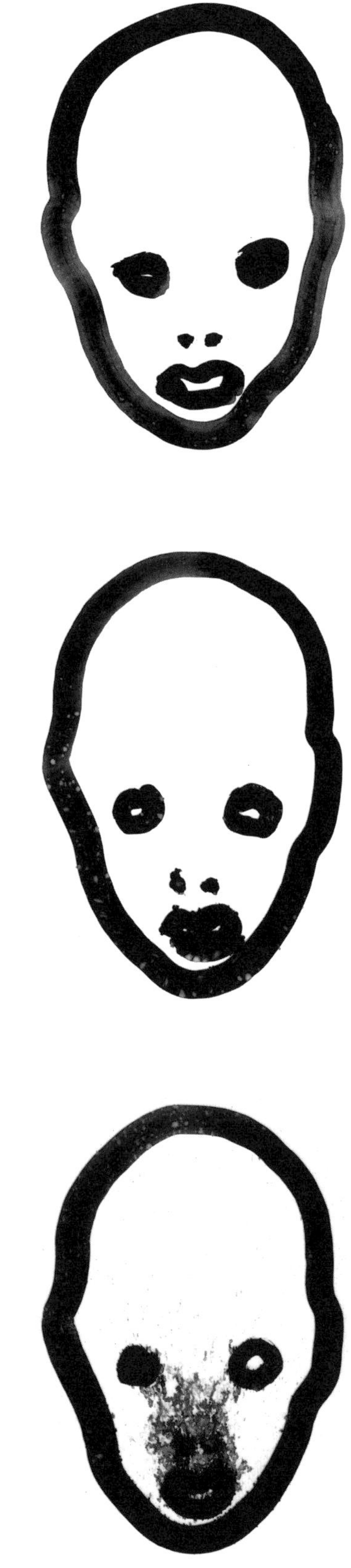

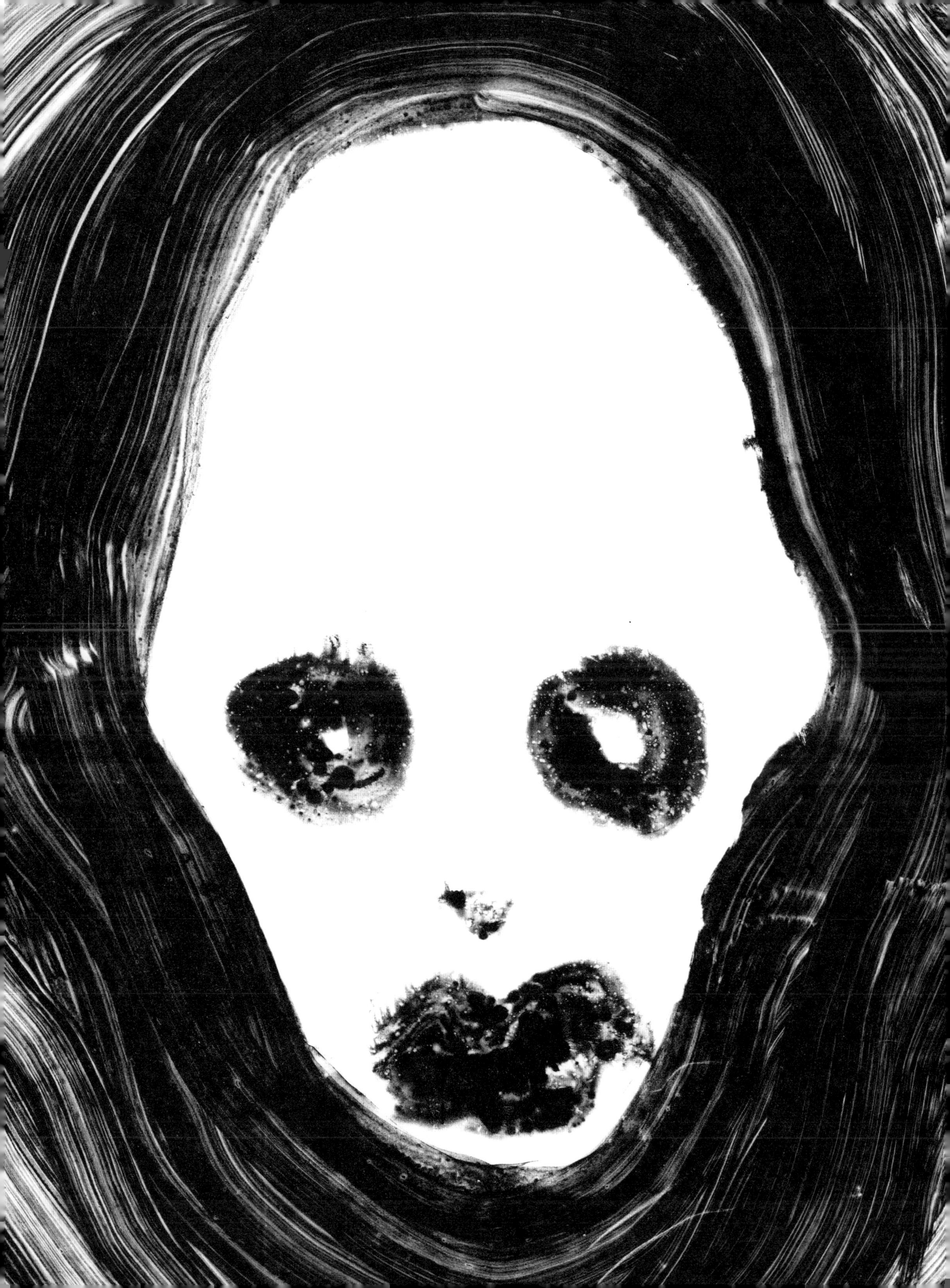

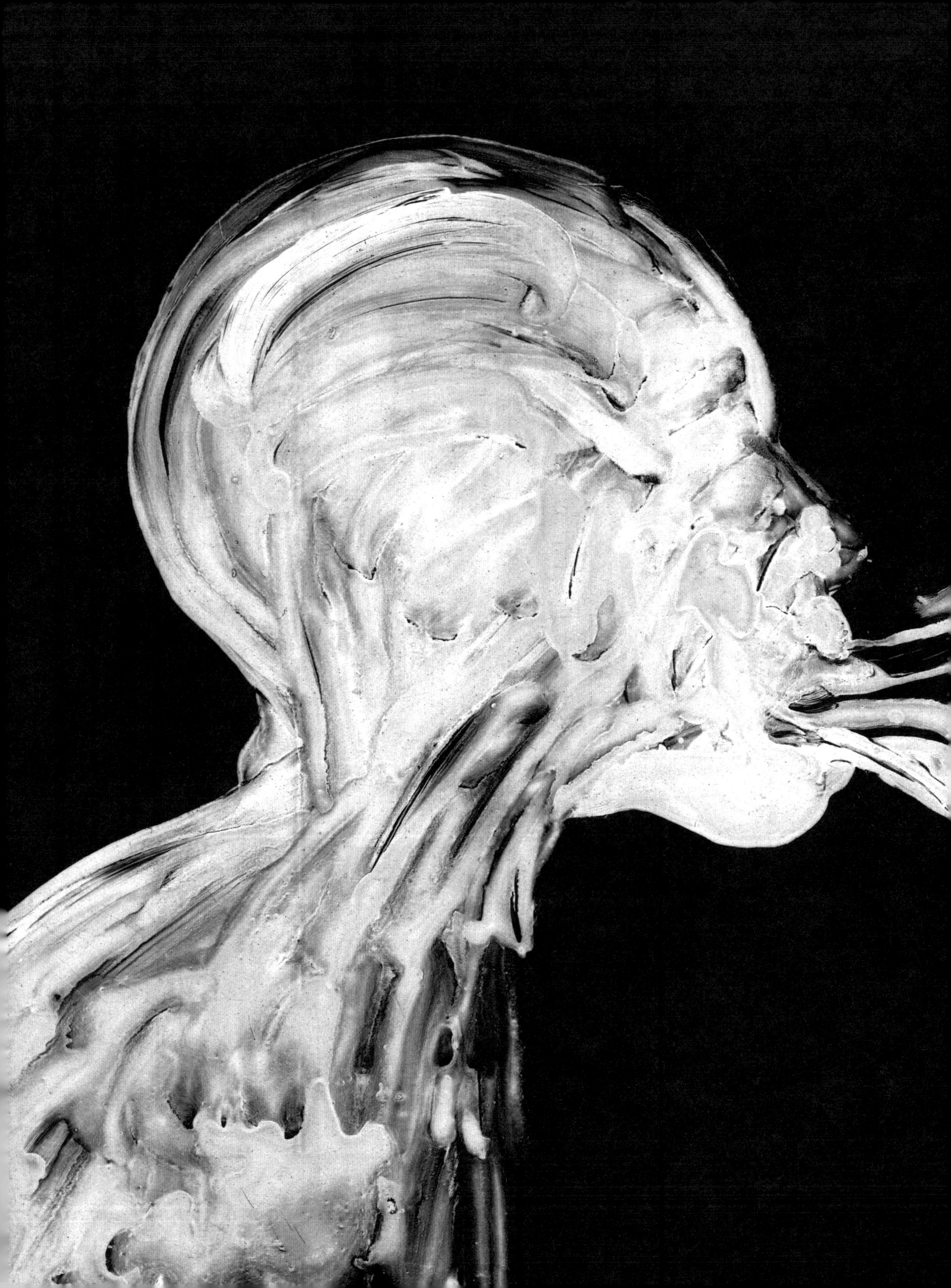

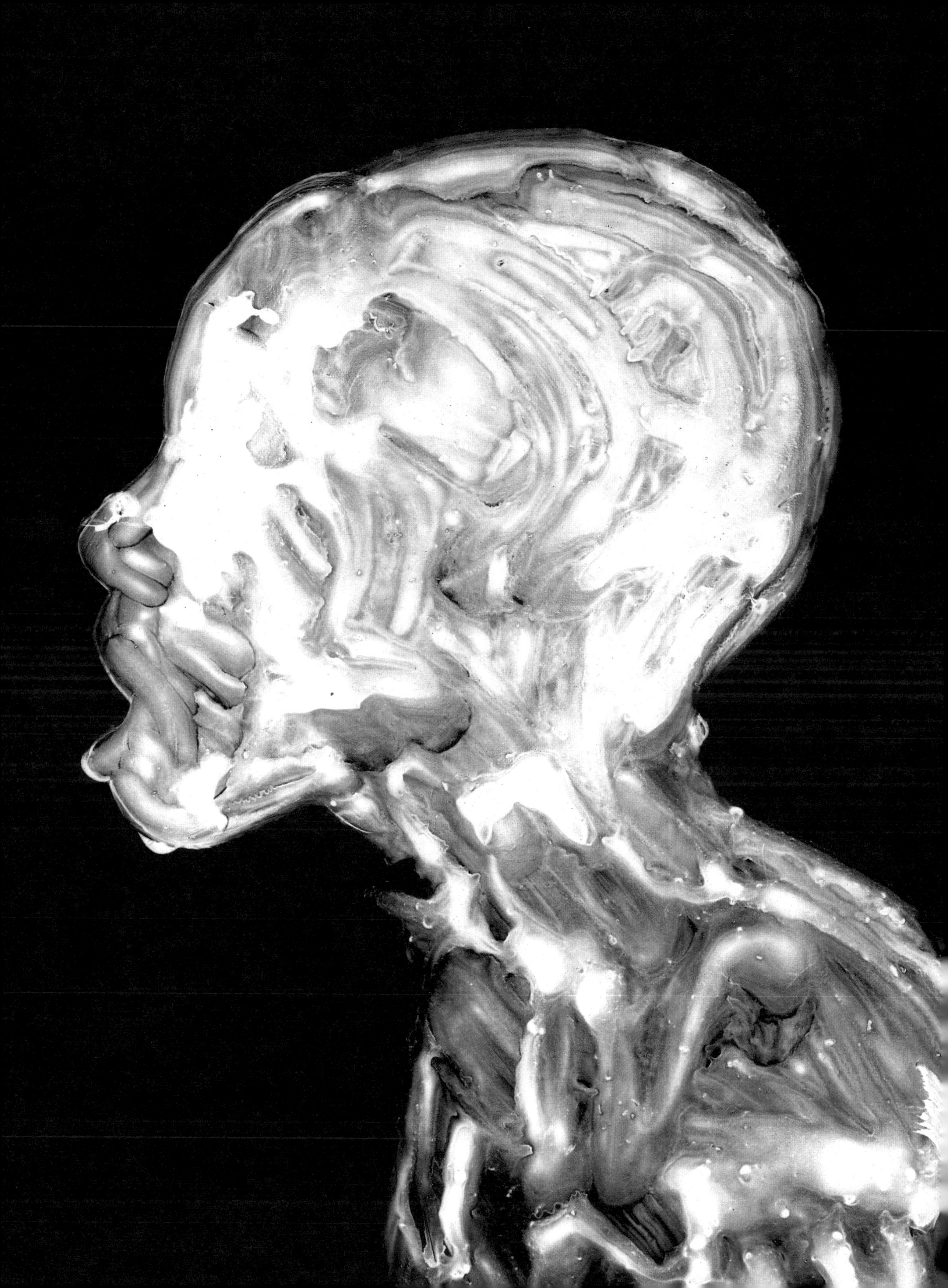

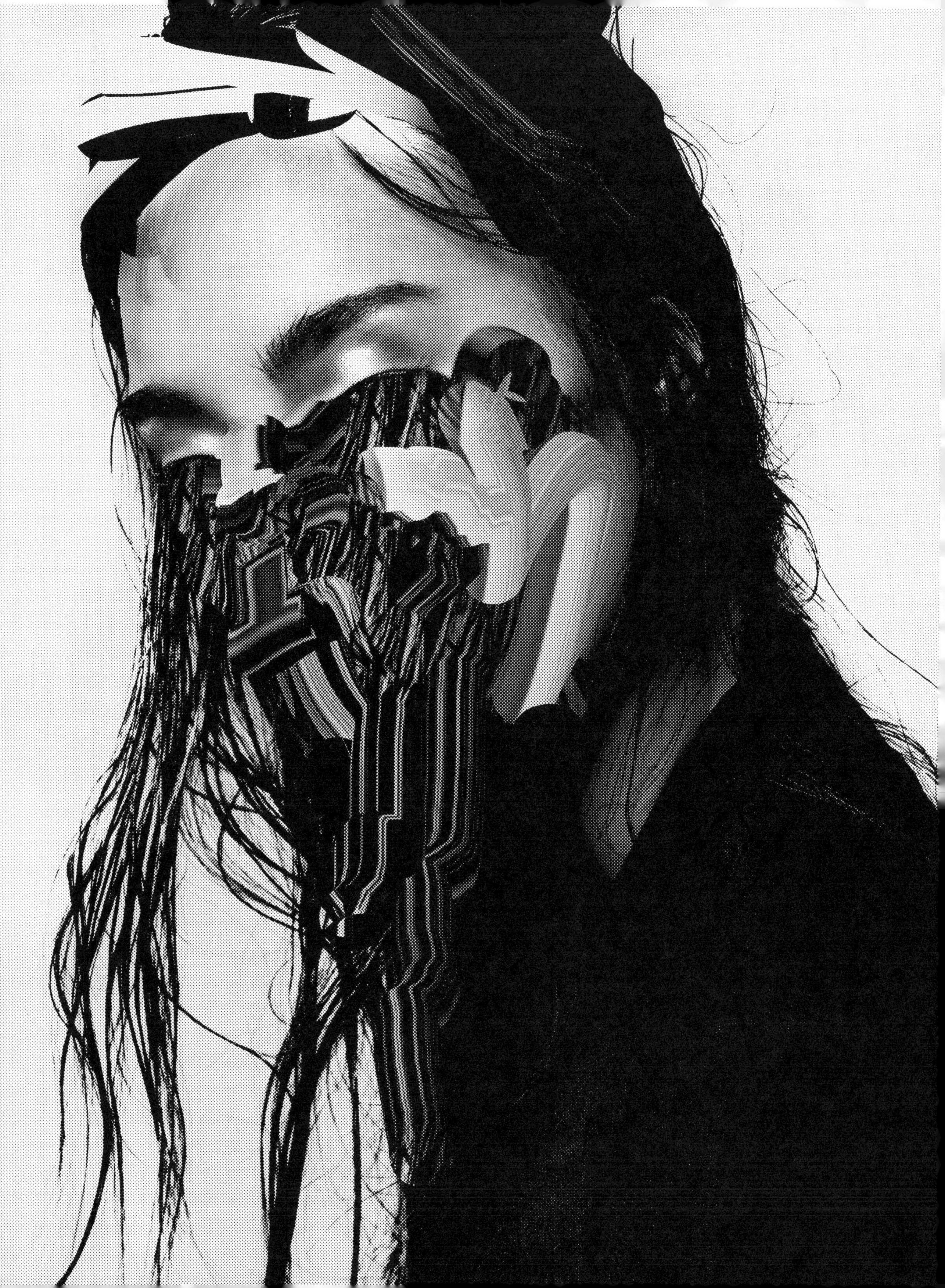

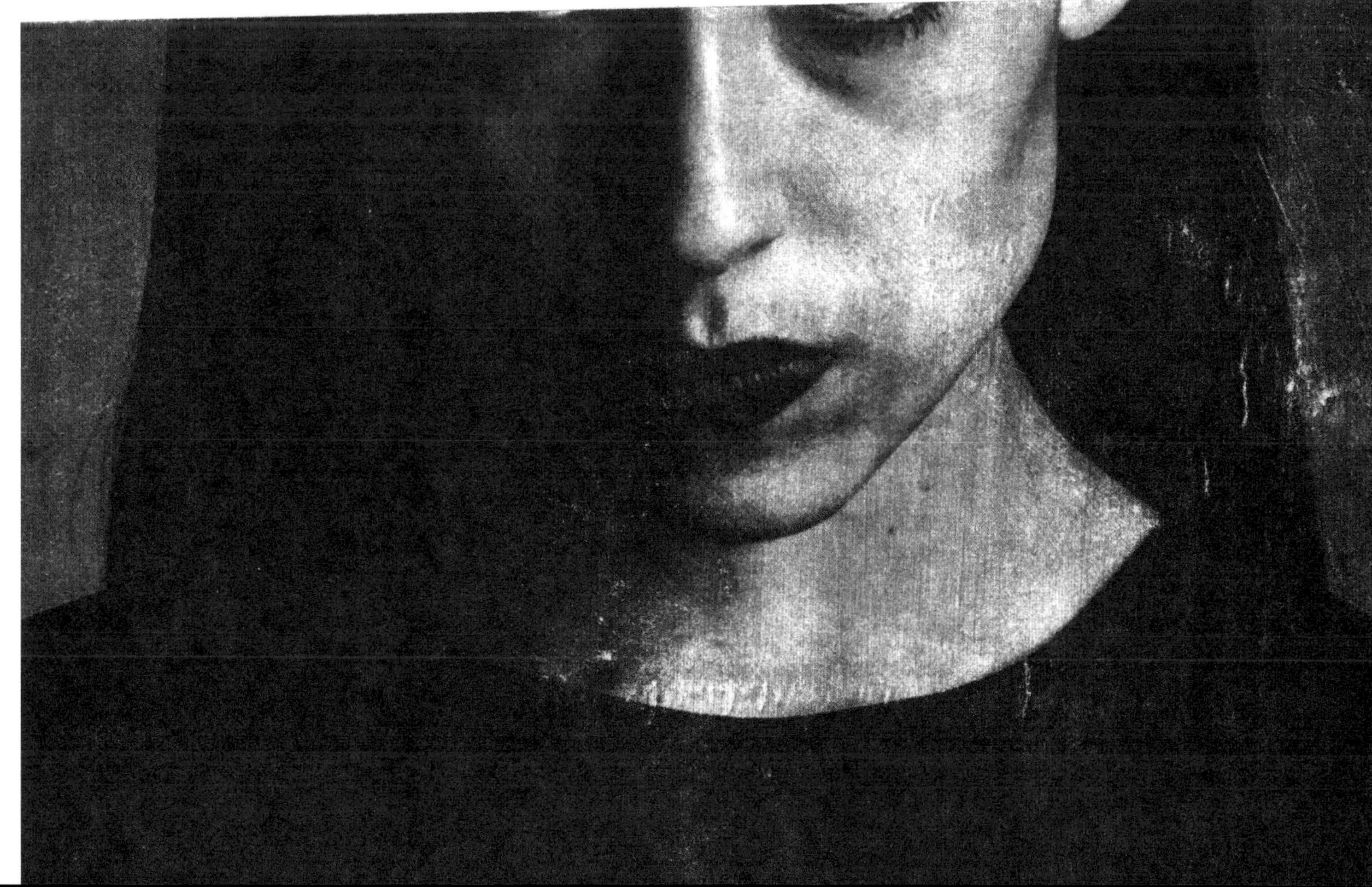

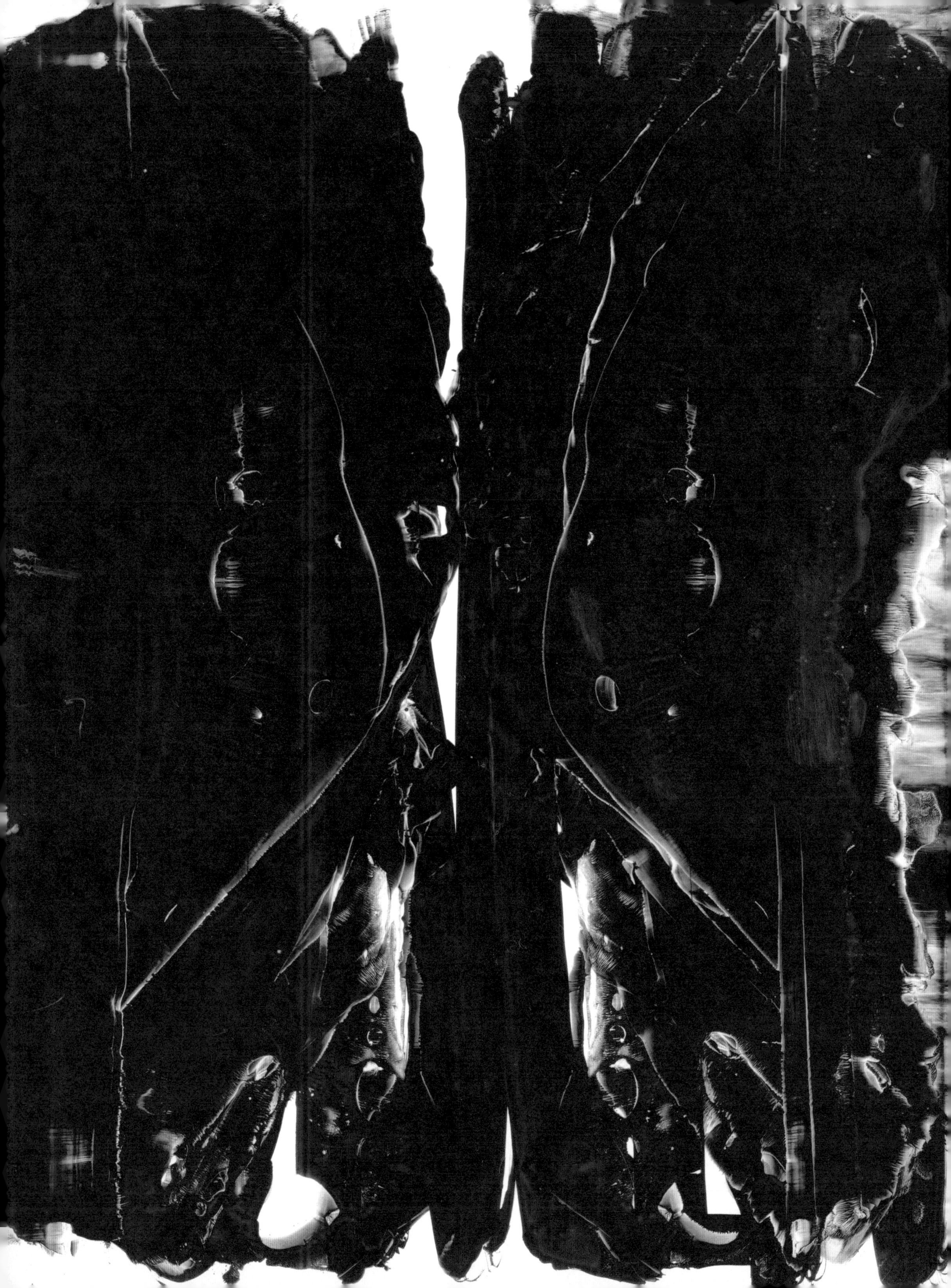

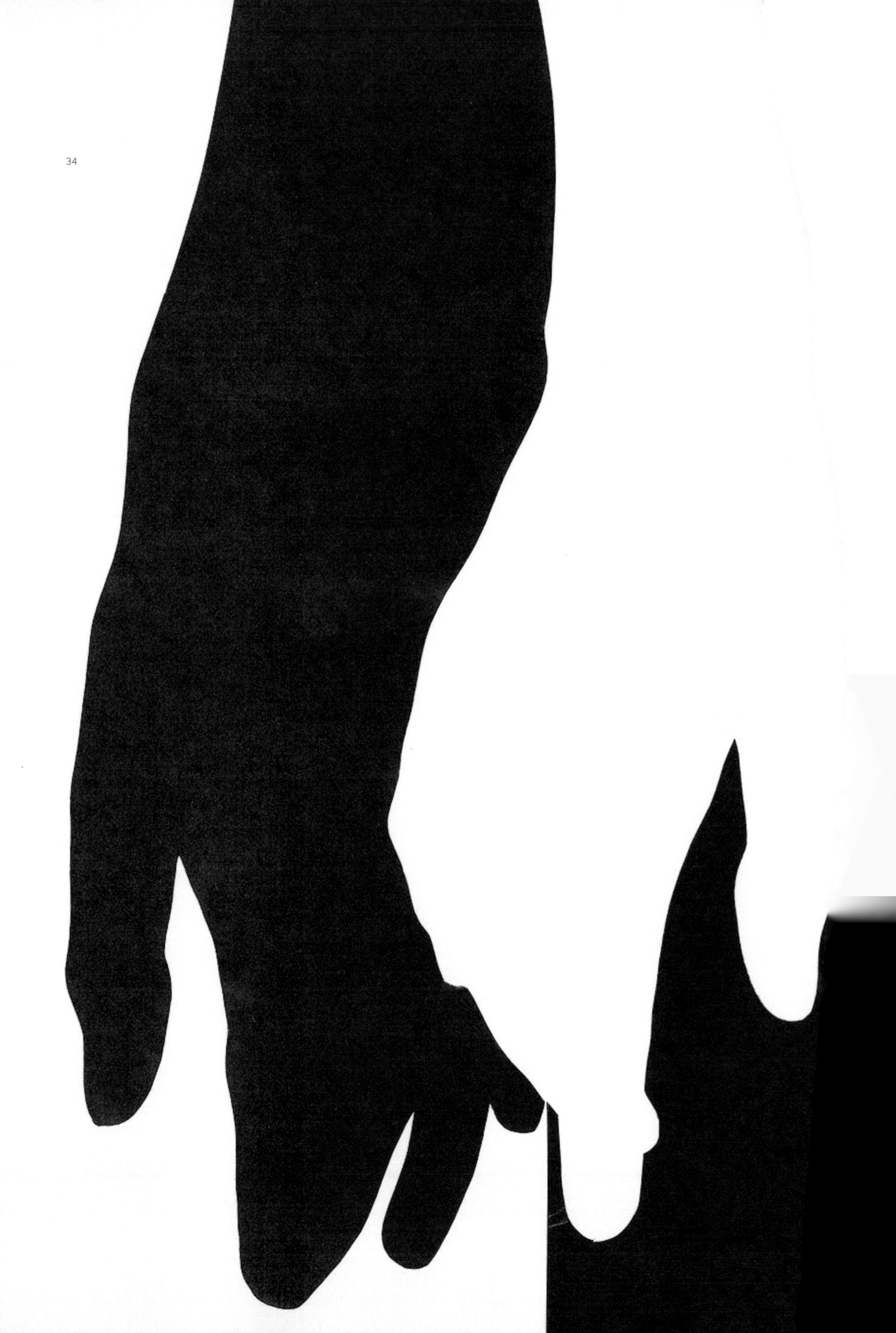

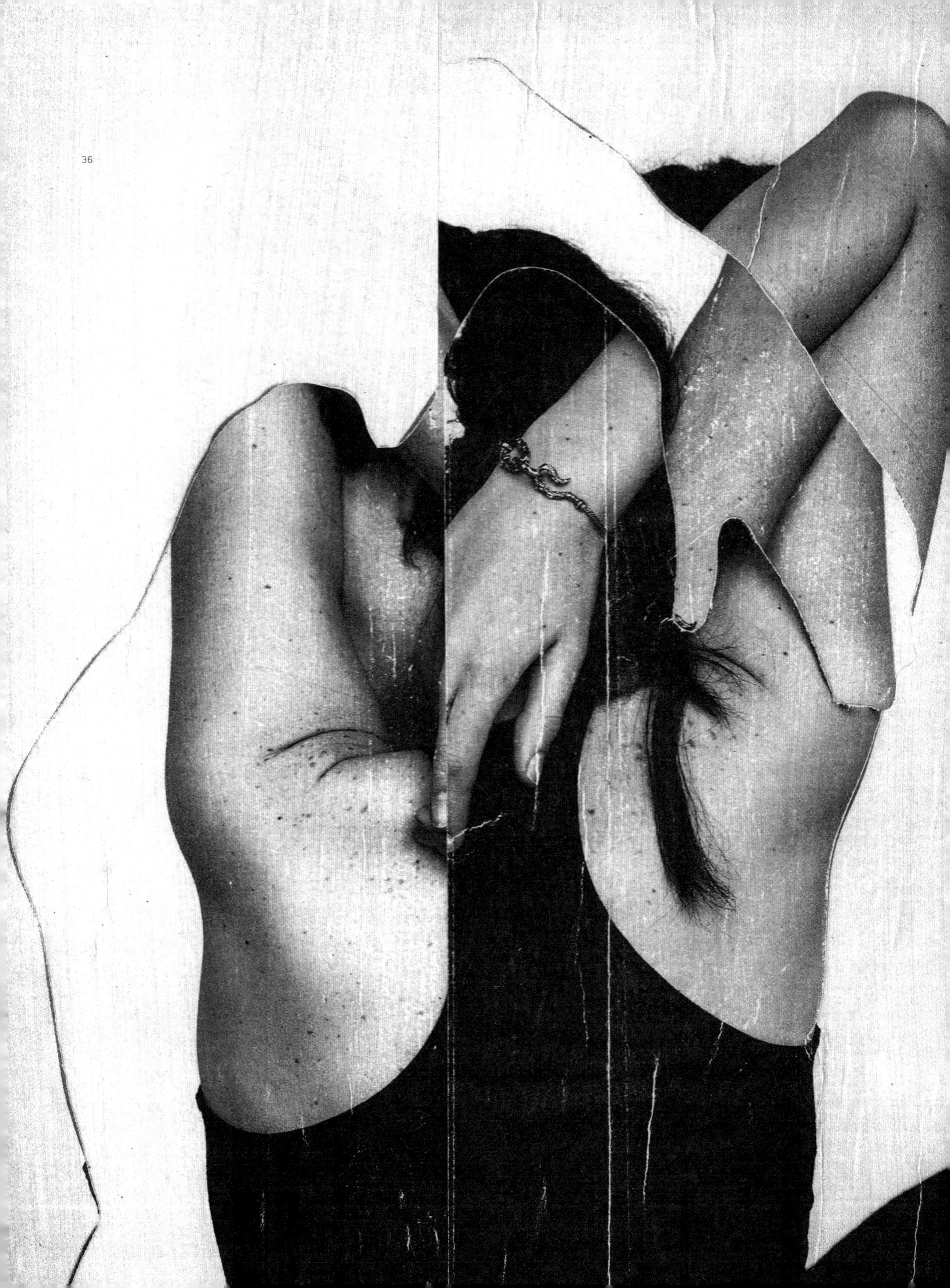

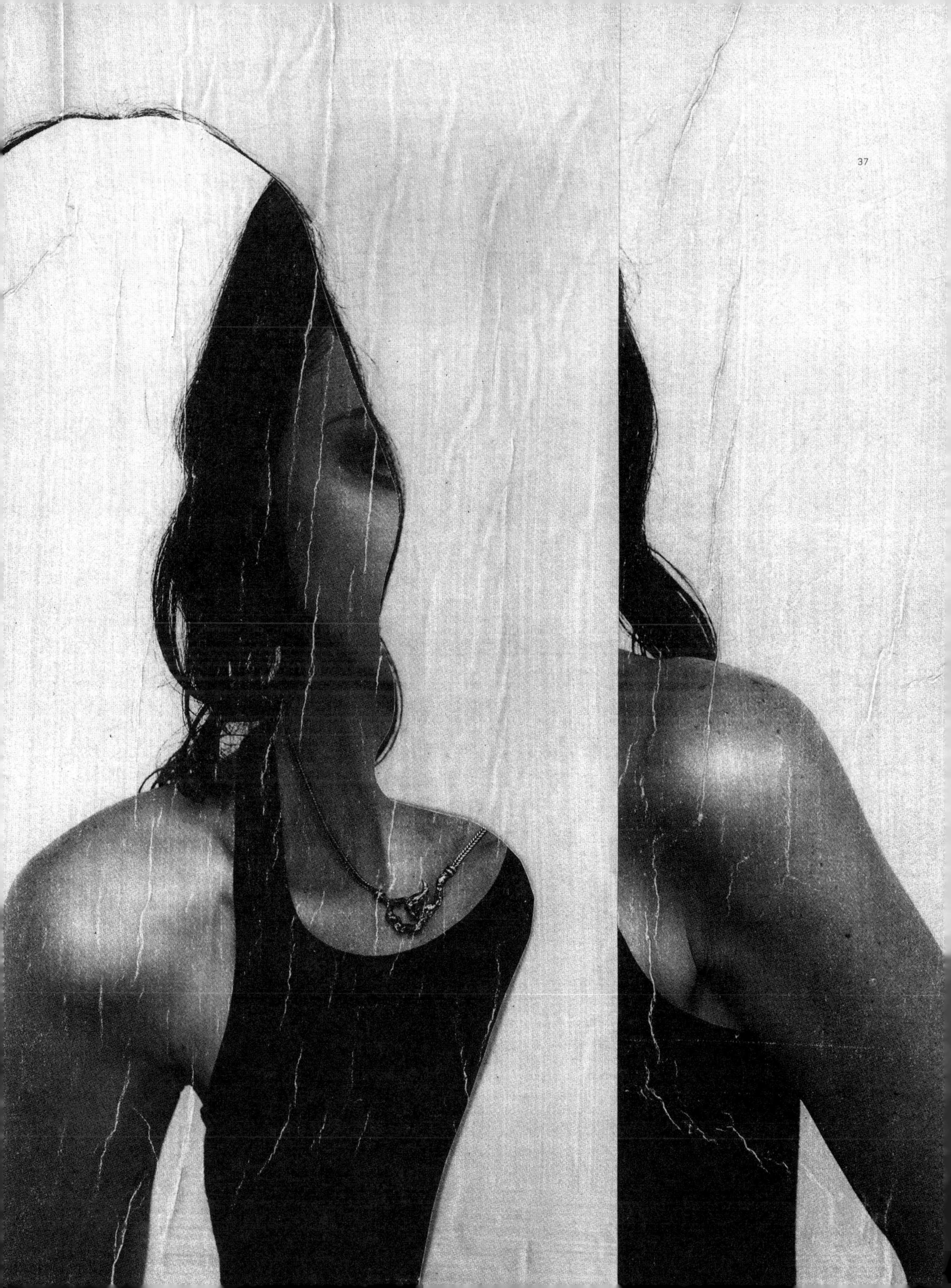

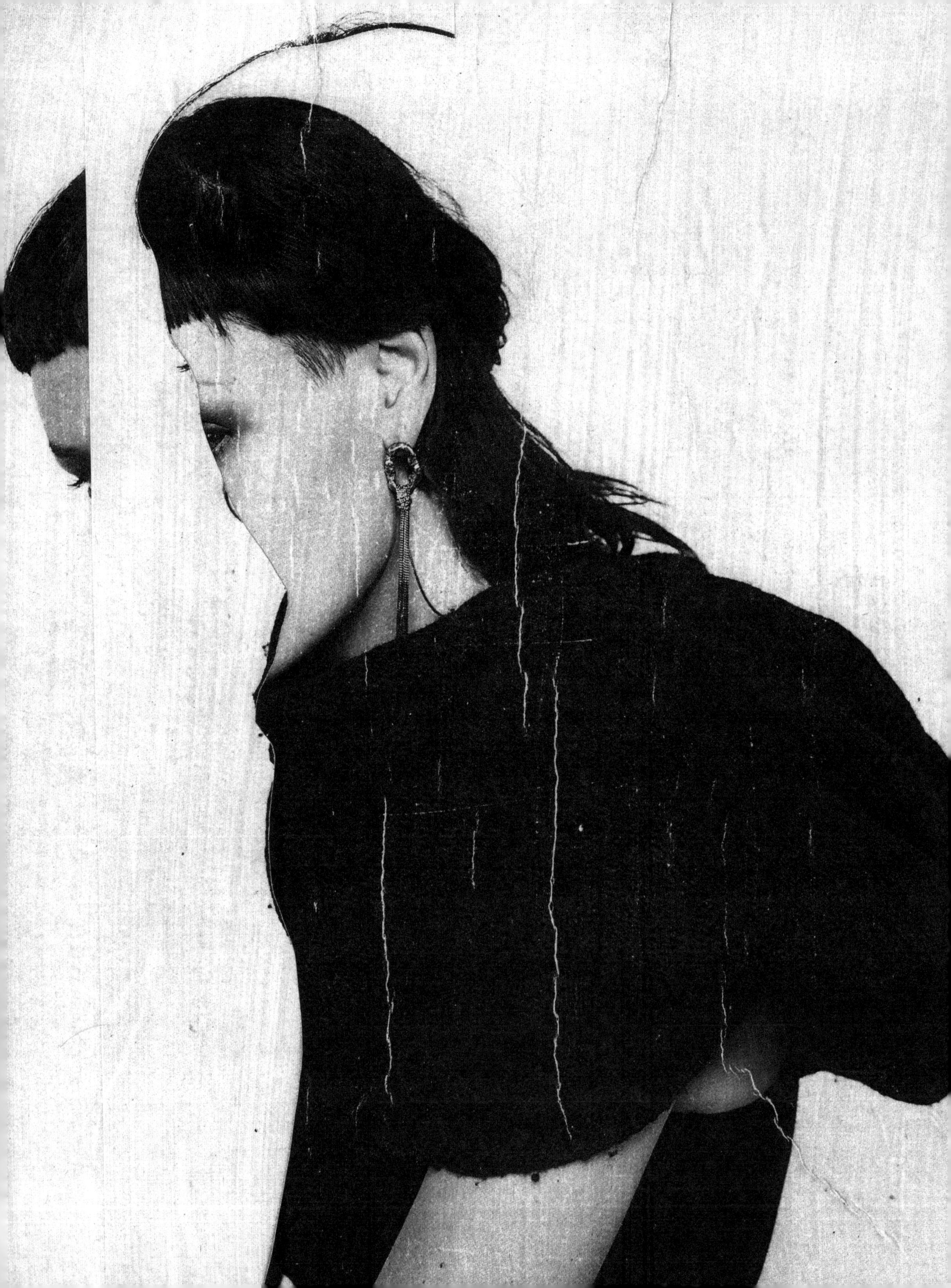

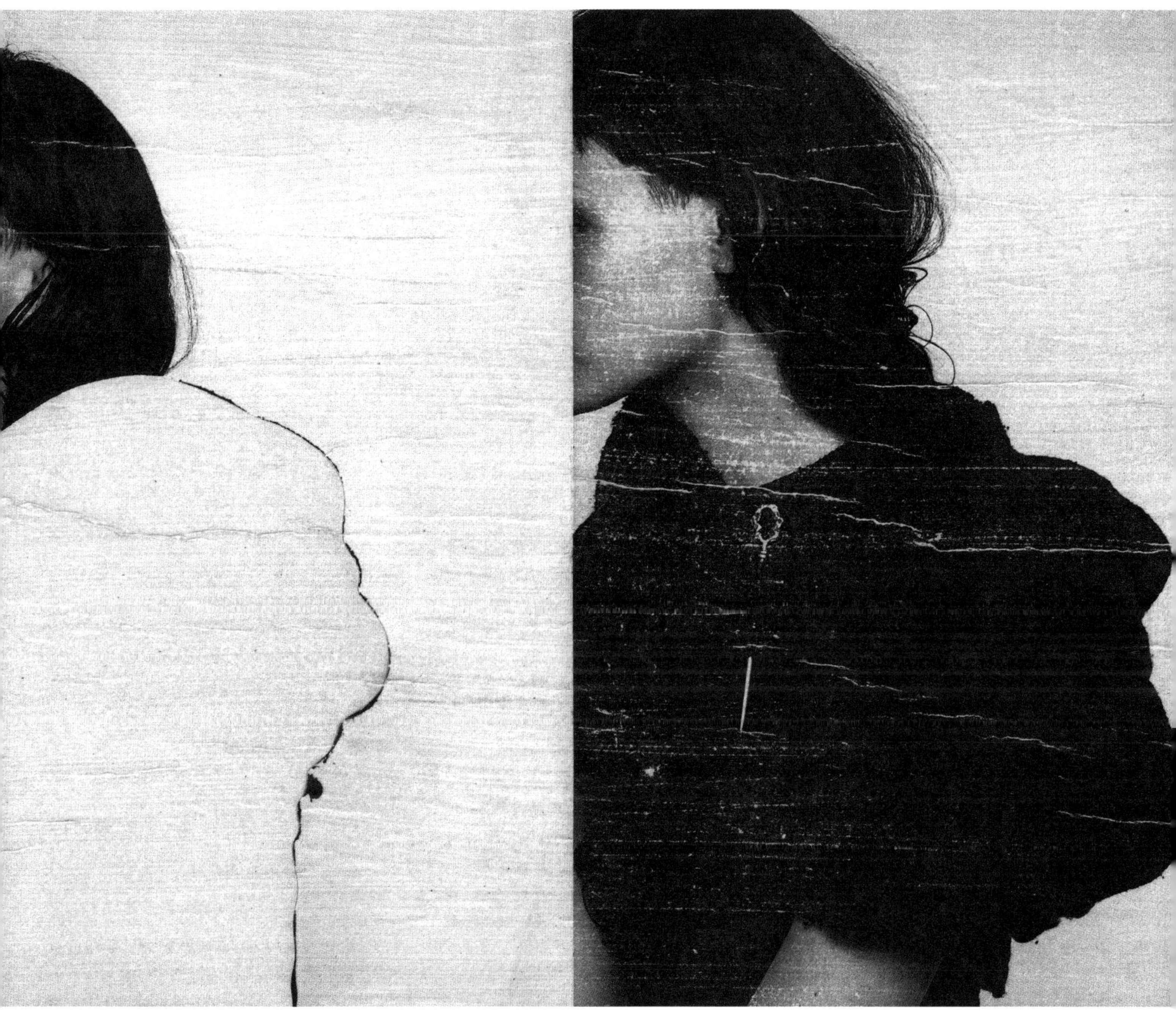

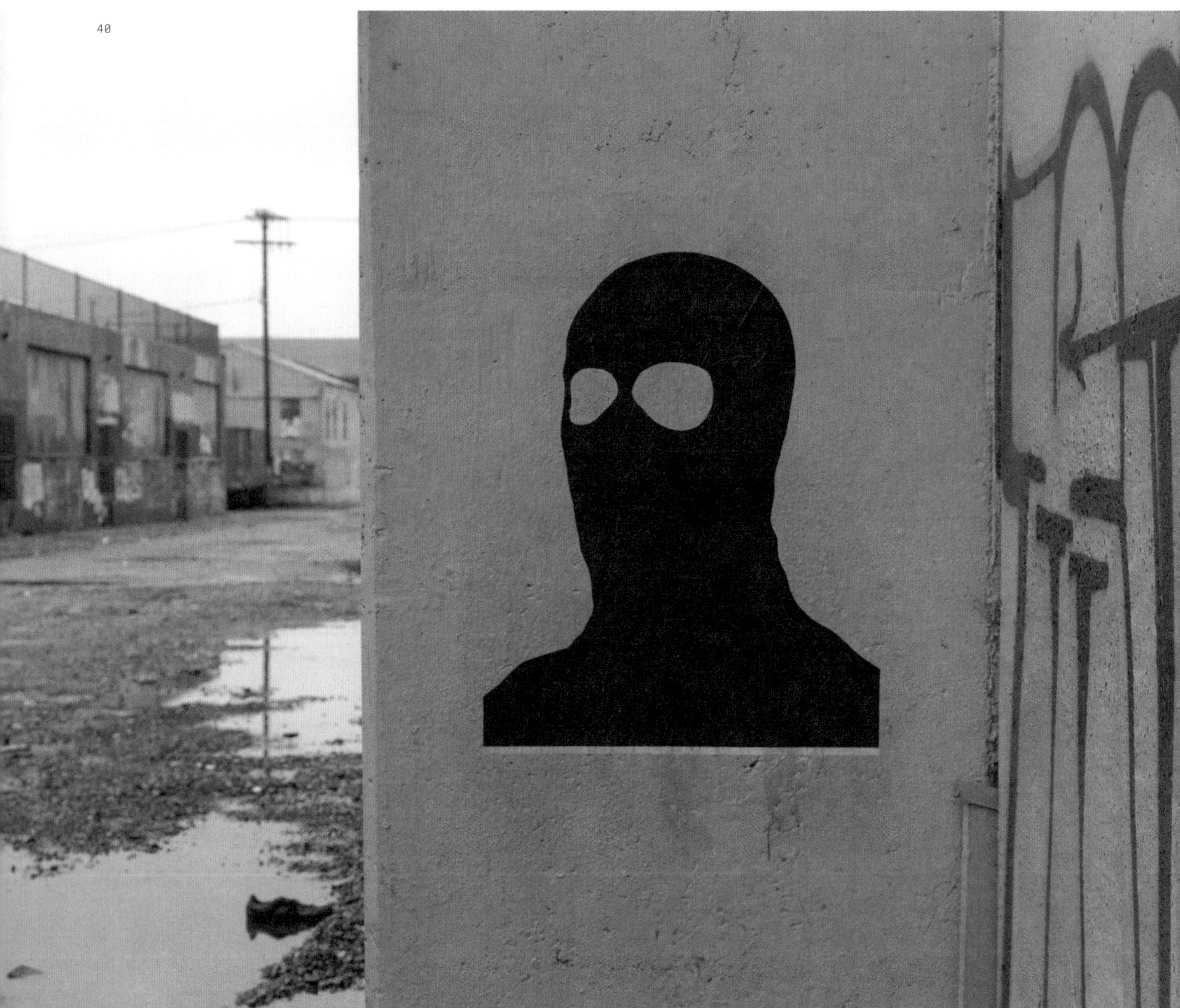

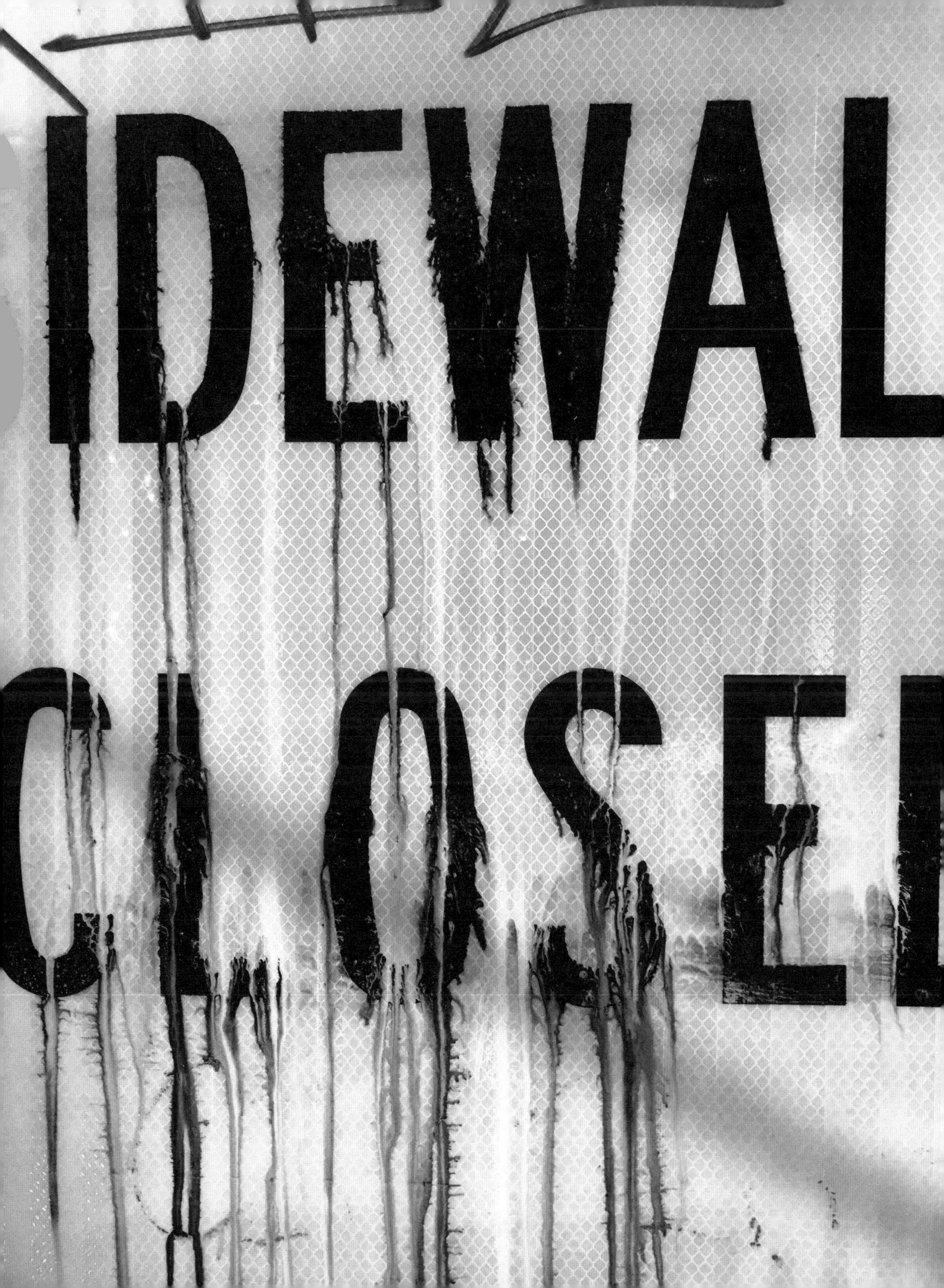

IDEWAL
CLOSED

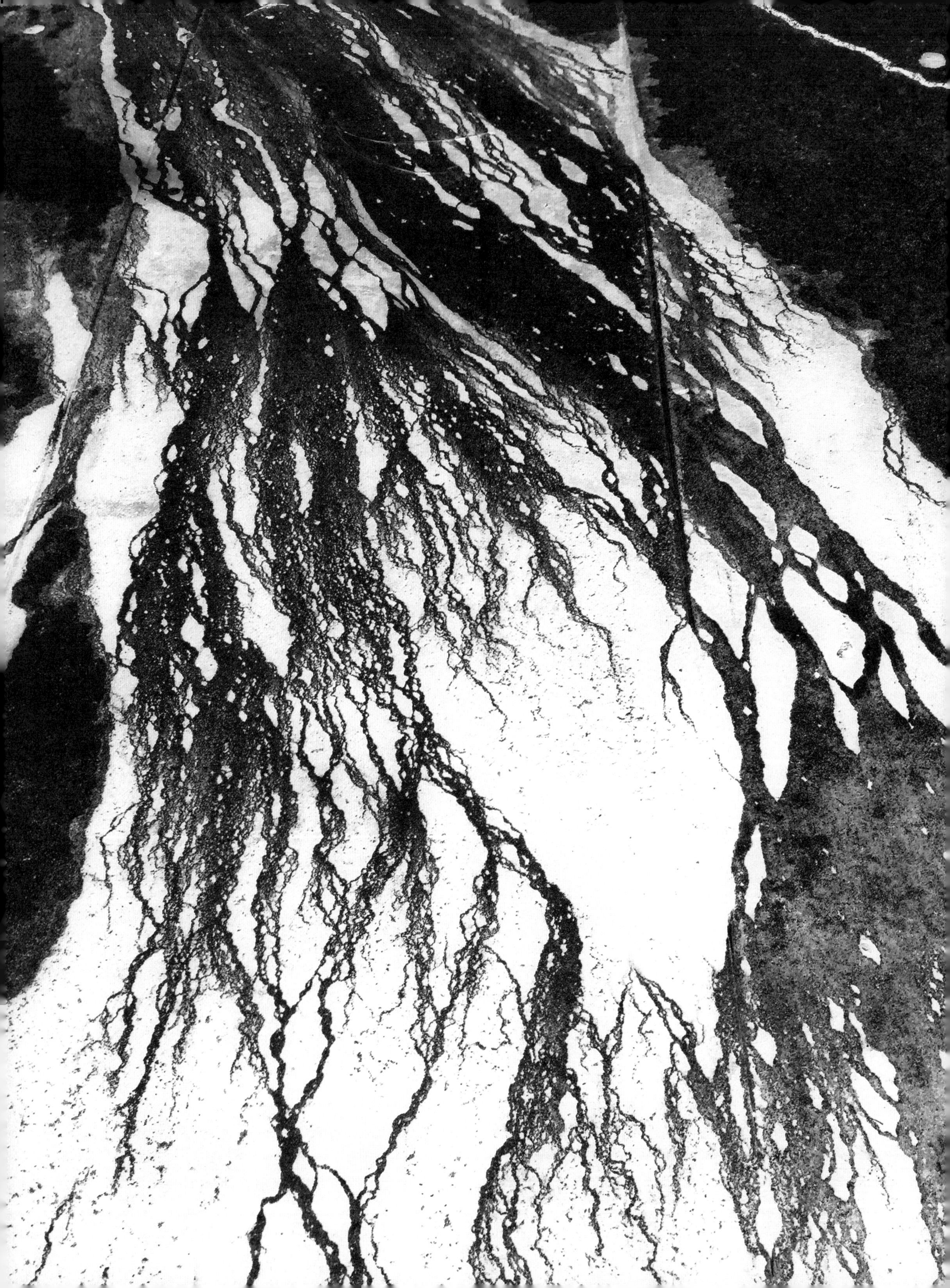

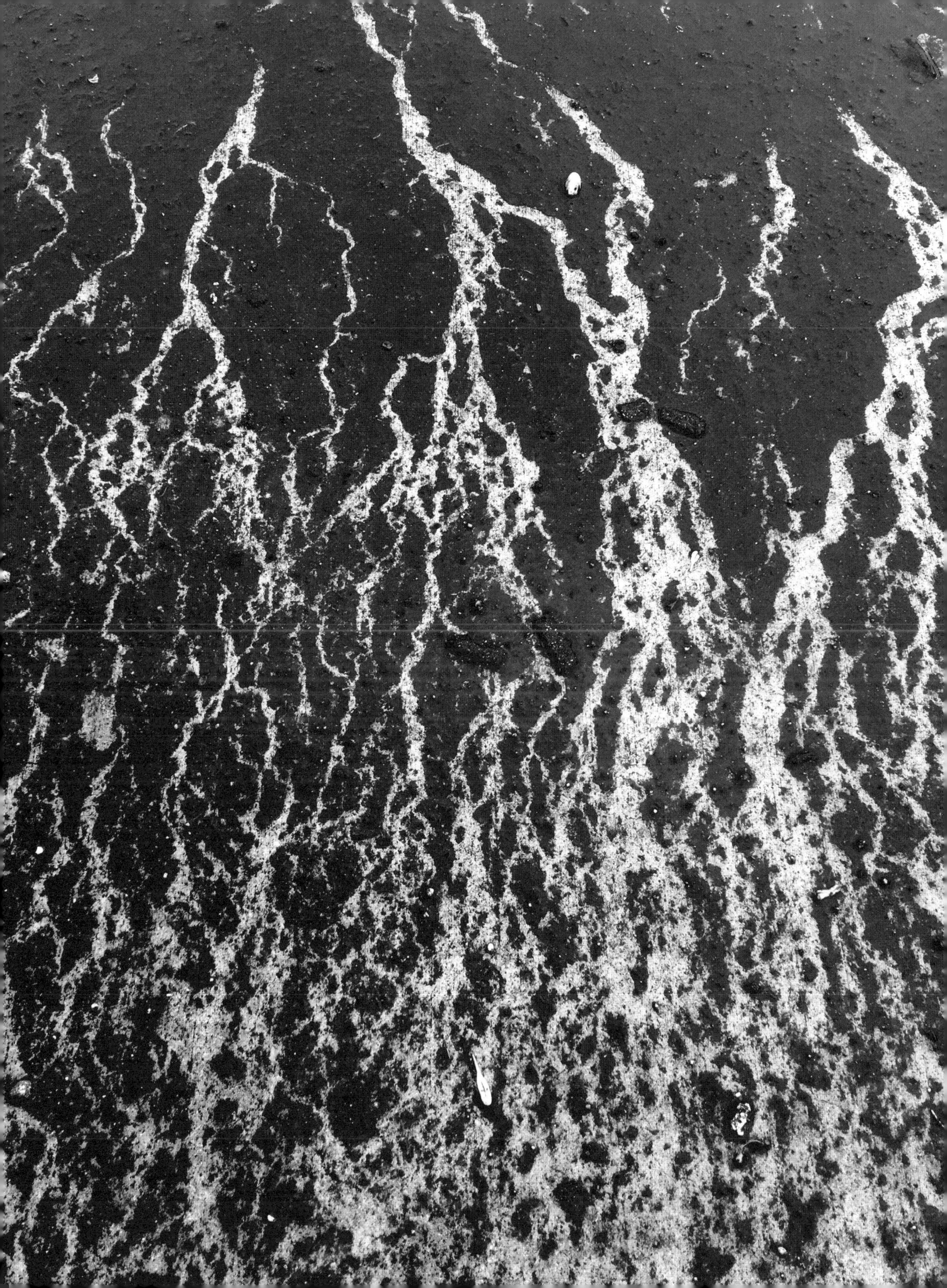

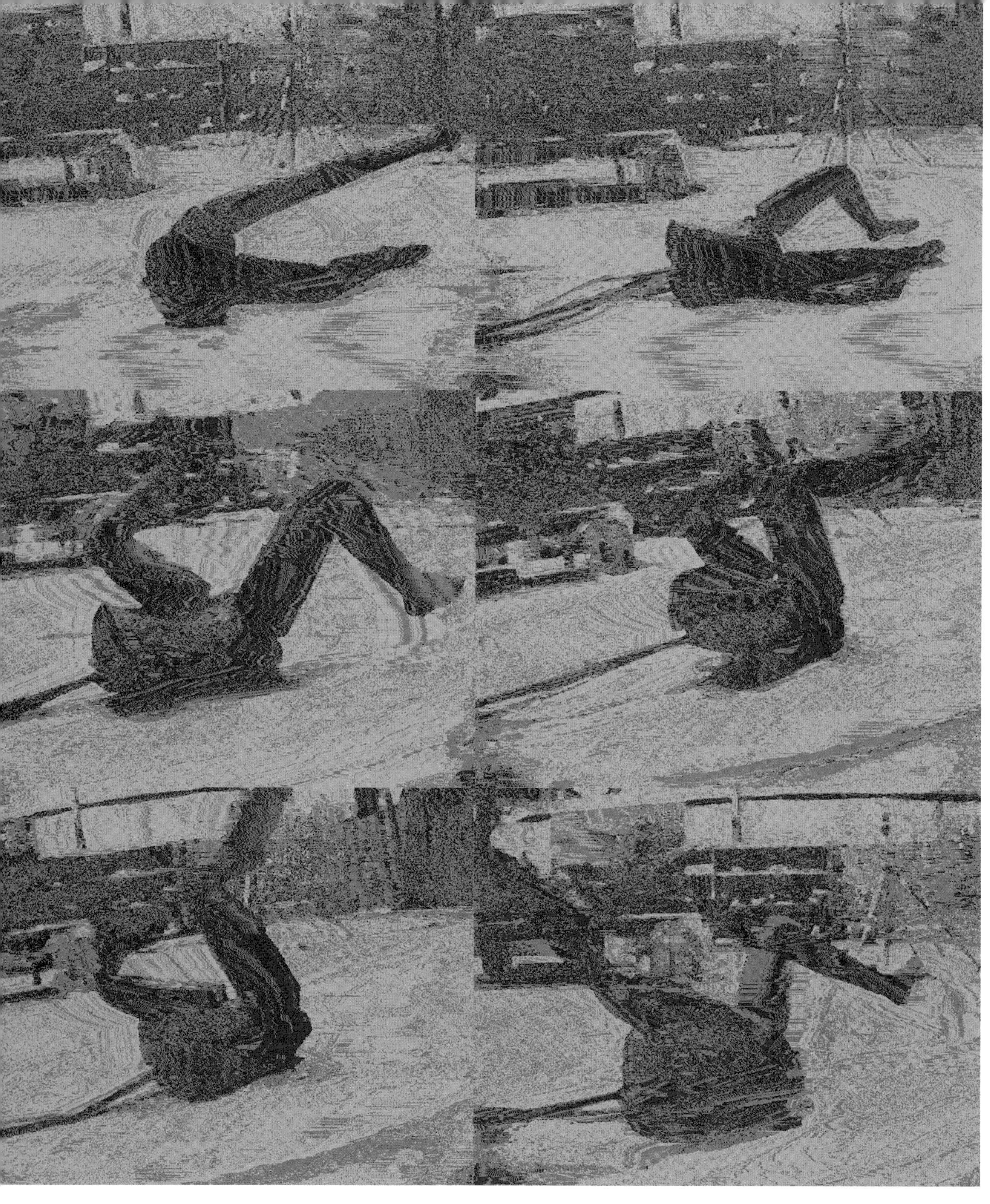

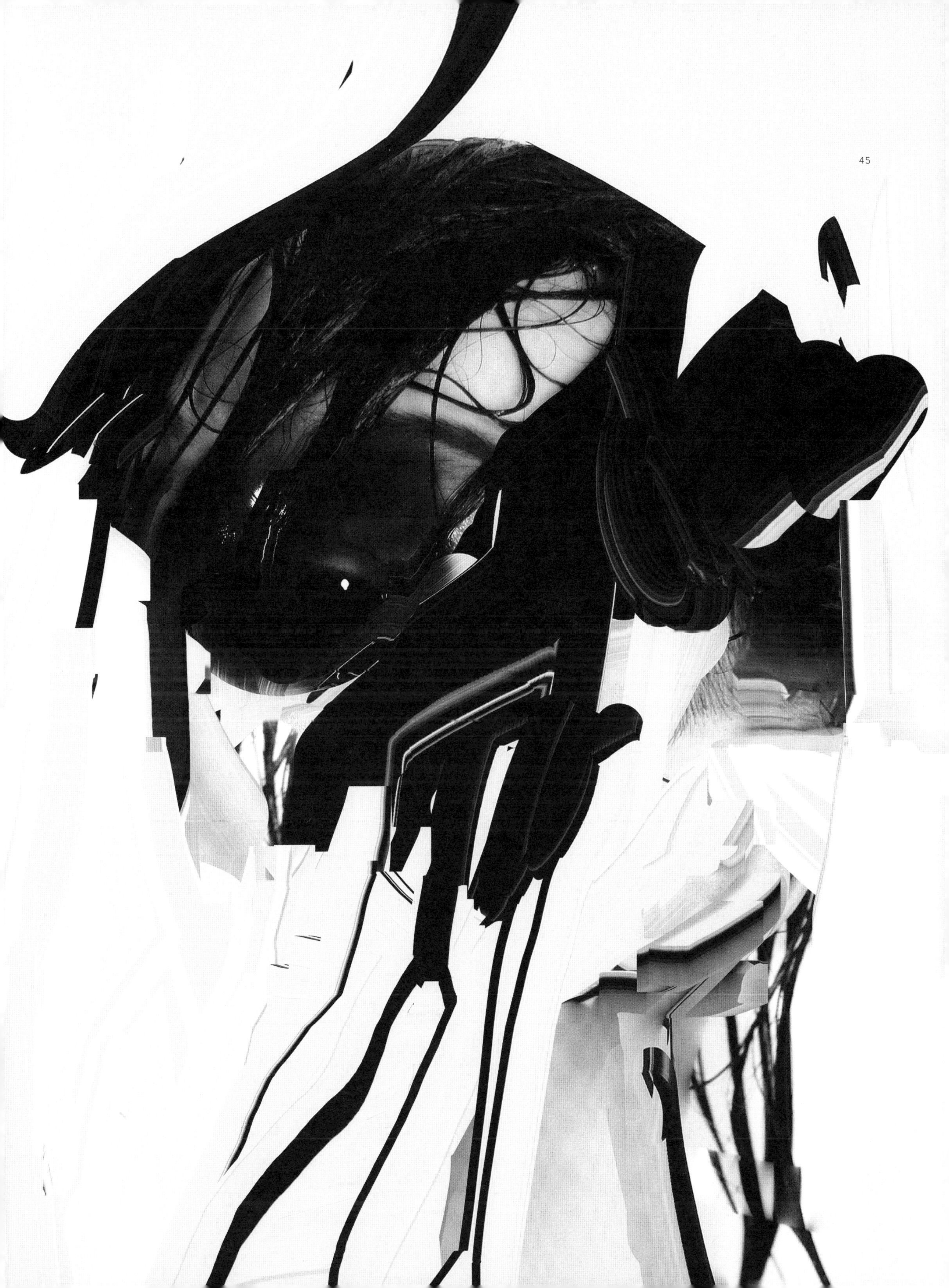

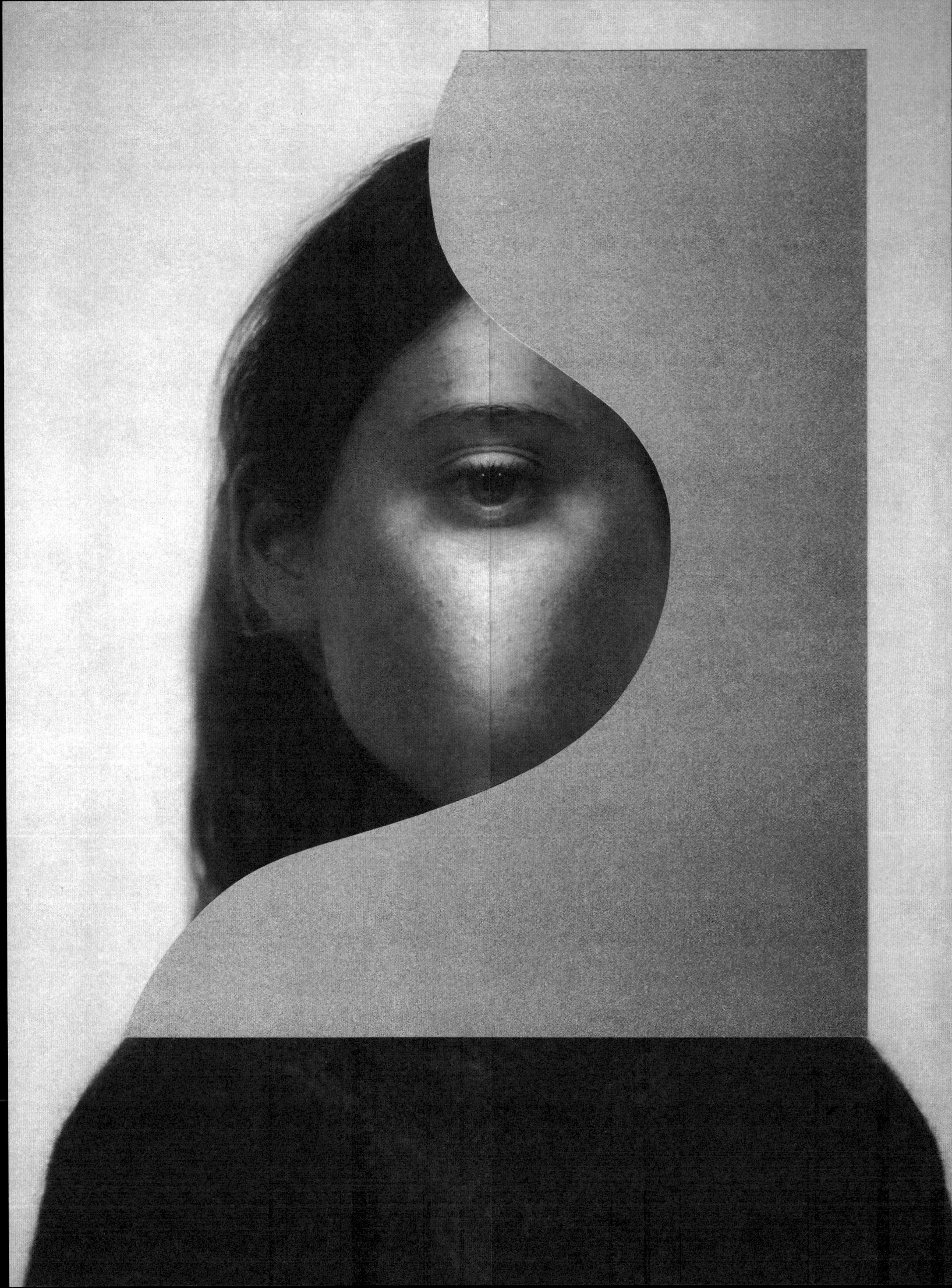

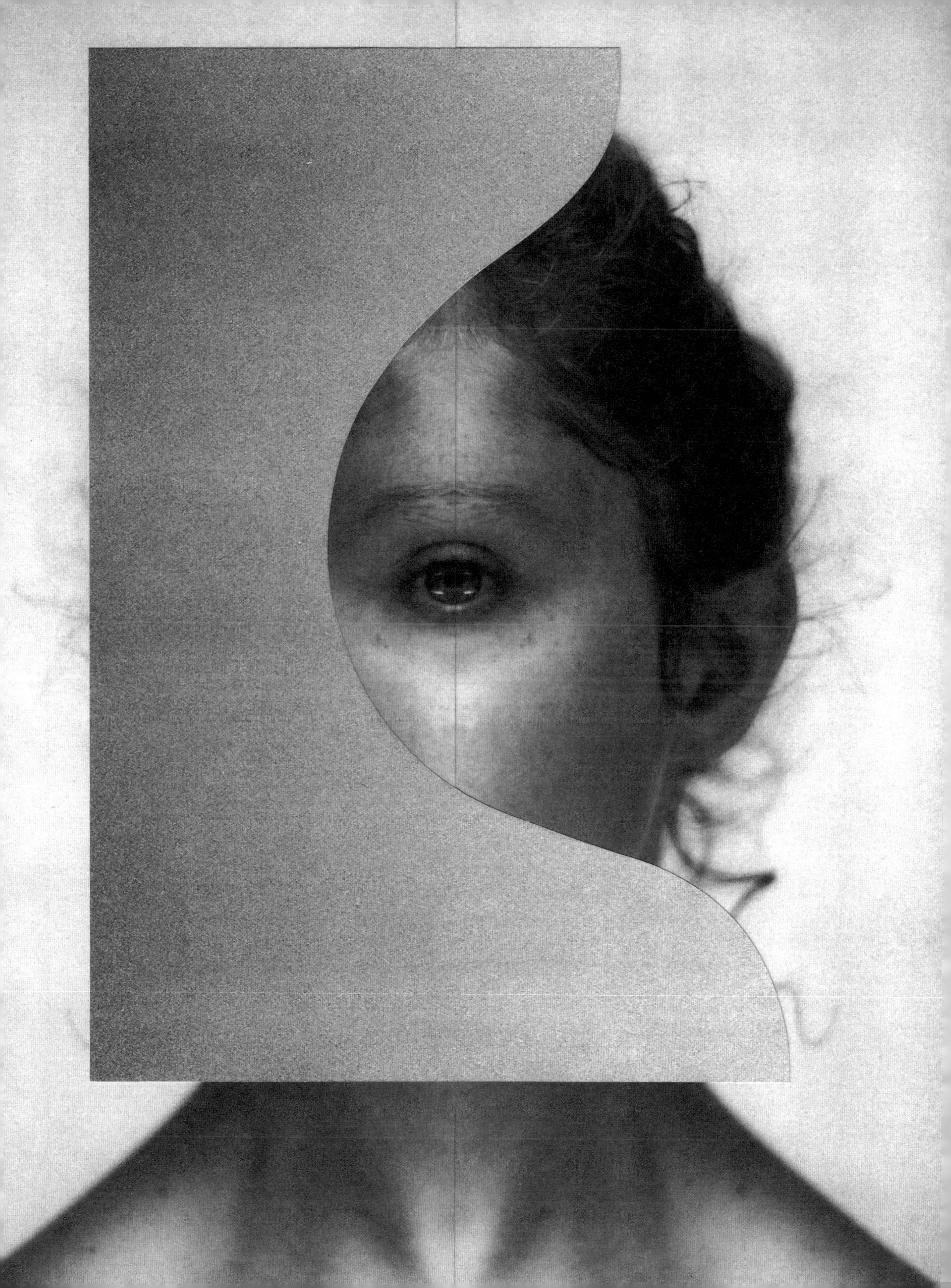

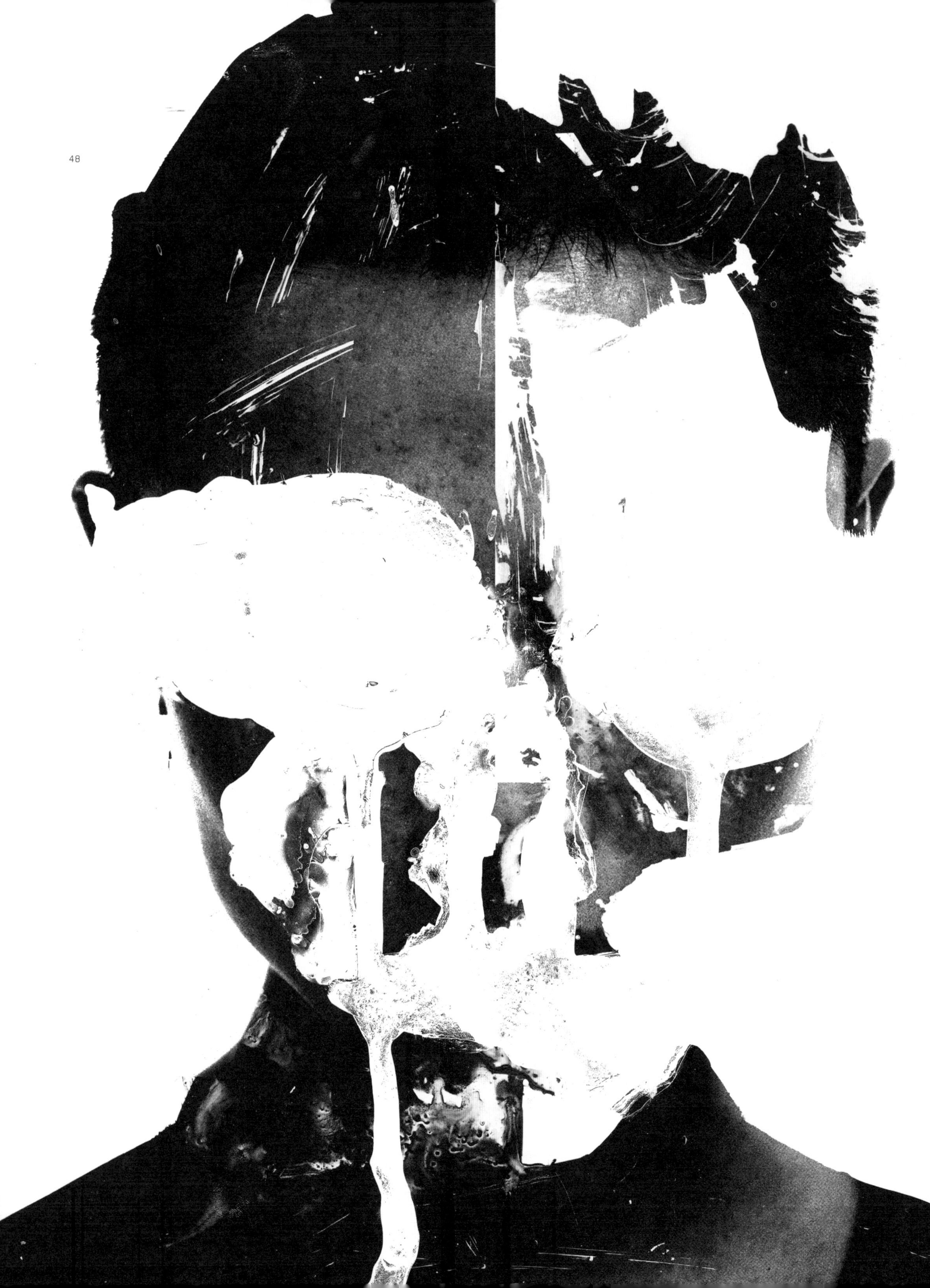

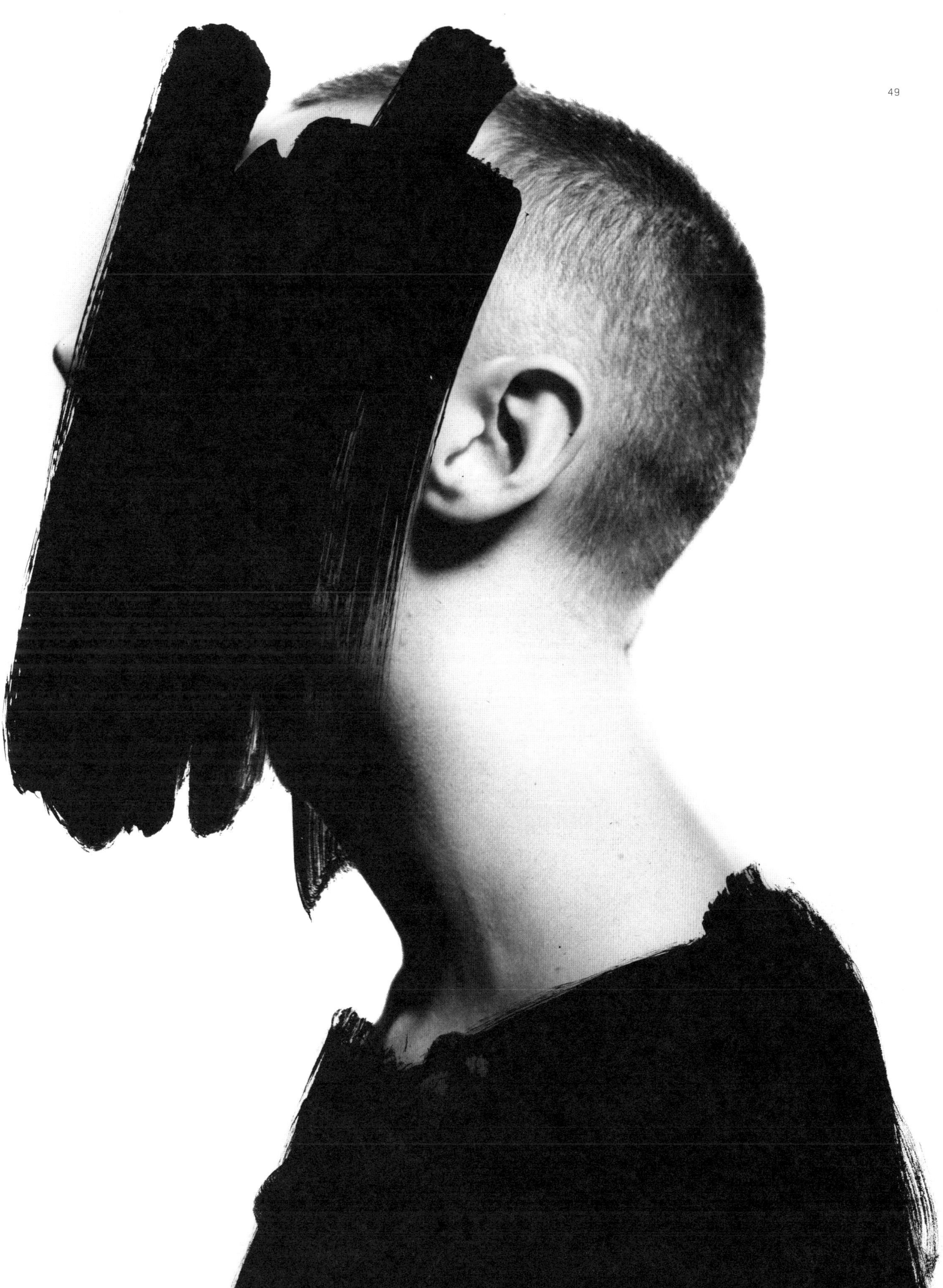

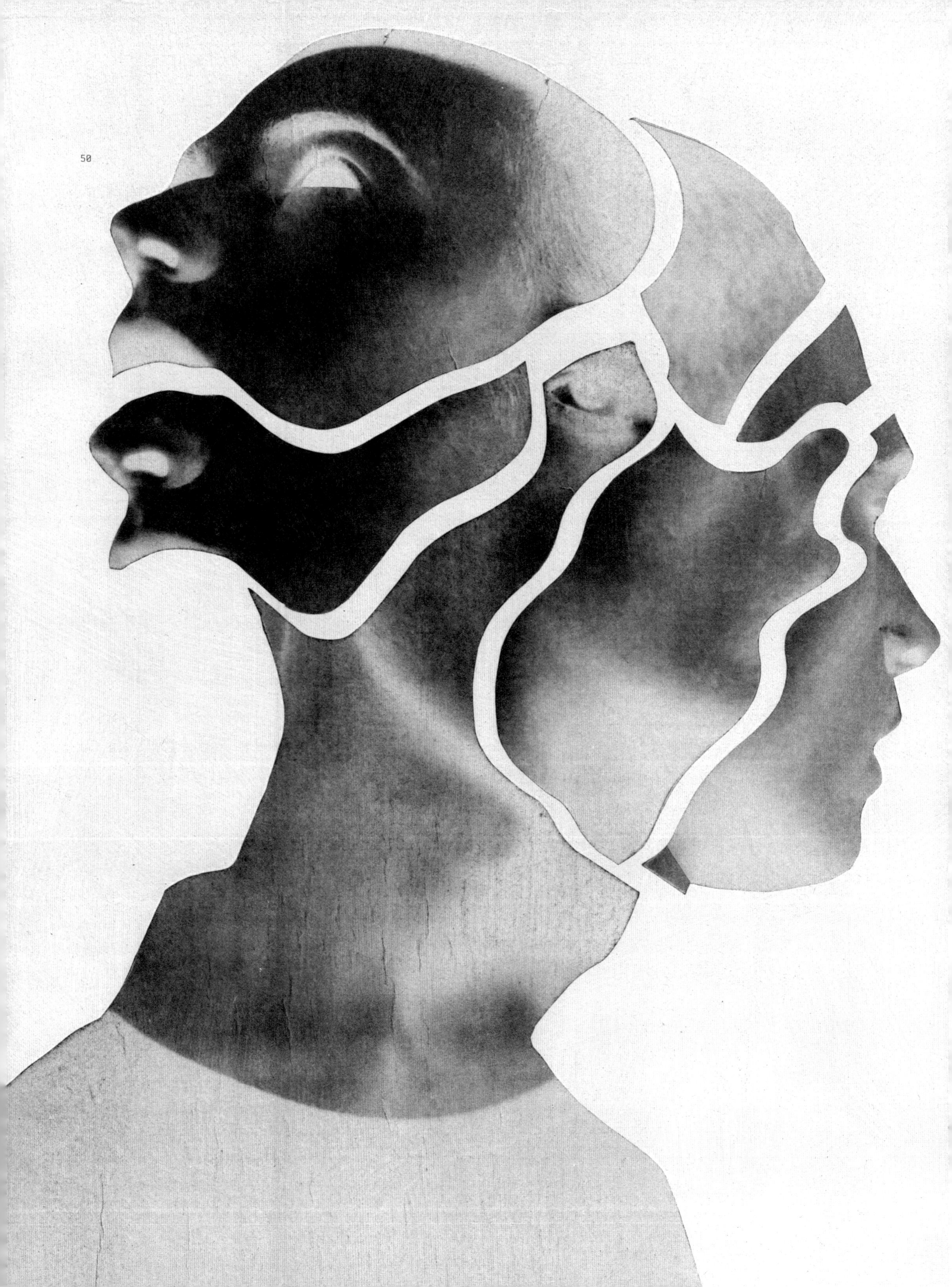

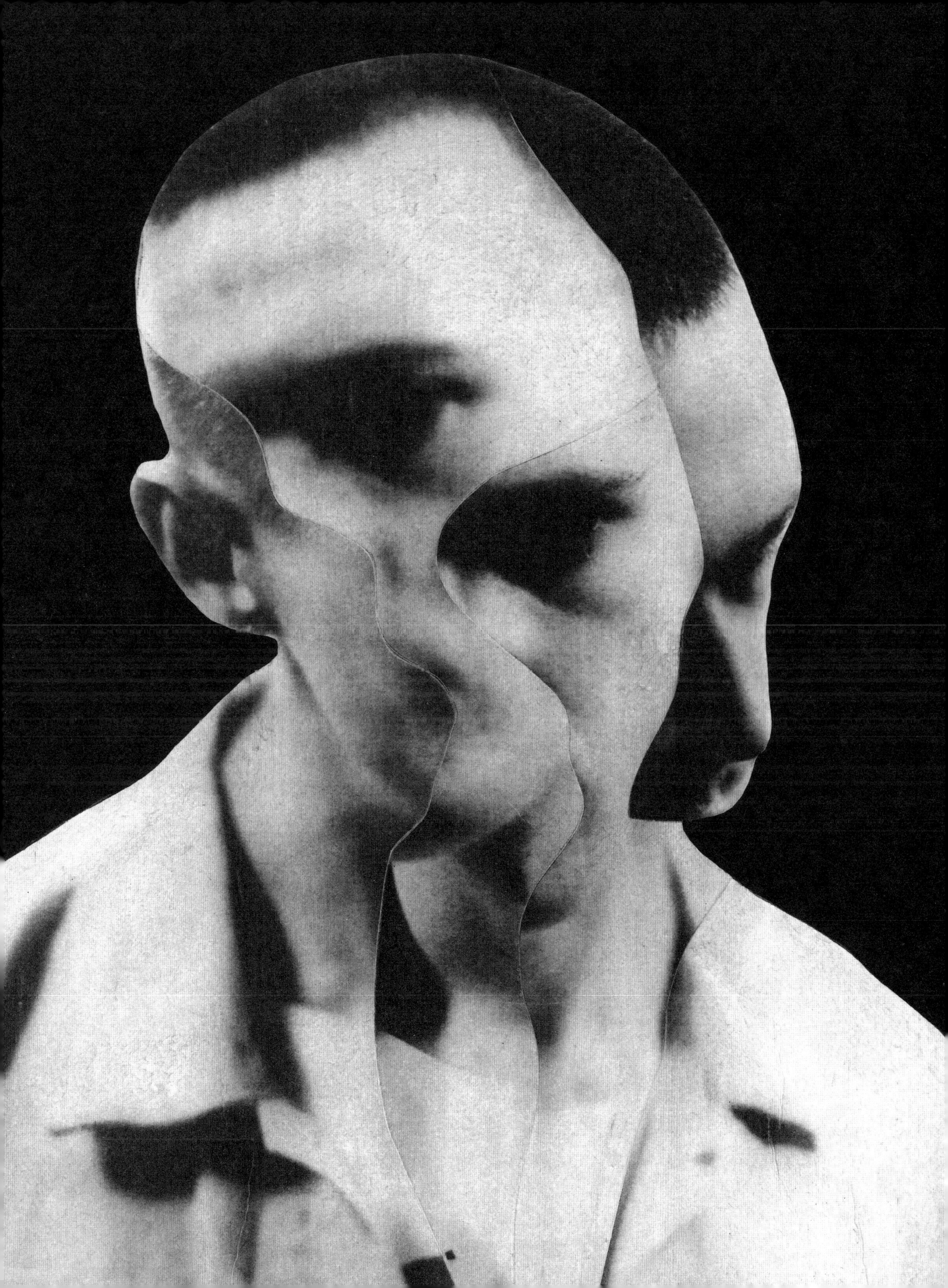

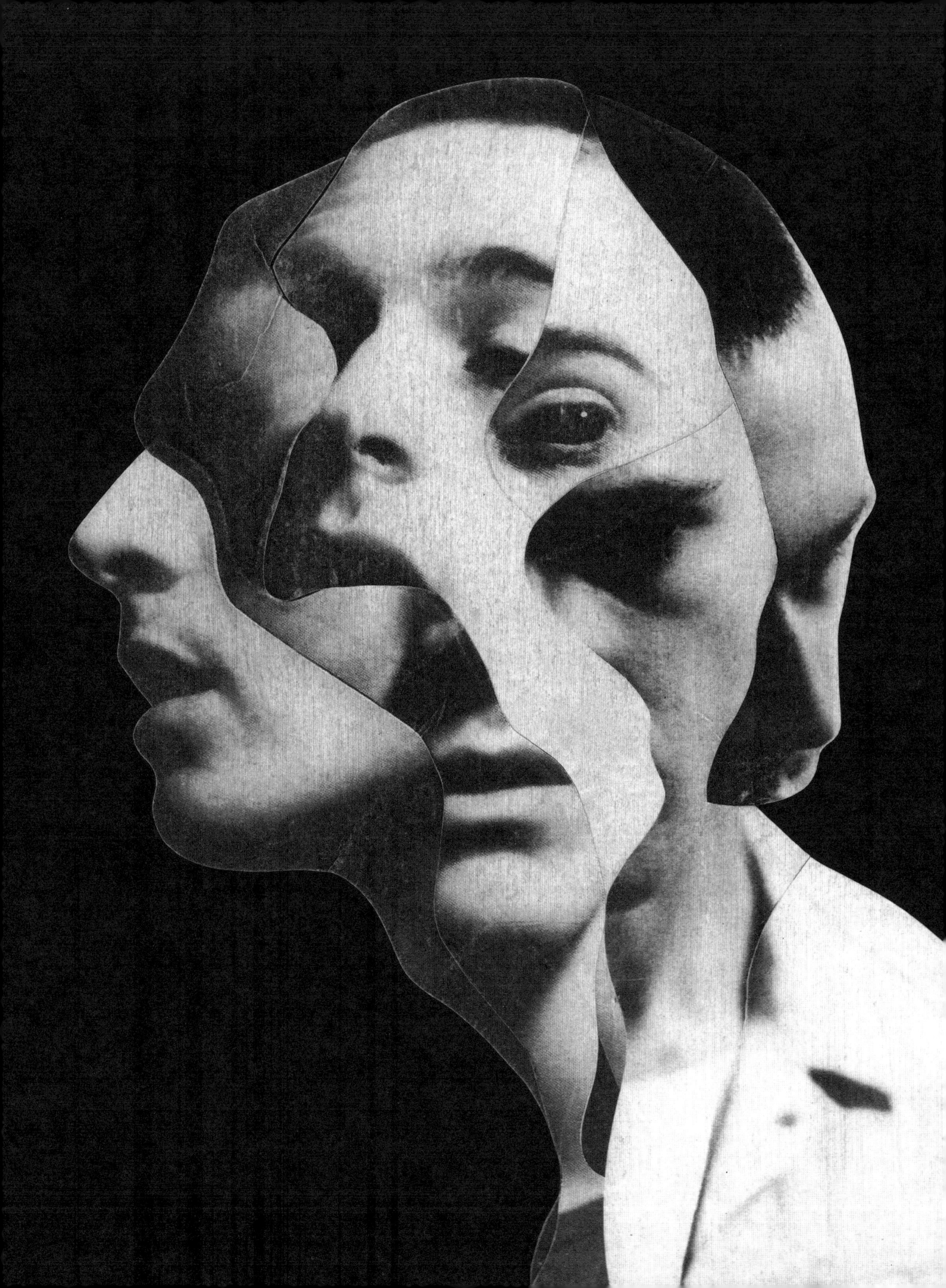

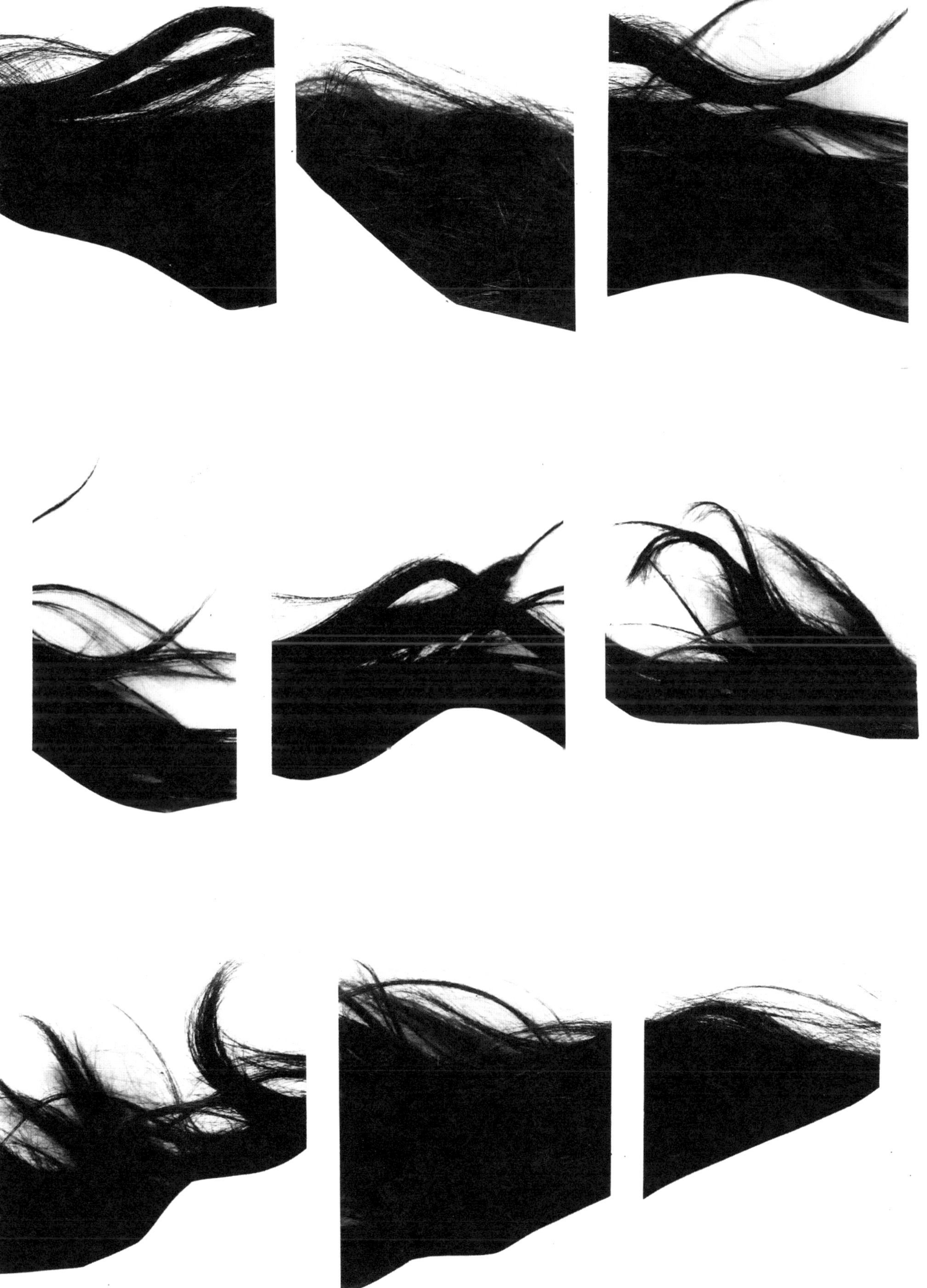

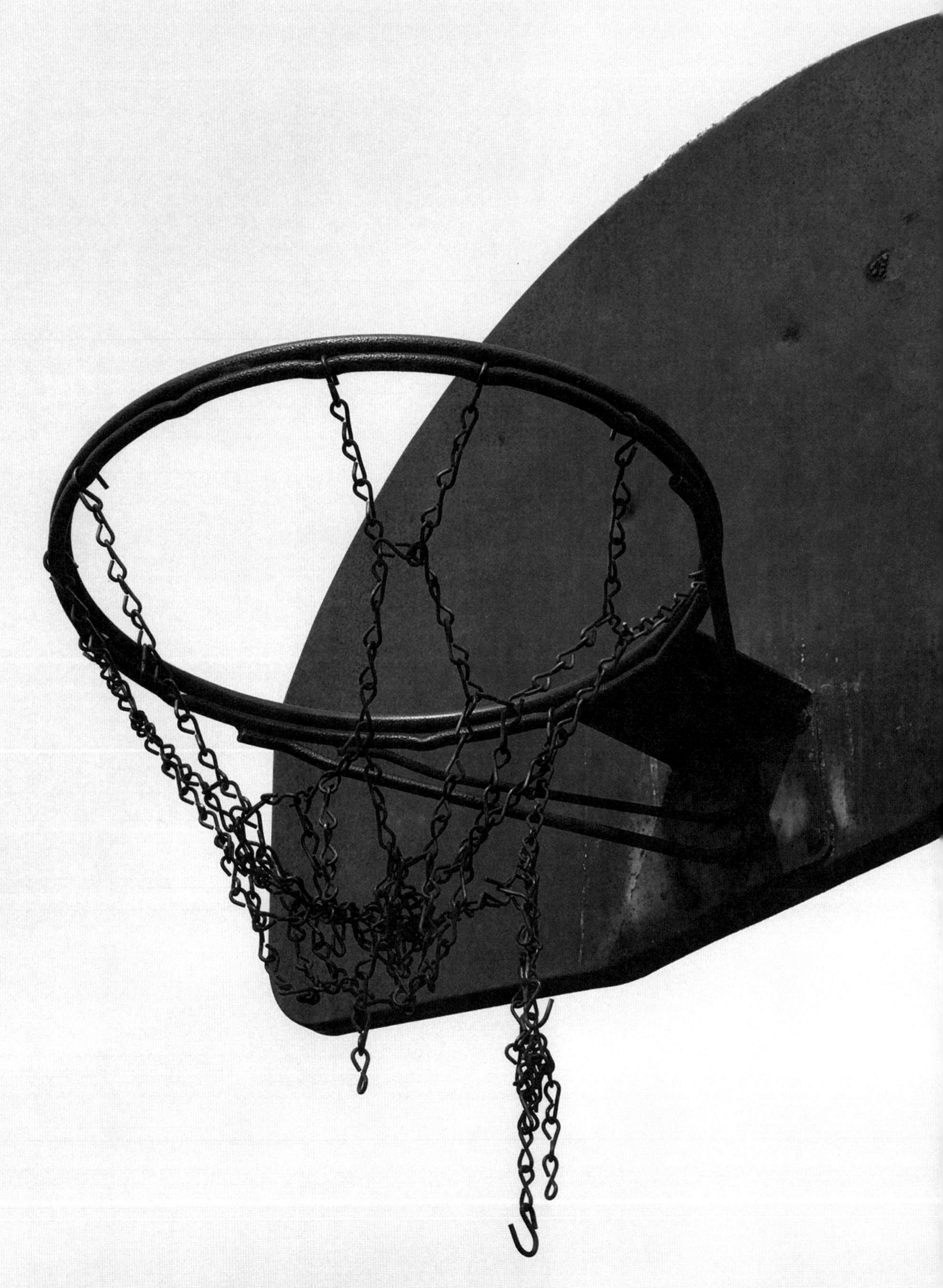

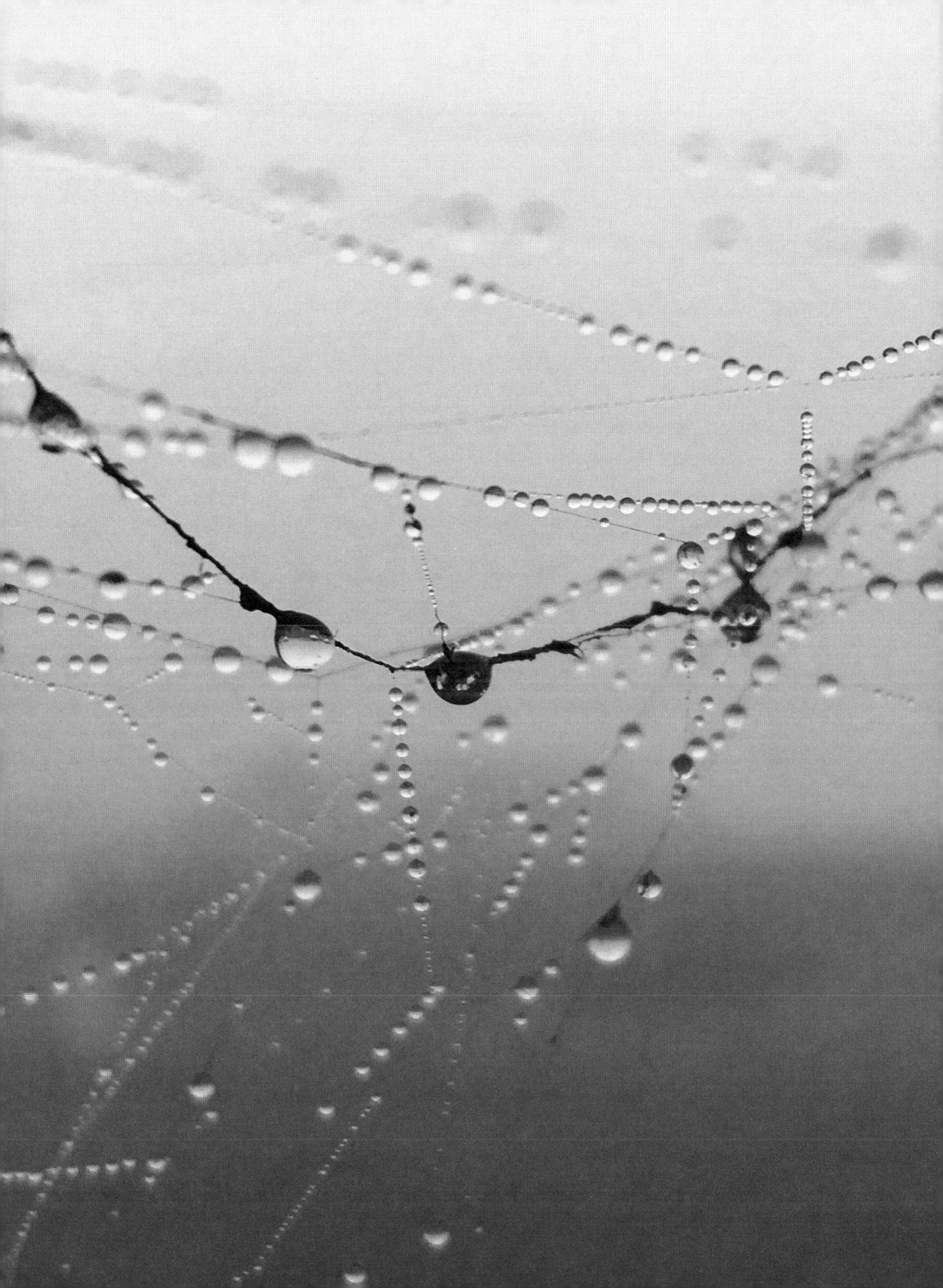

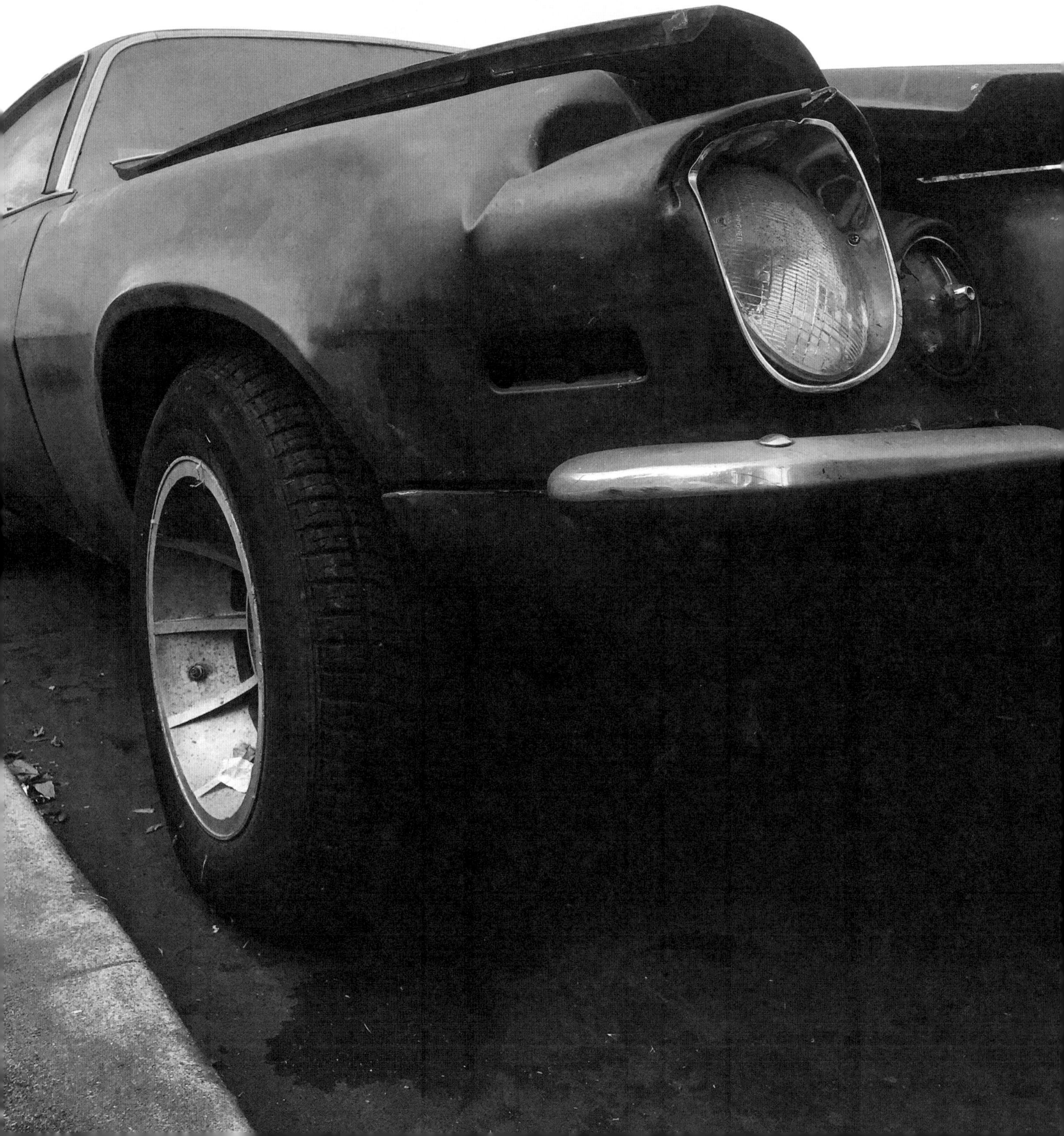

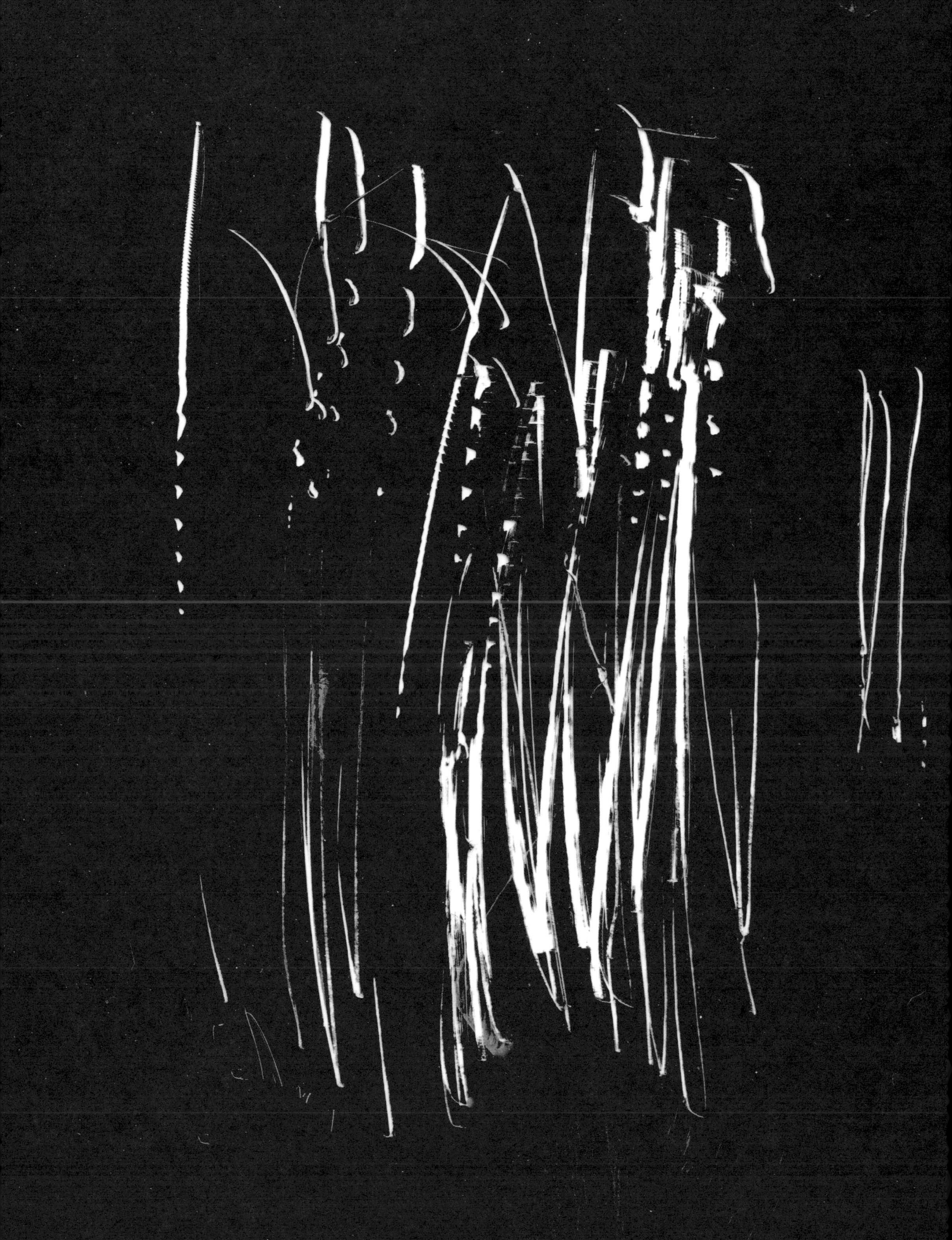

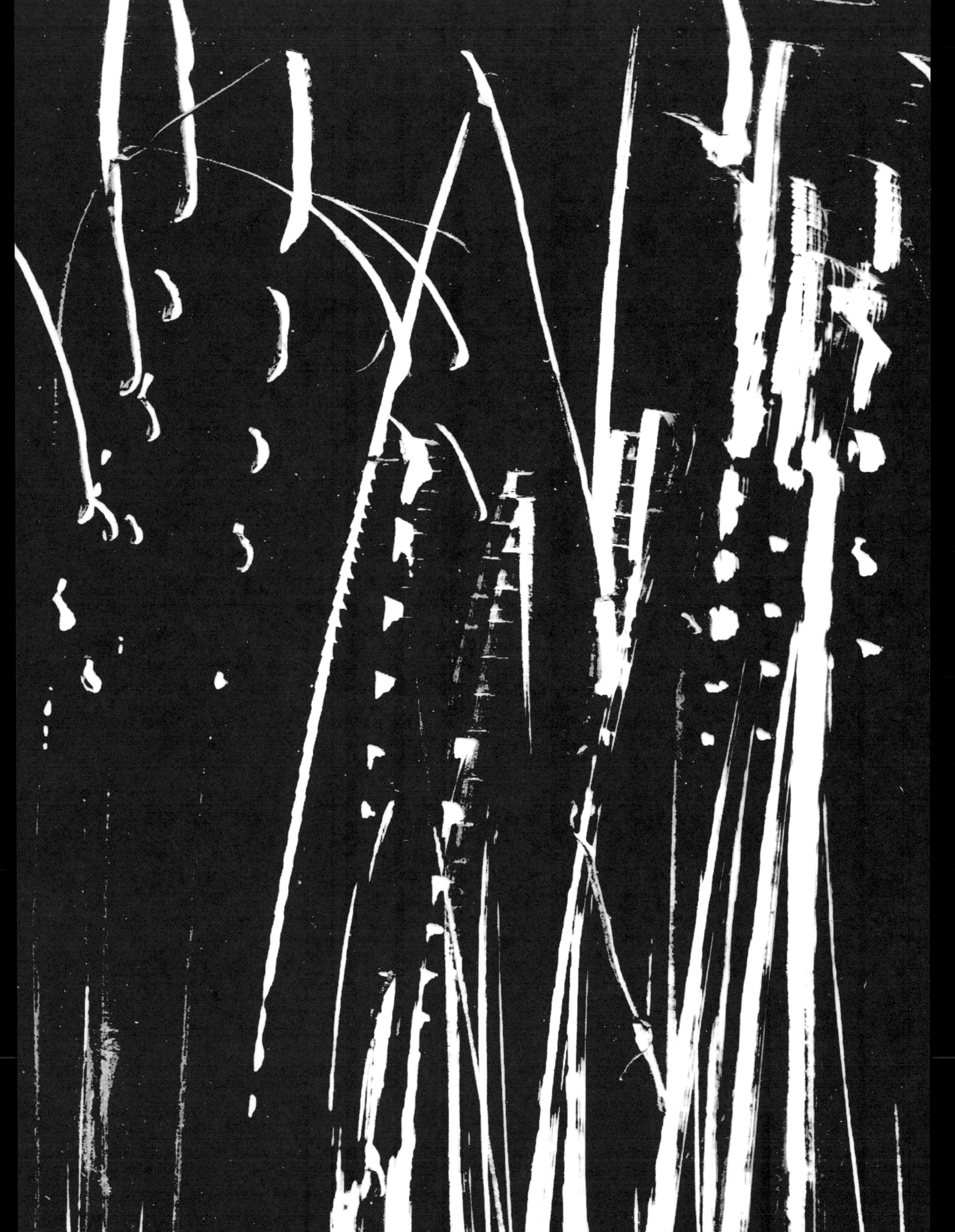

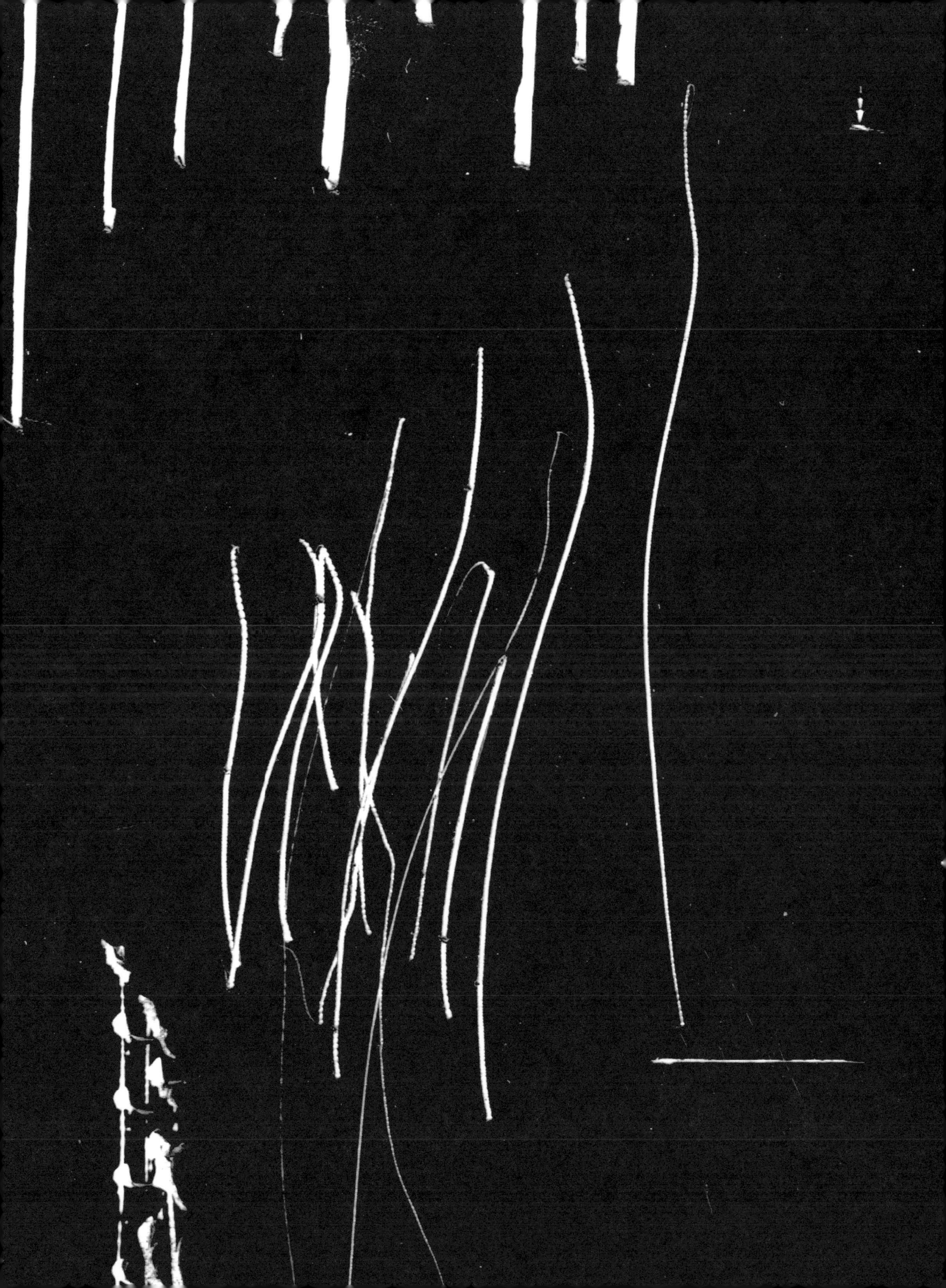

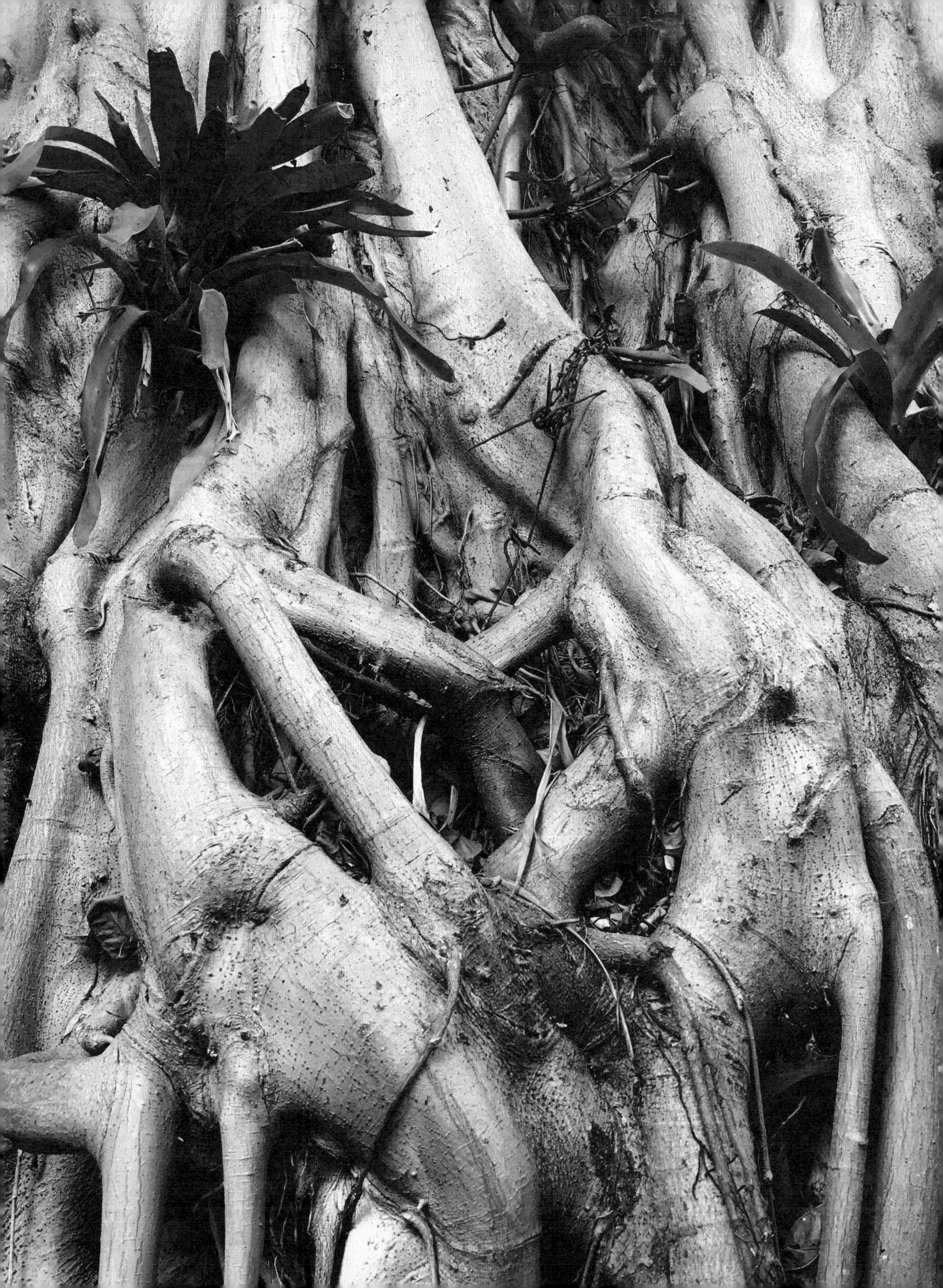

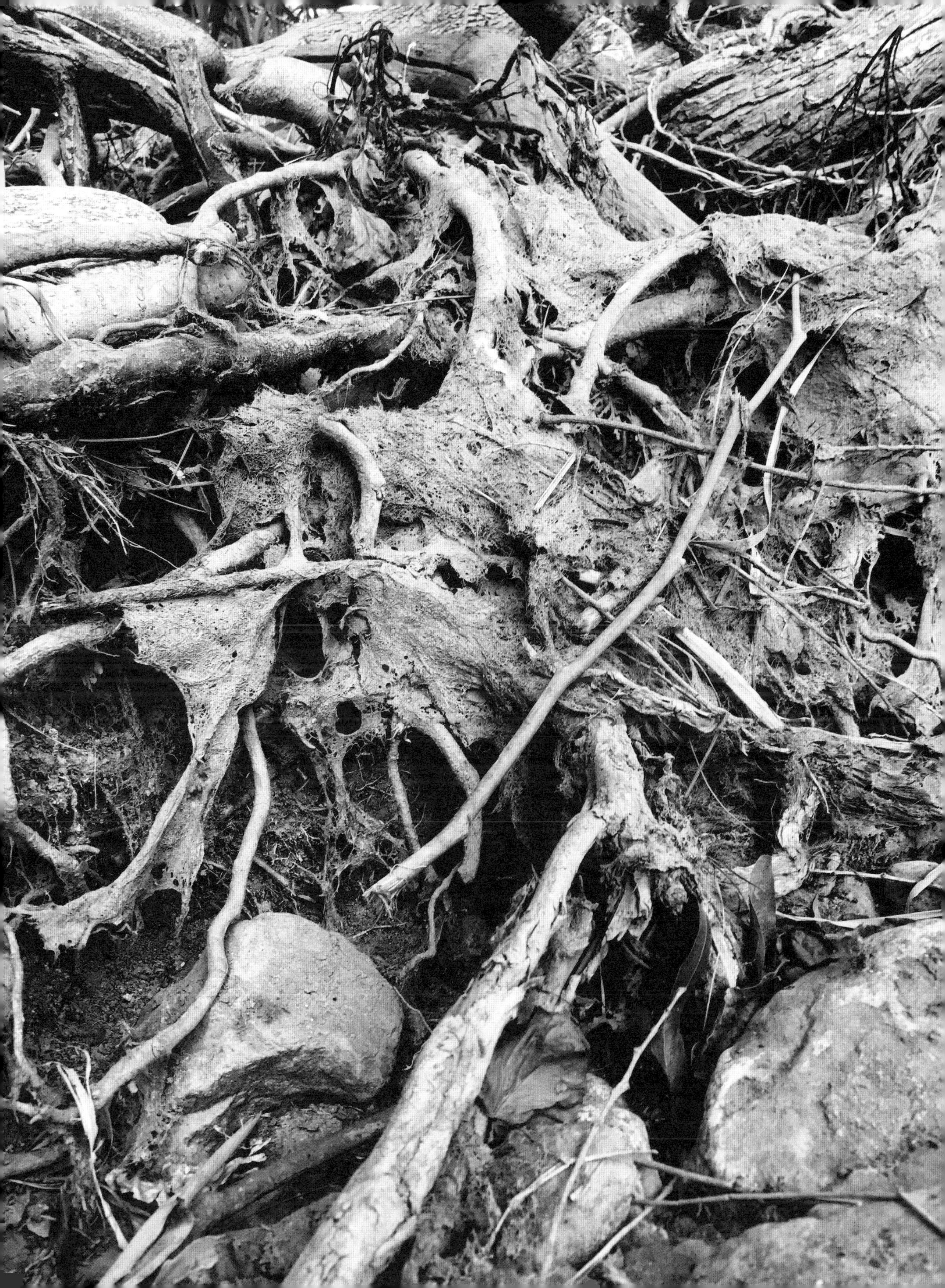

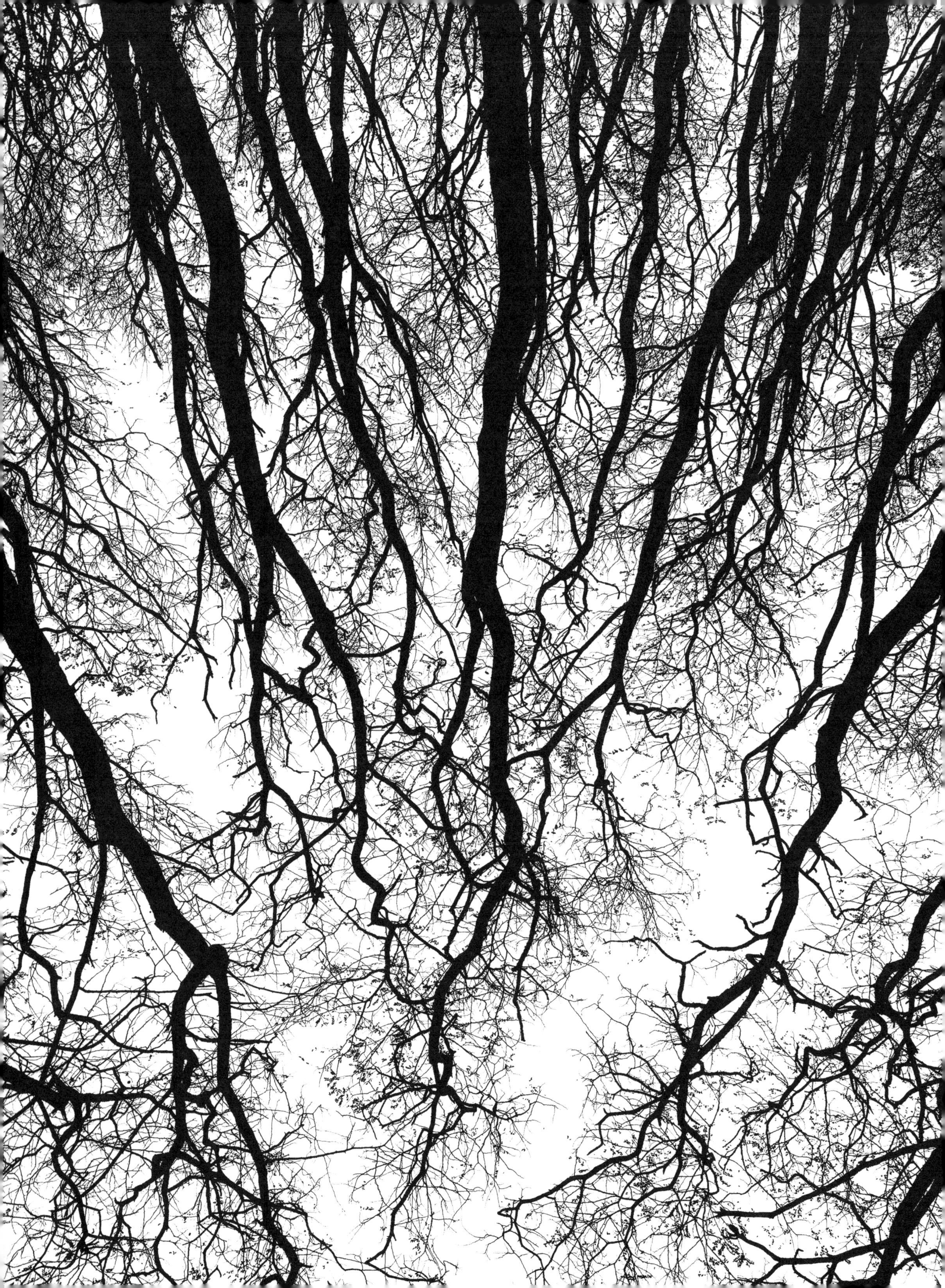

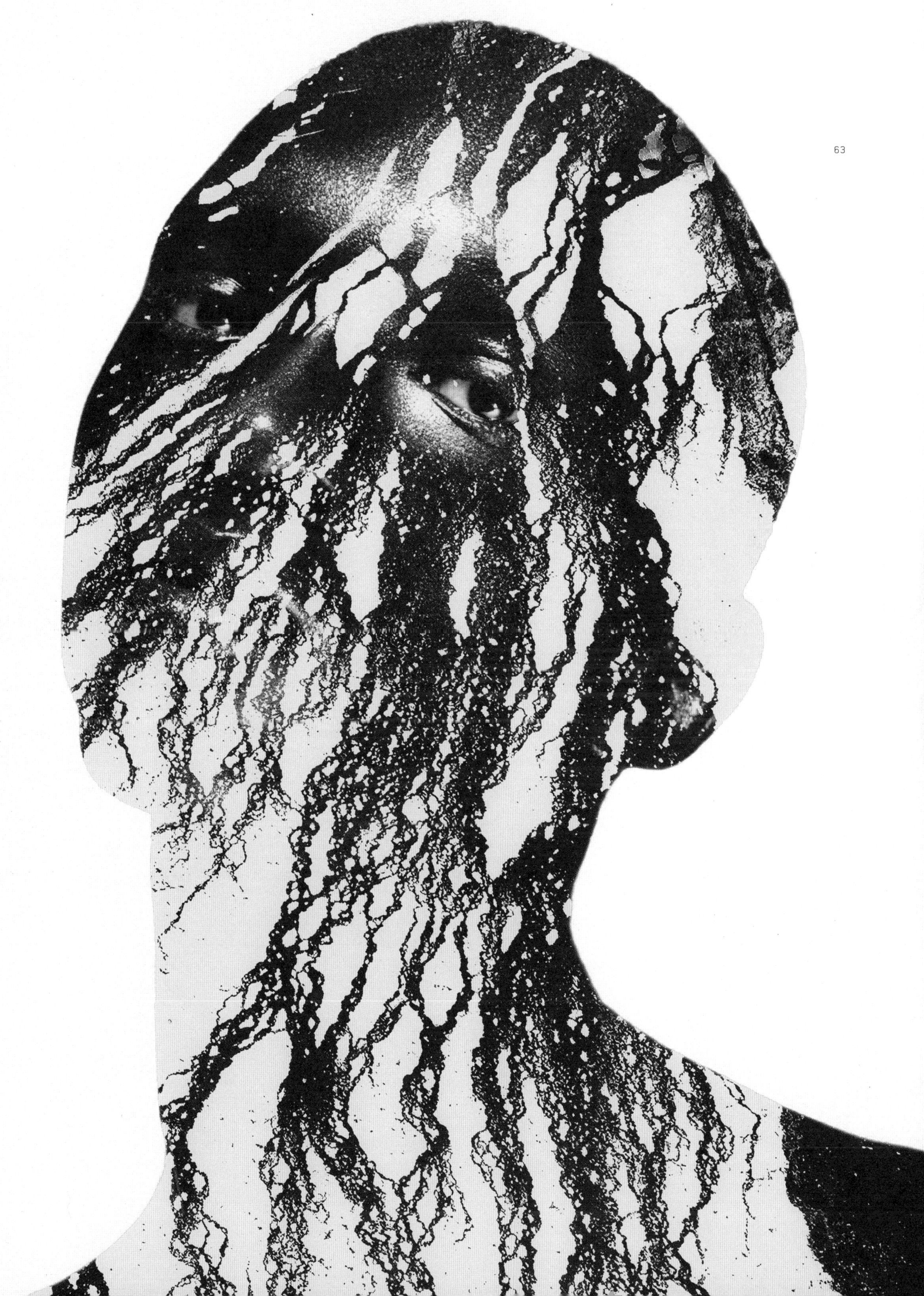

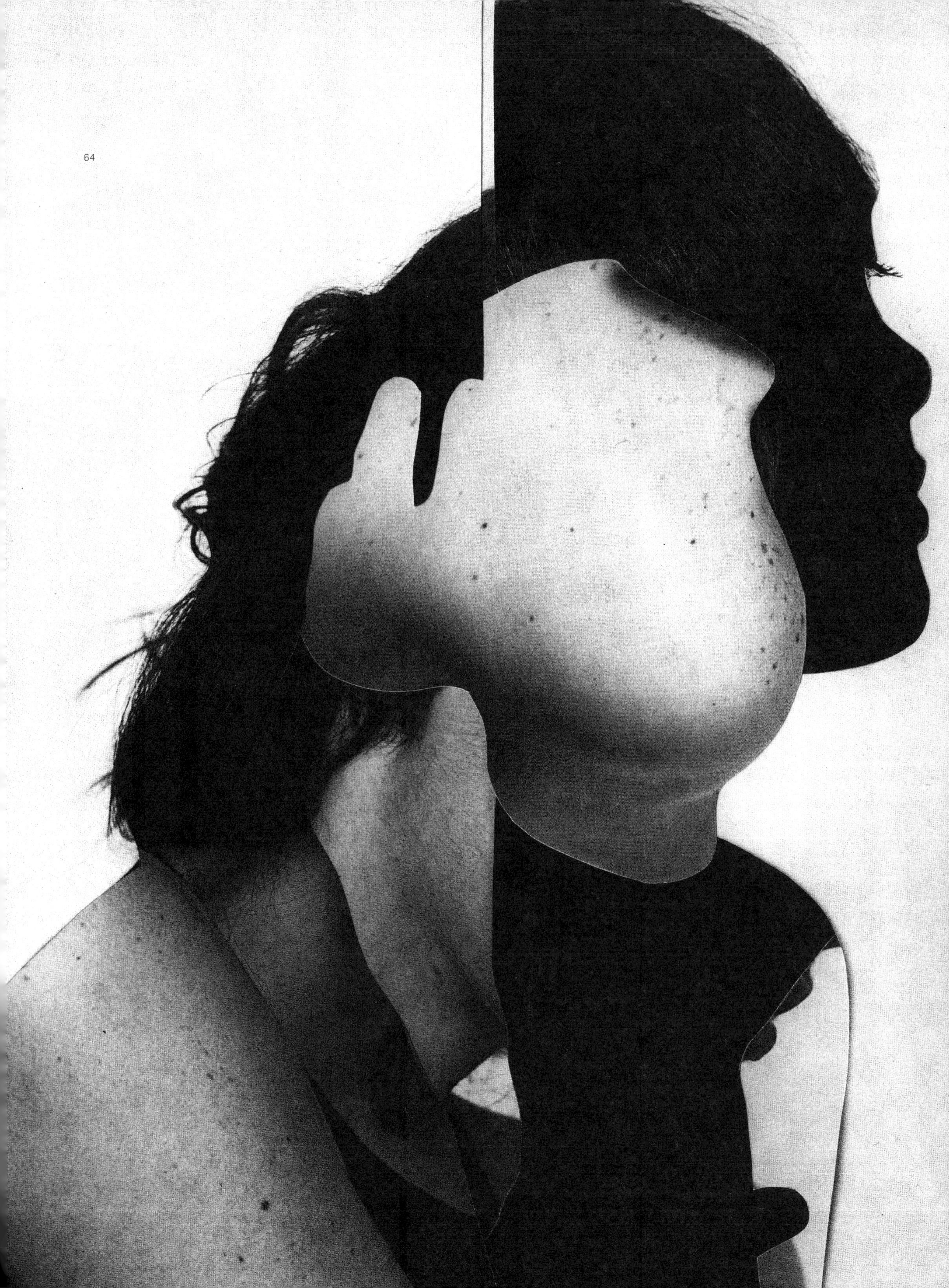

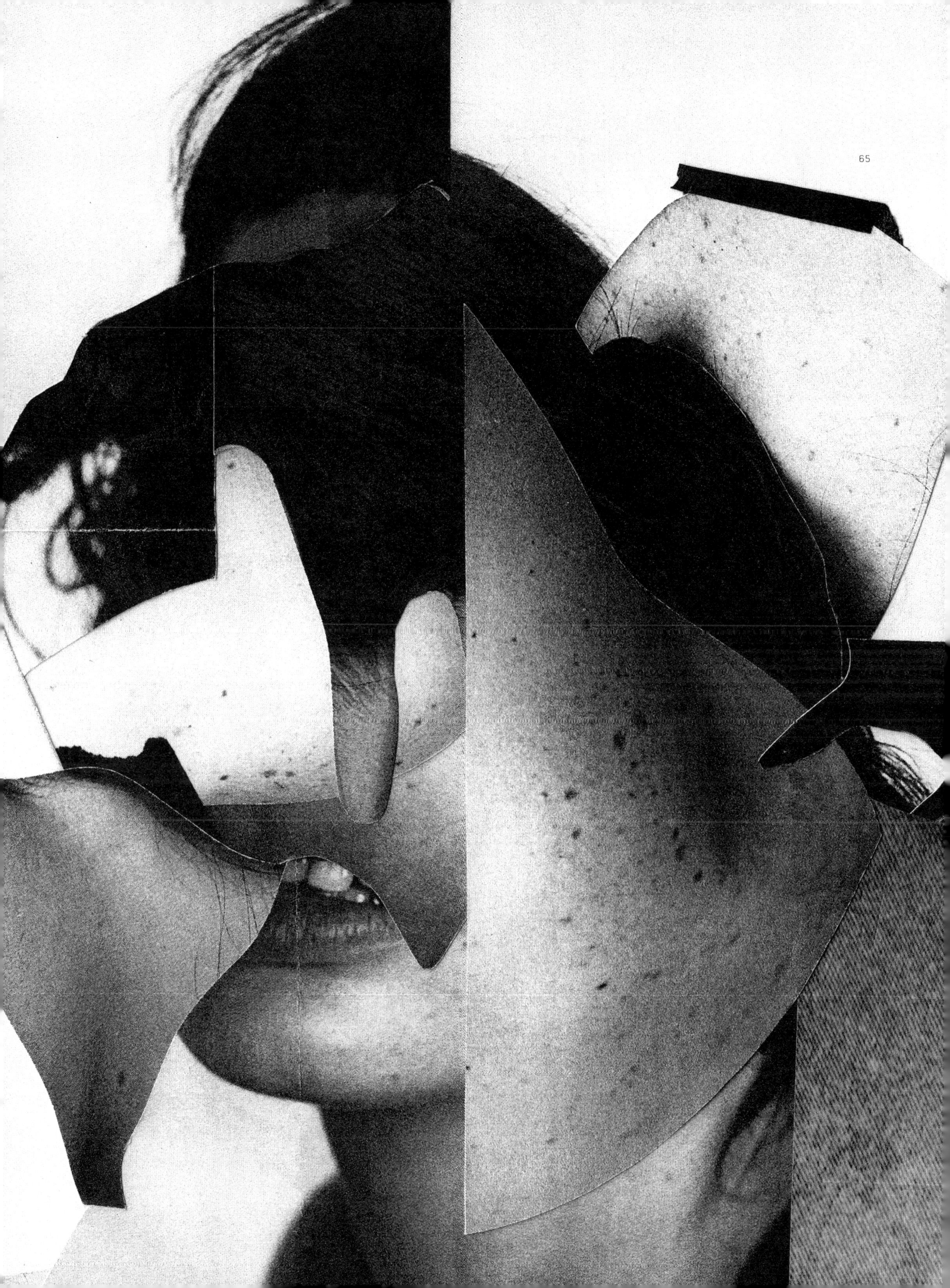

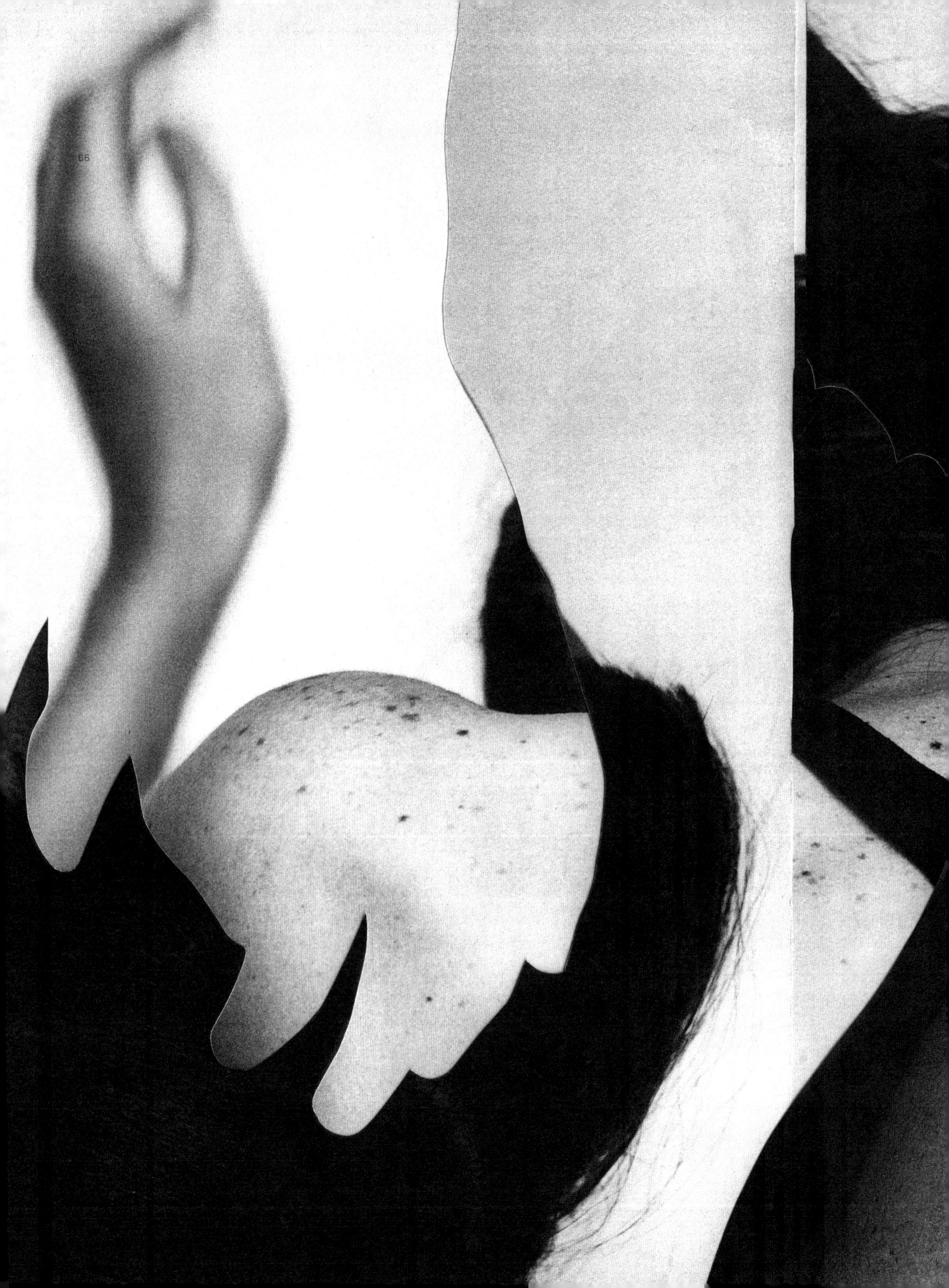

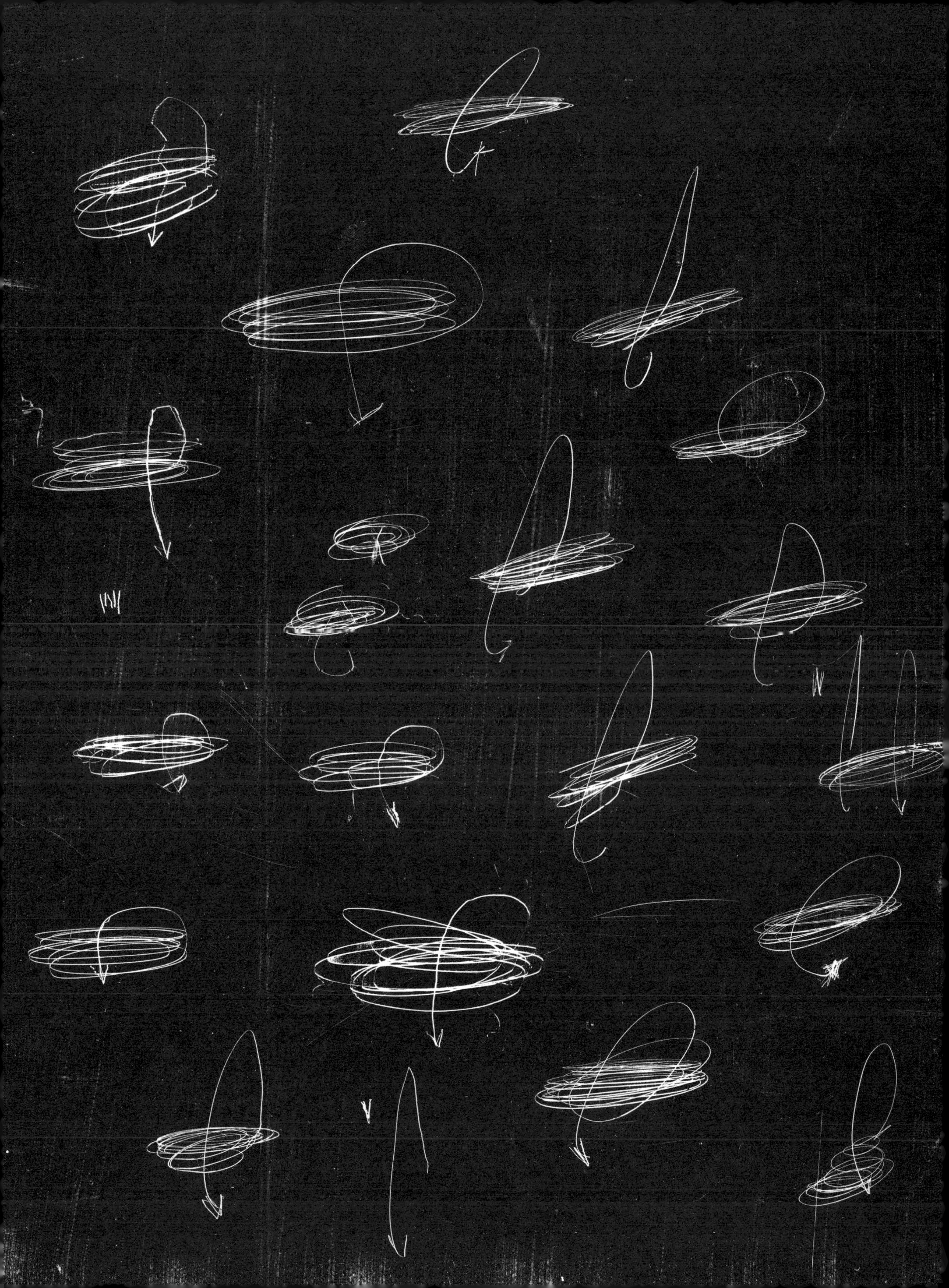

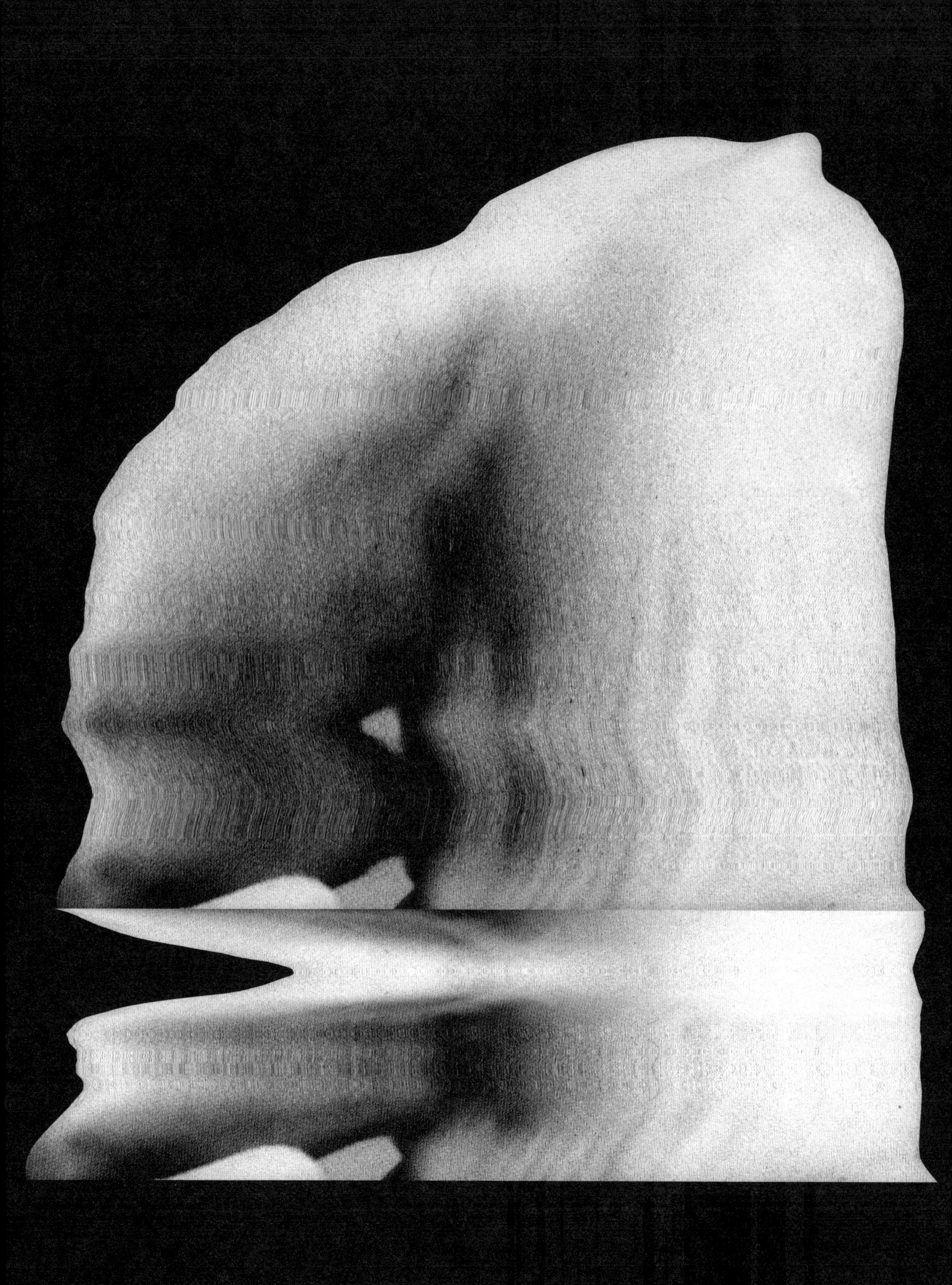

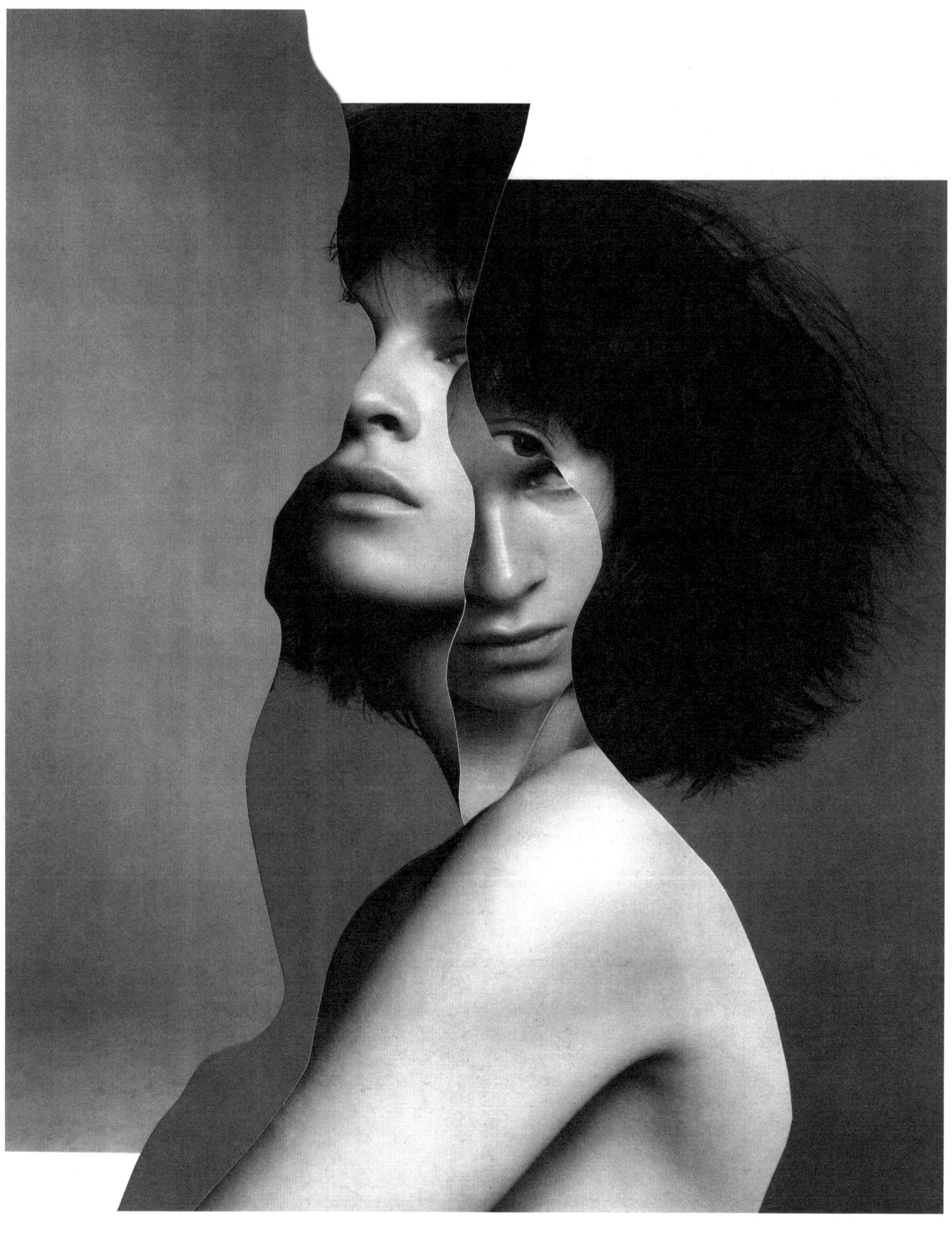

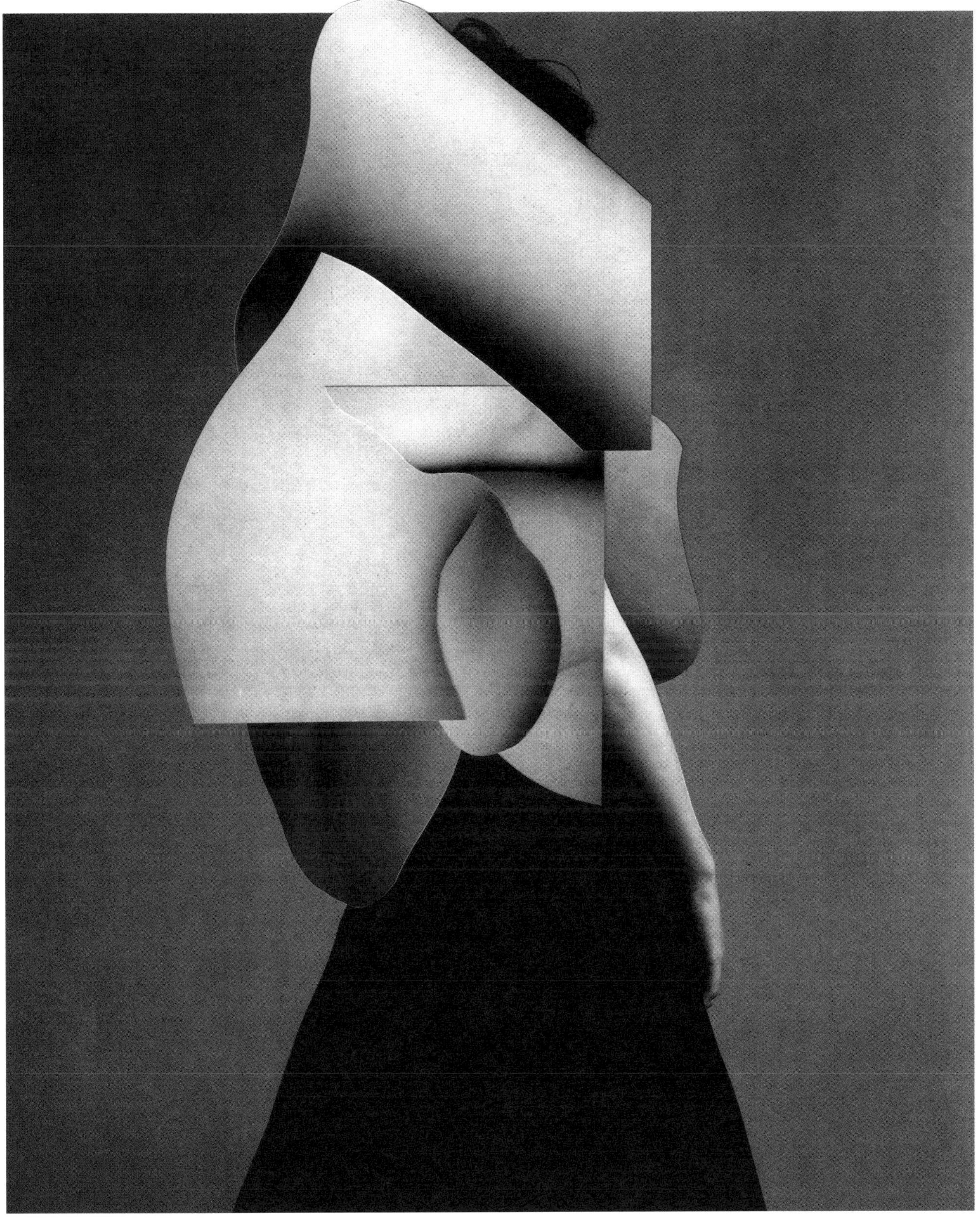

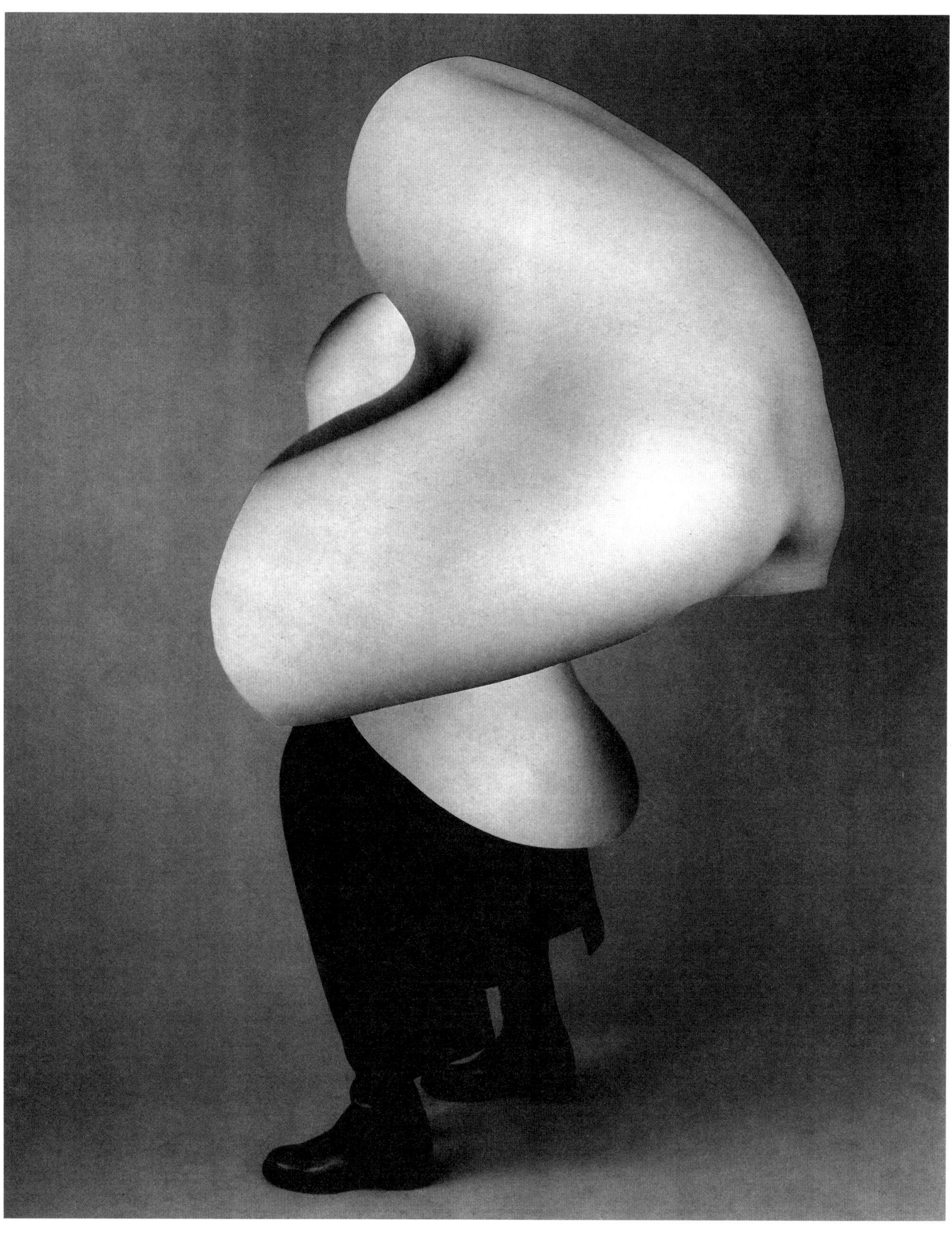

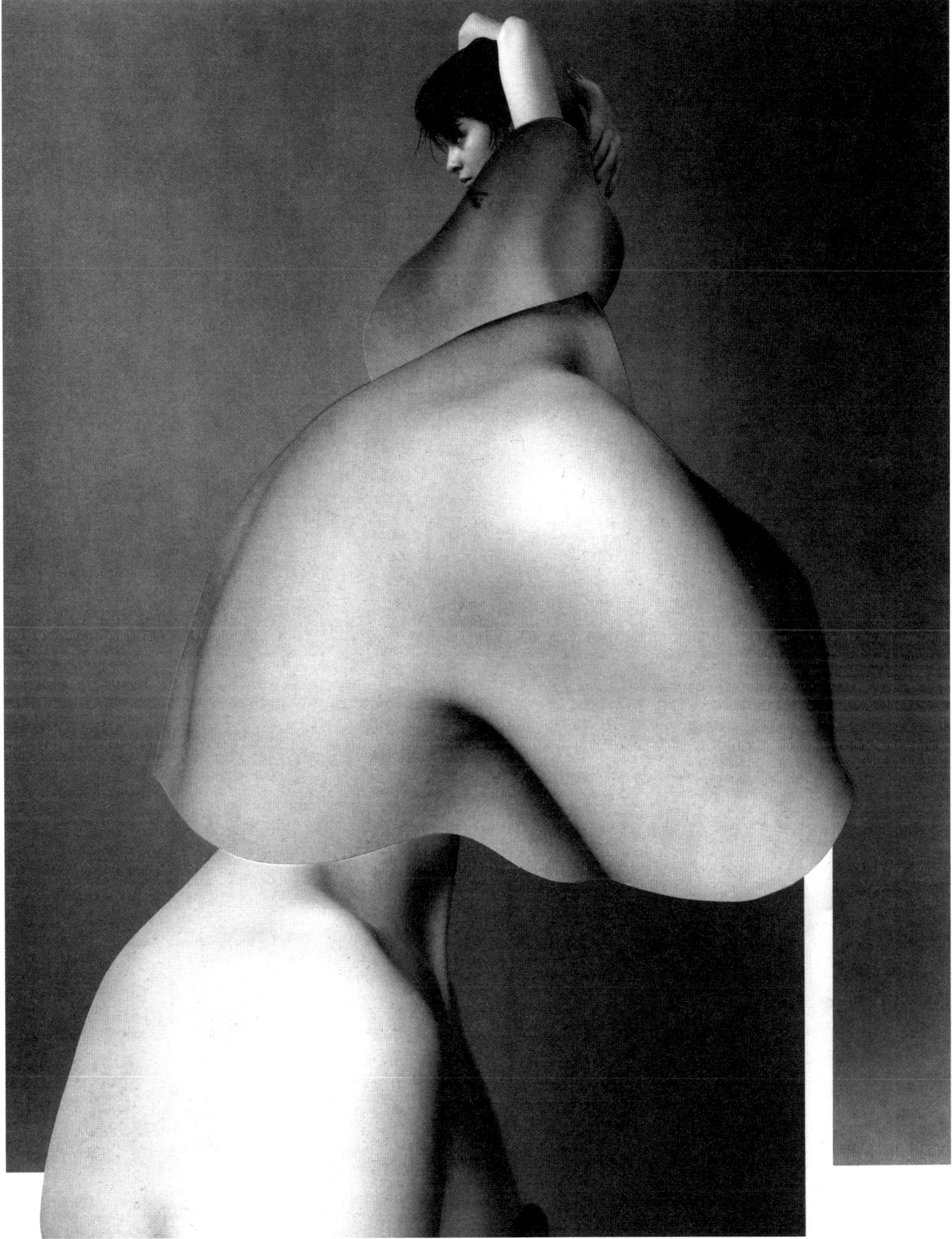

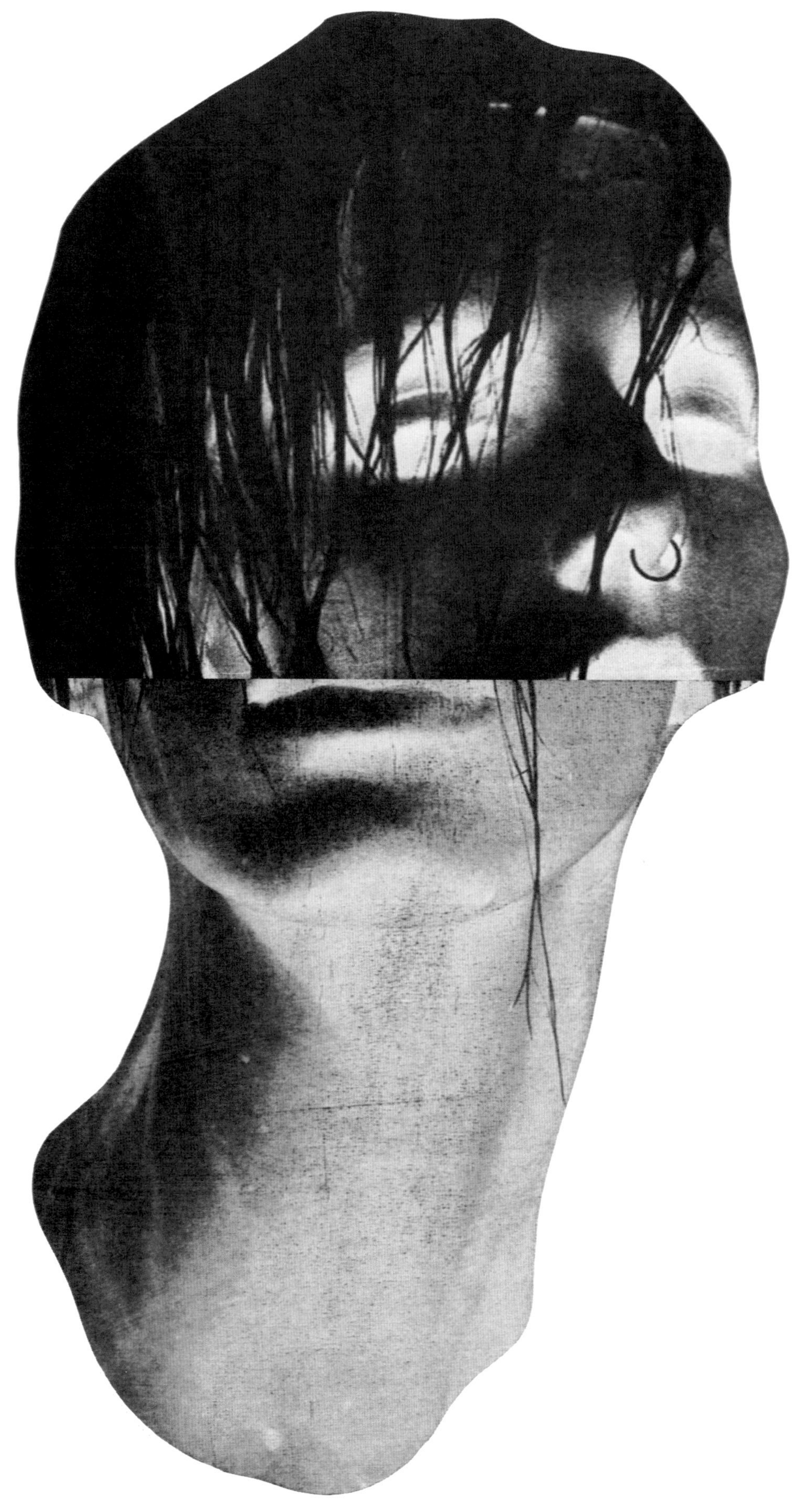

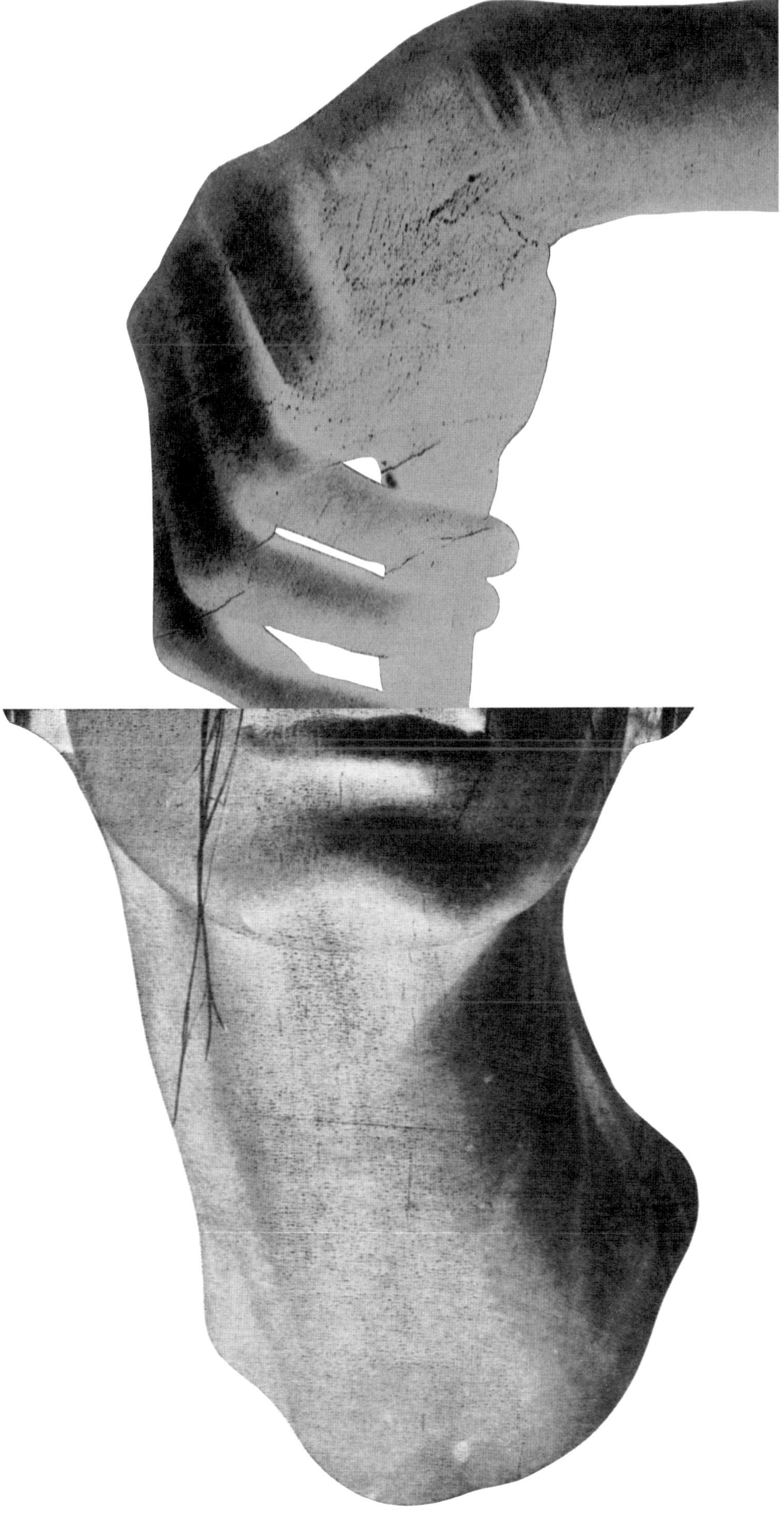

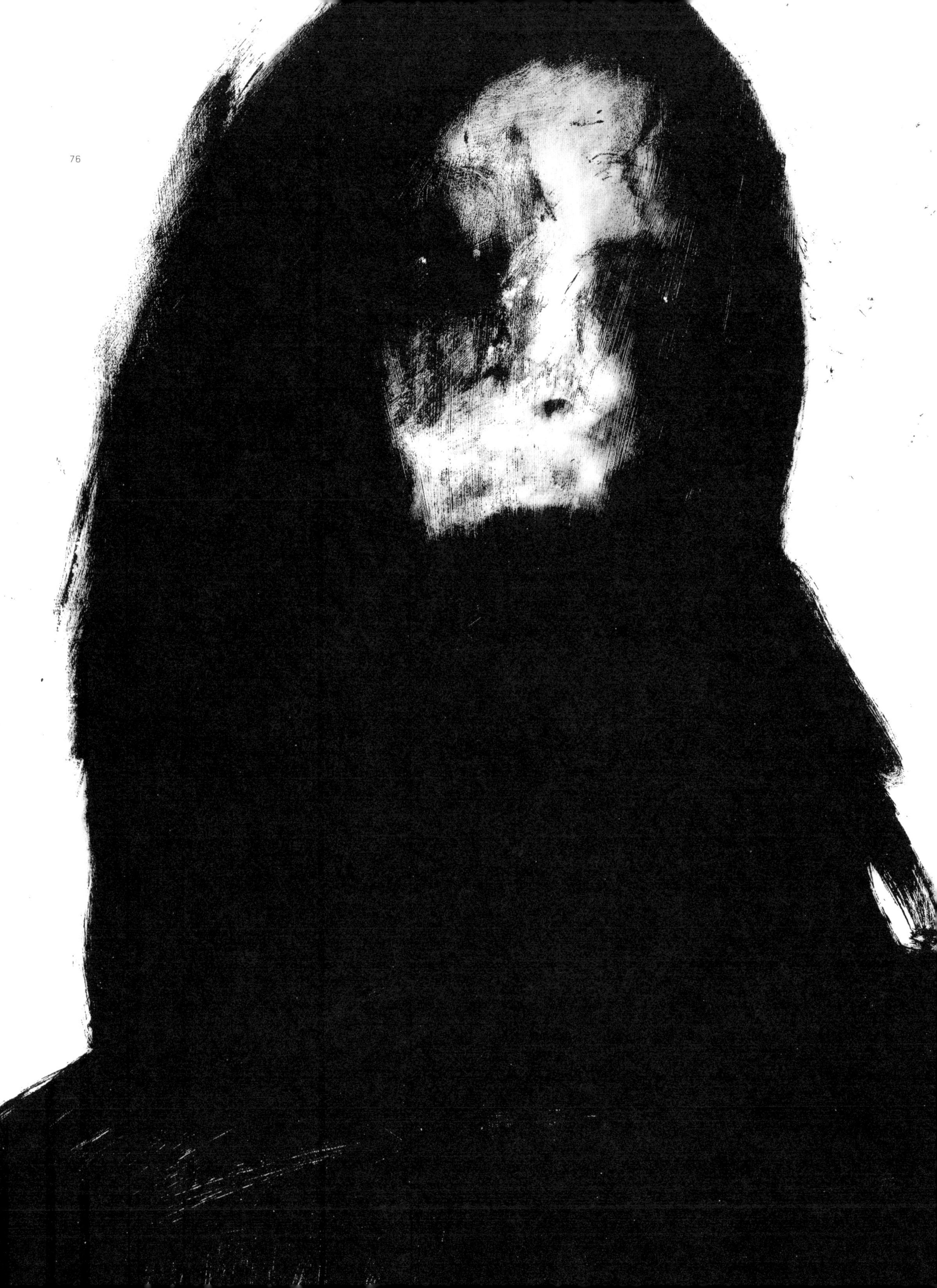

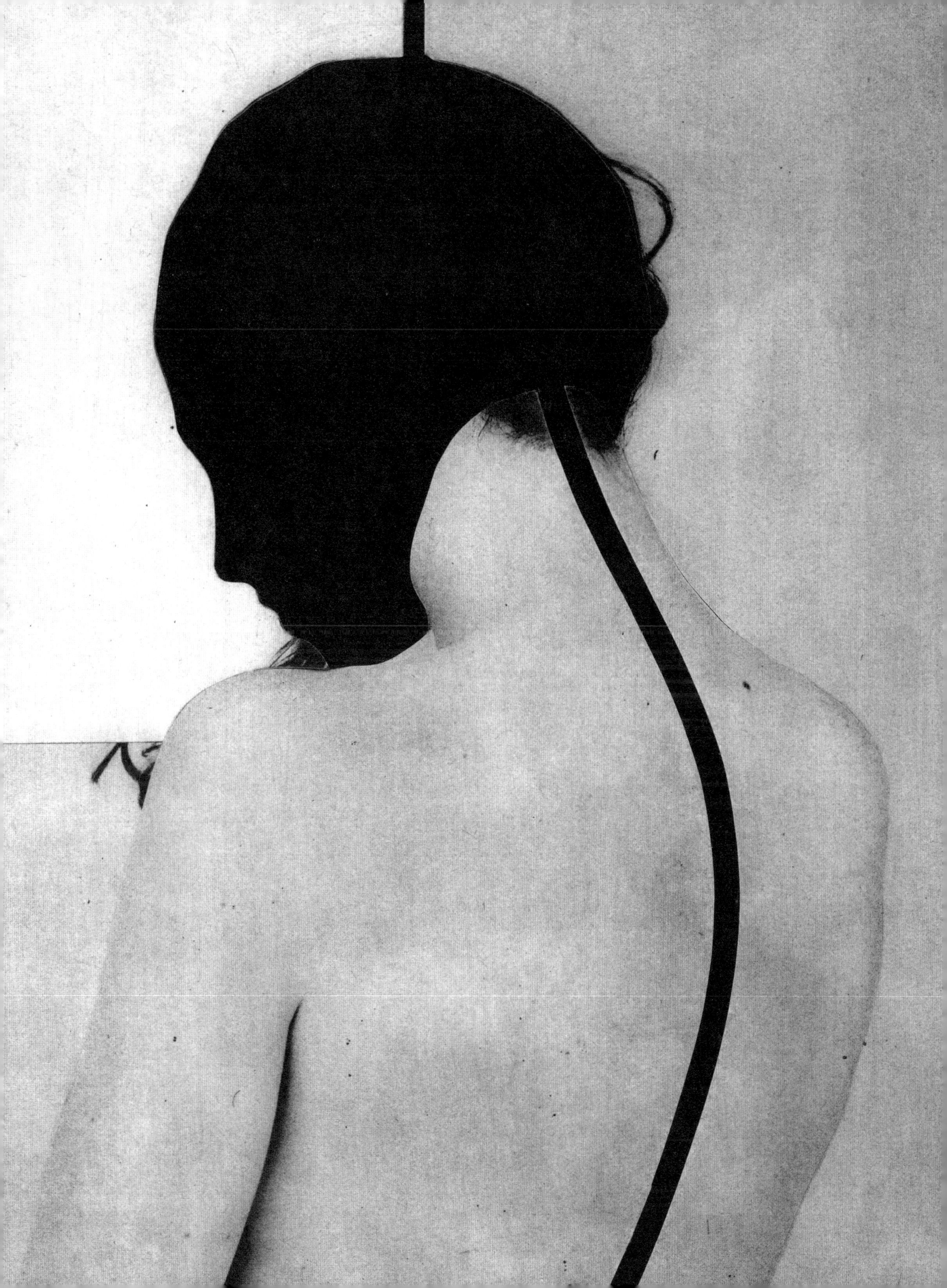

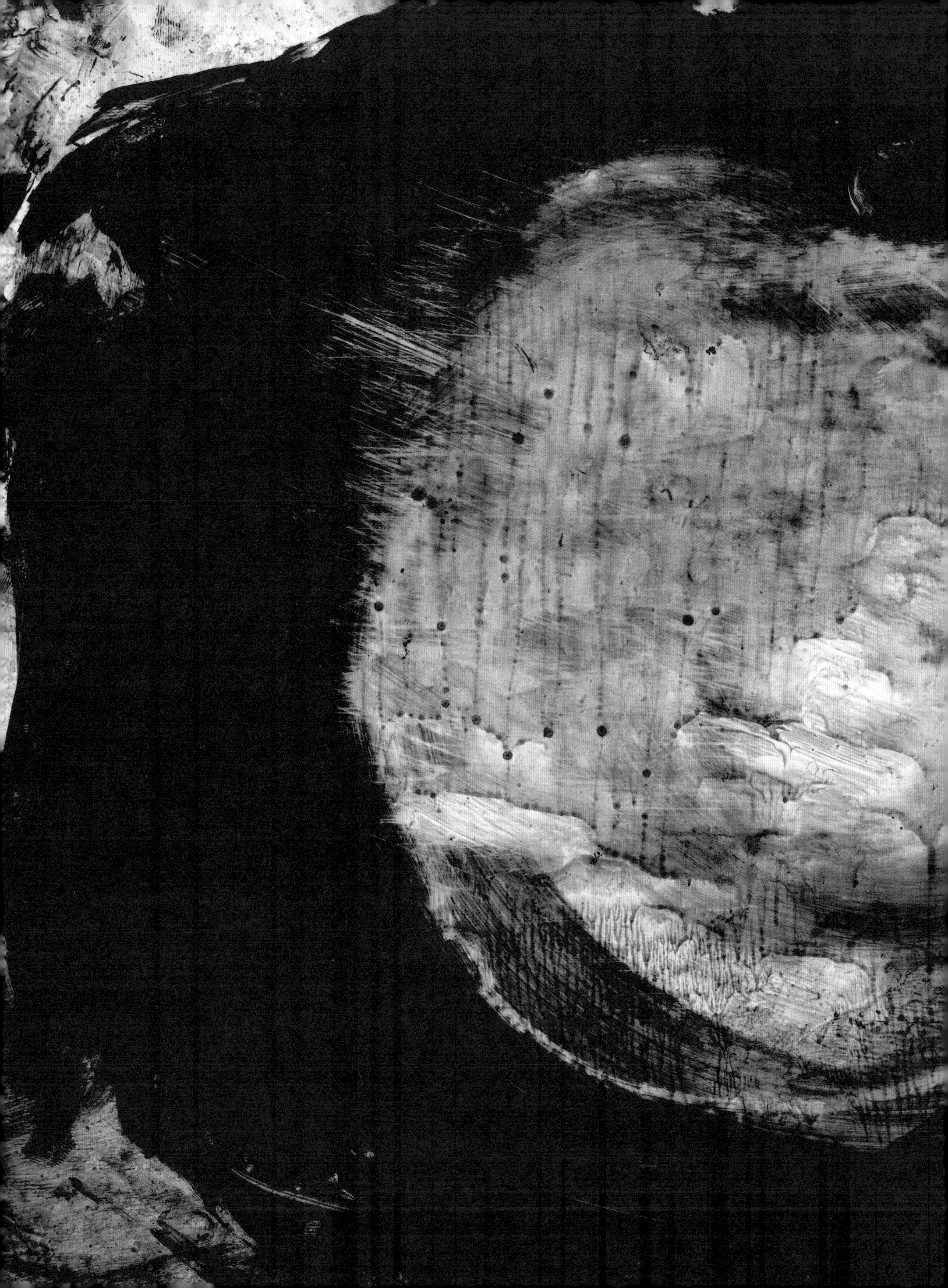

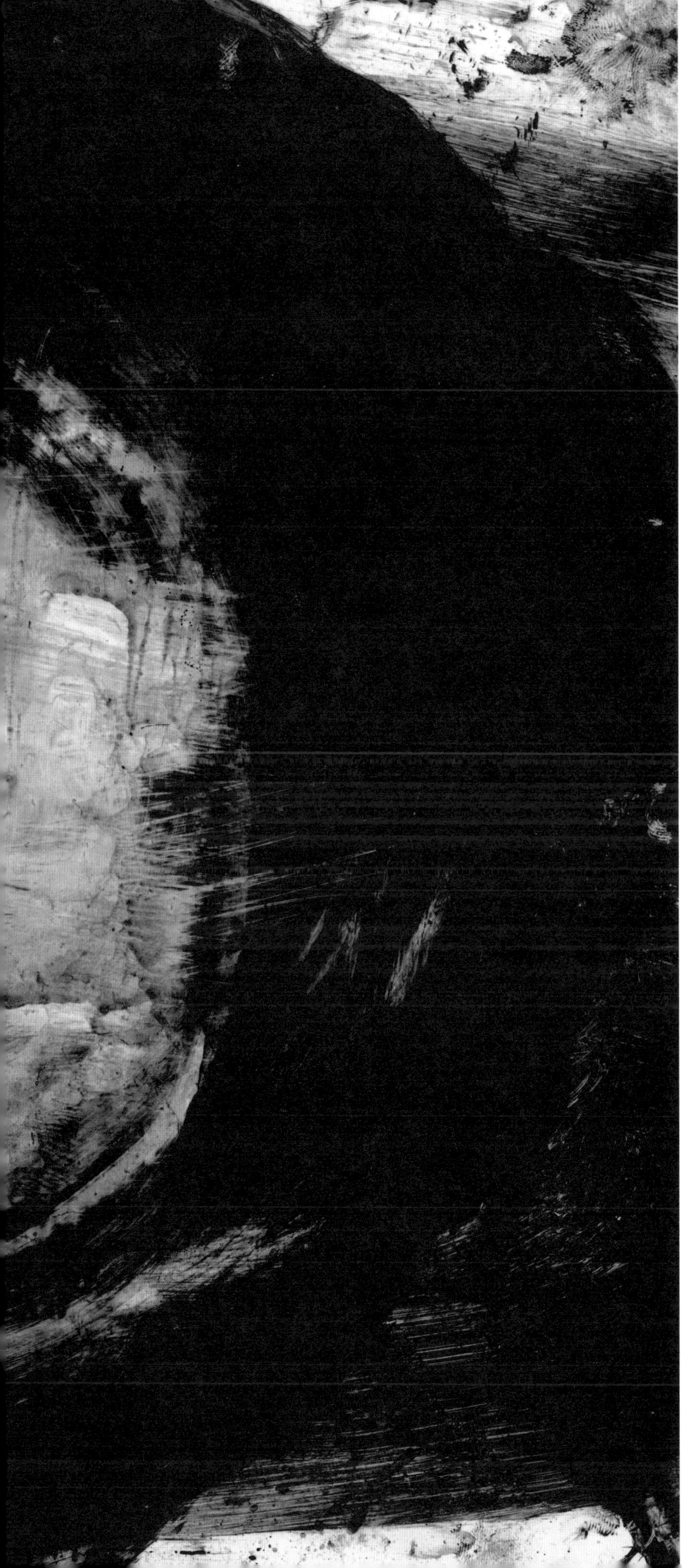

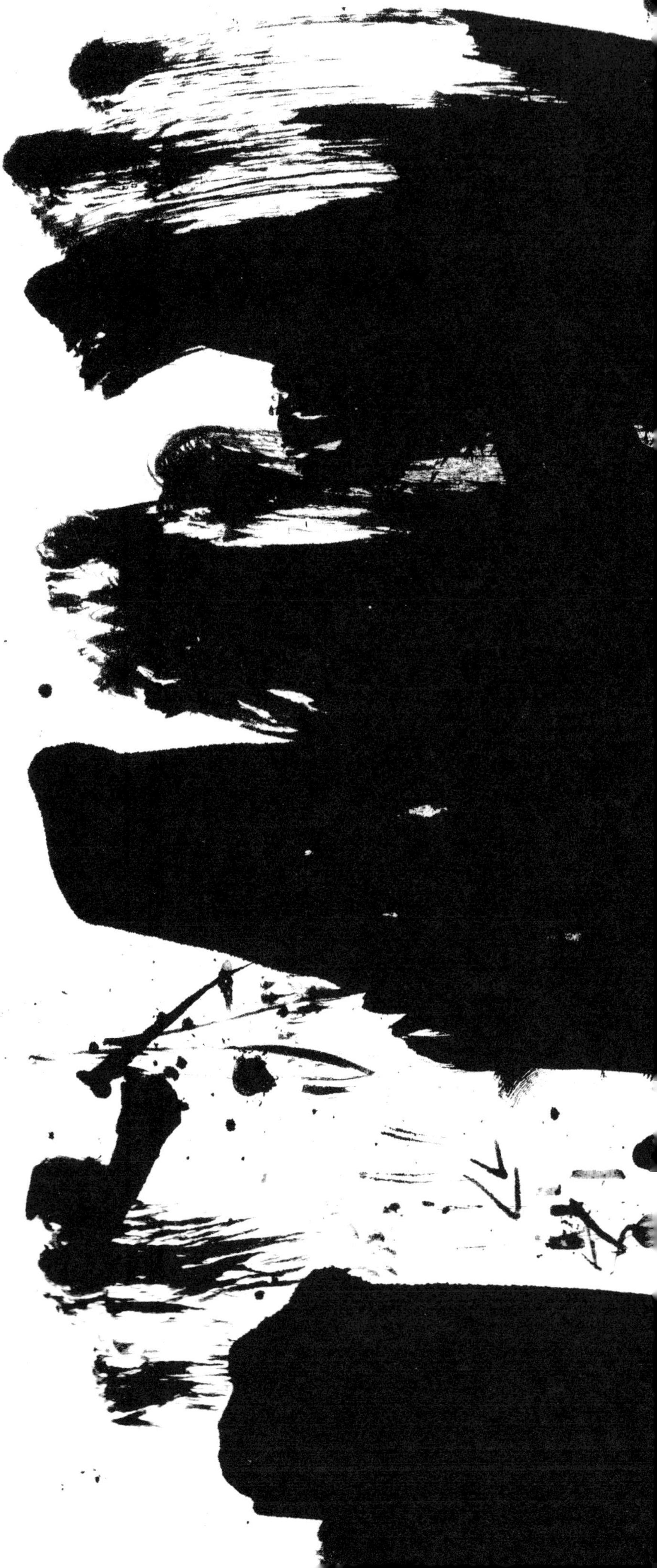

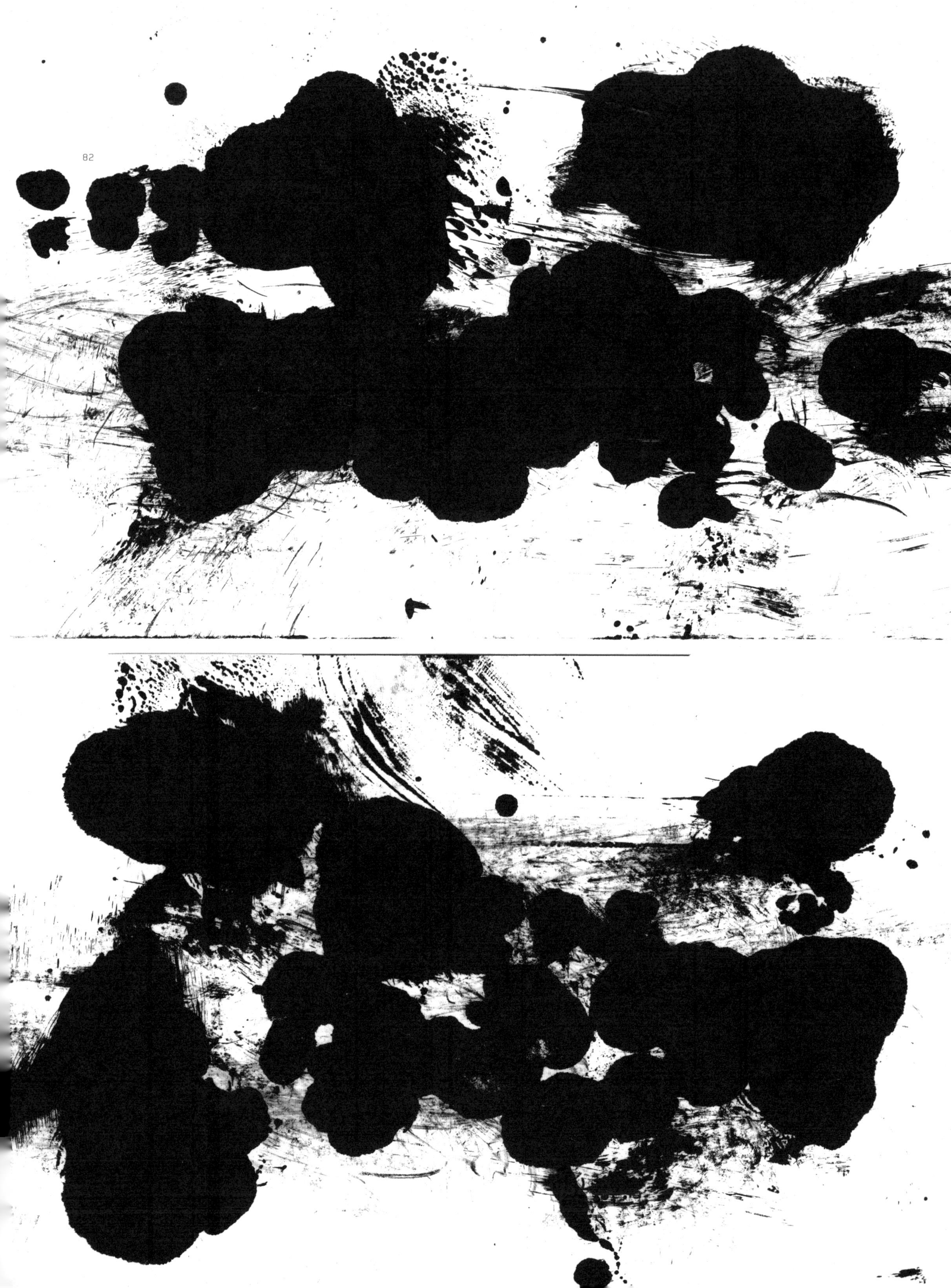

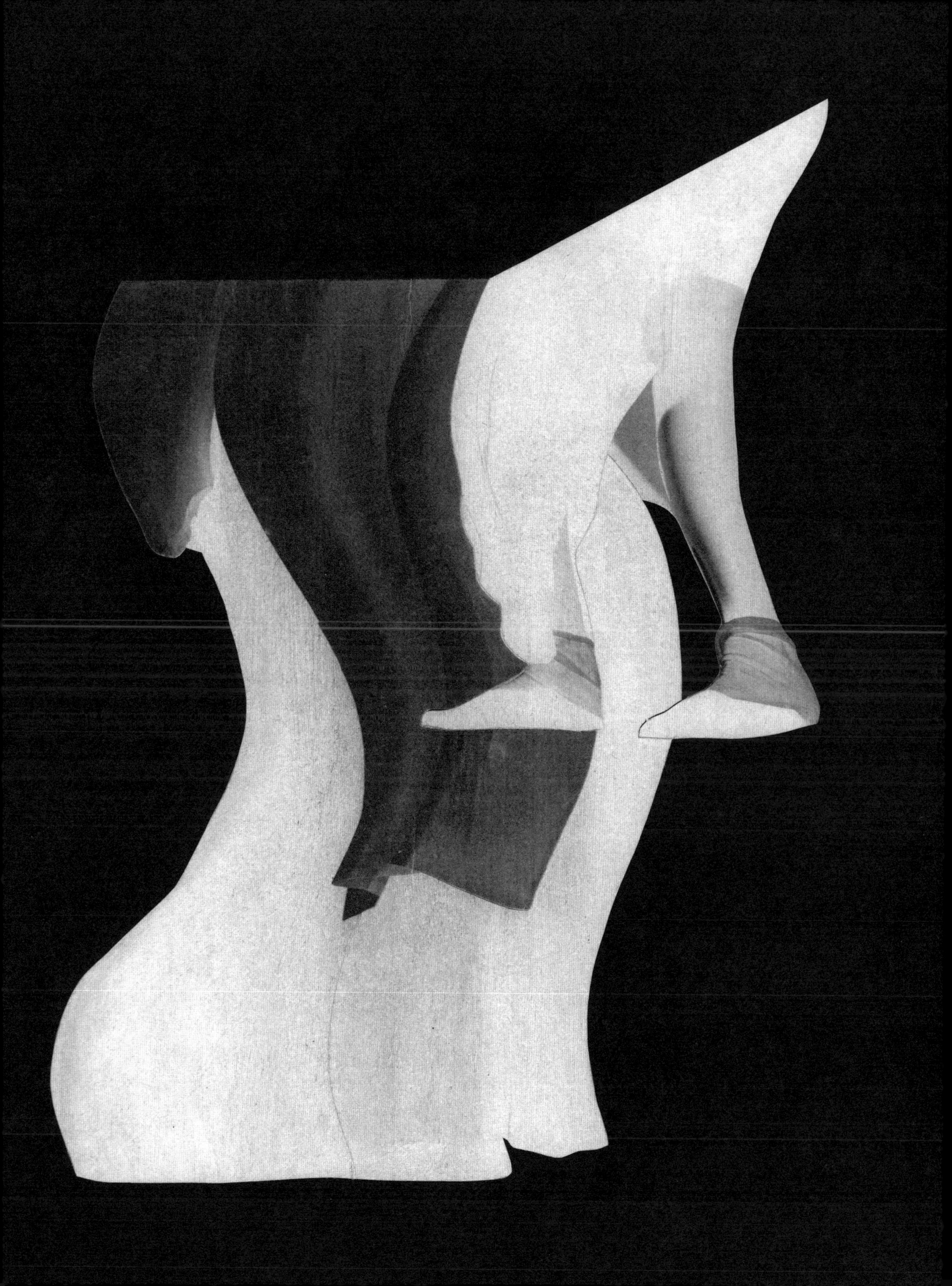

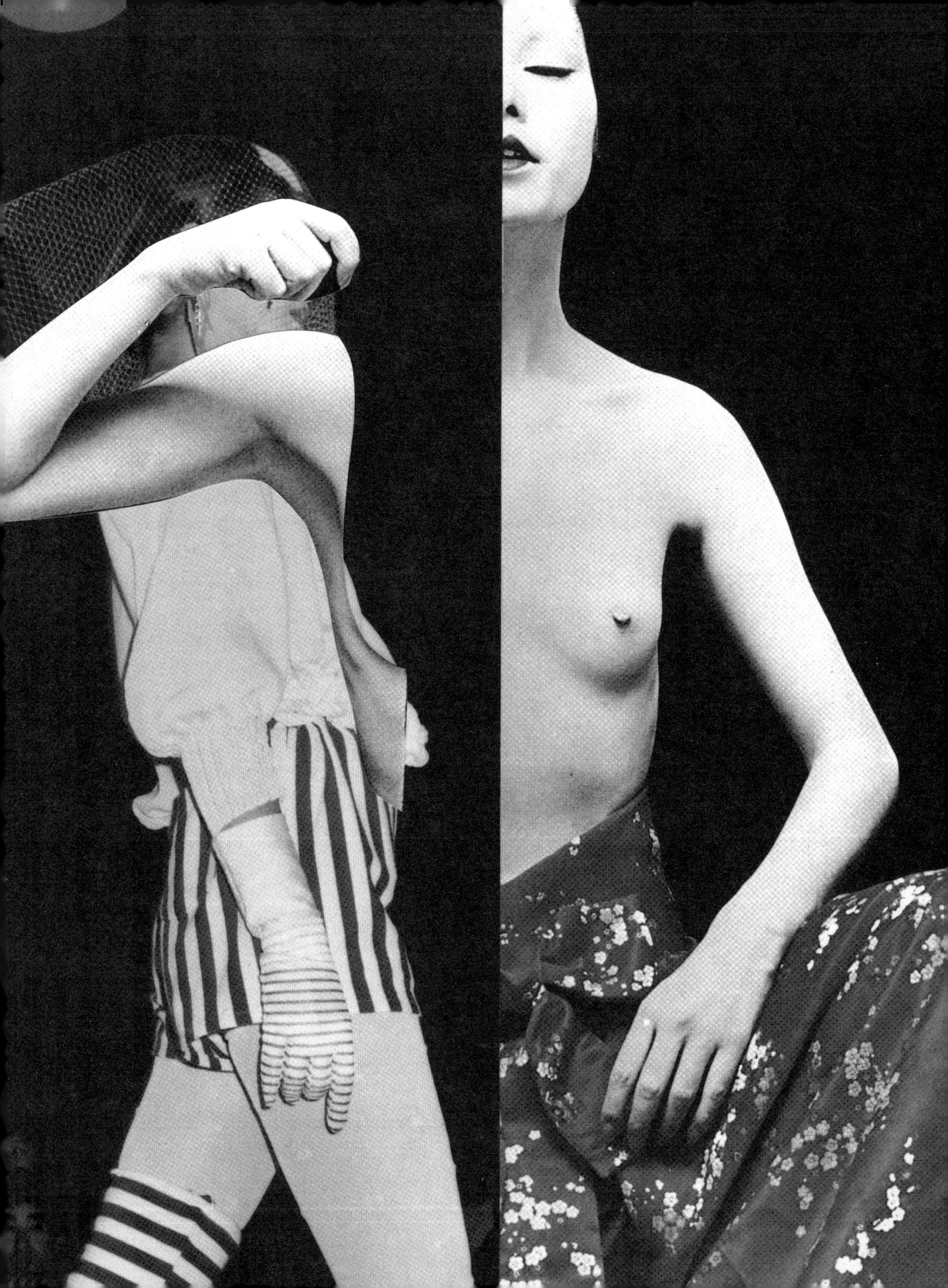

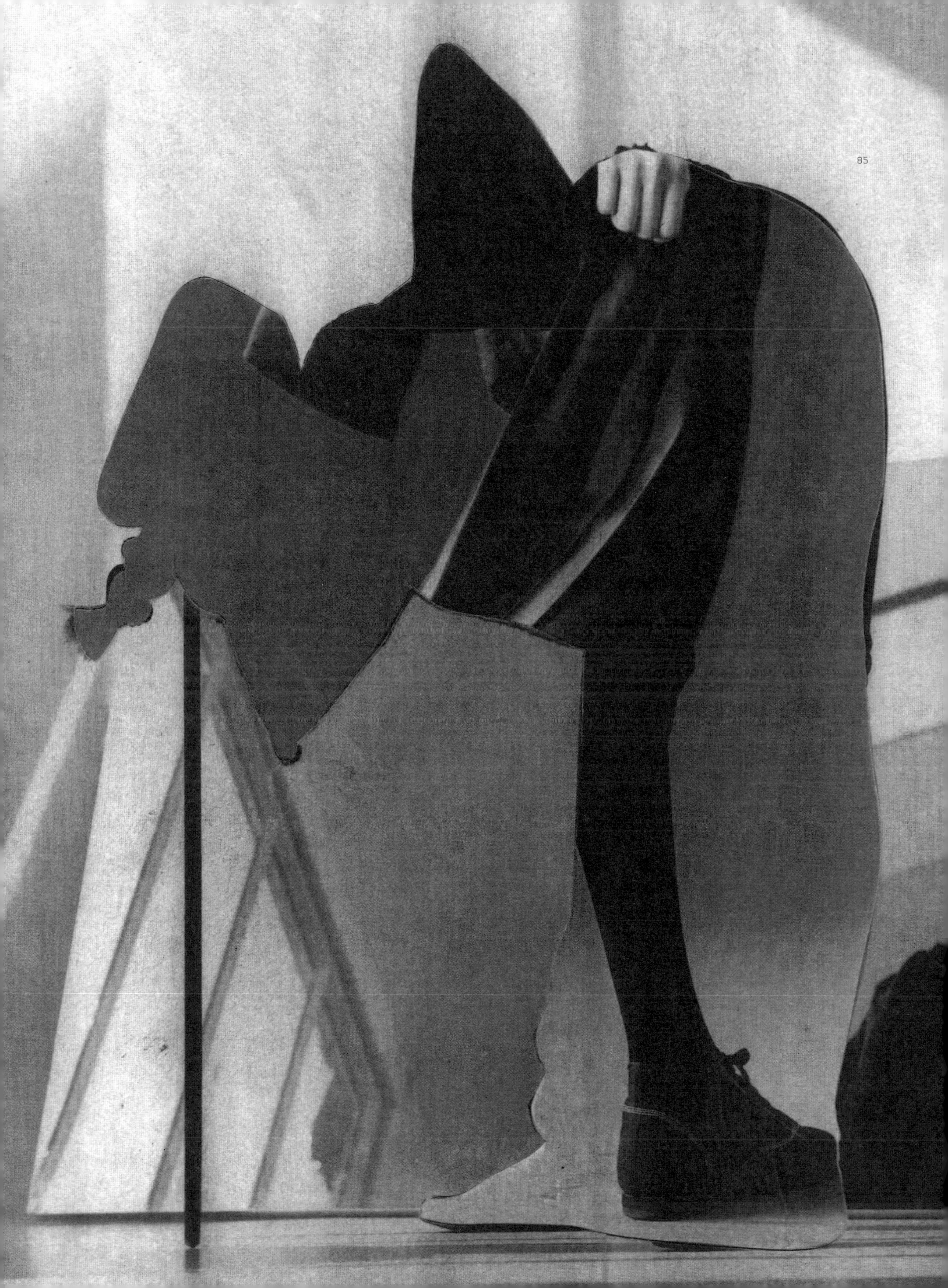

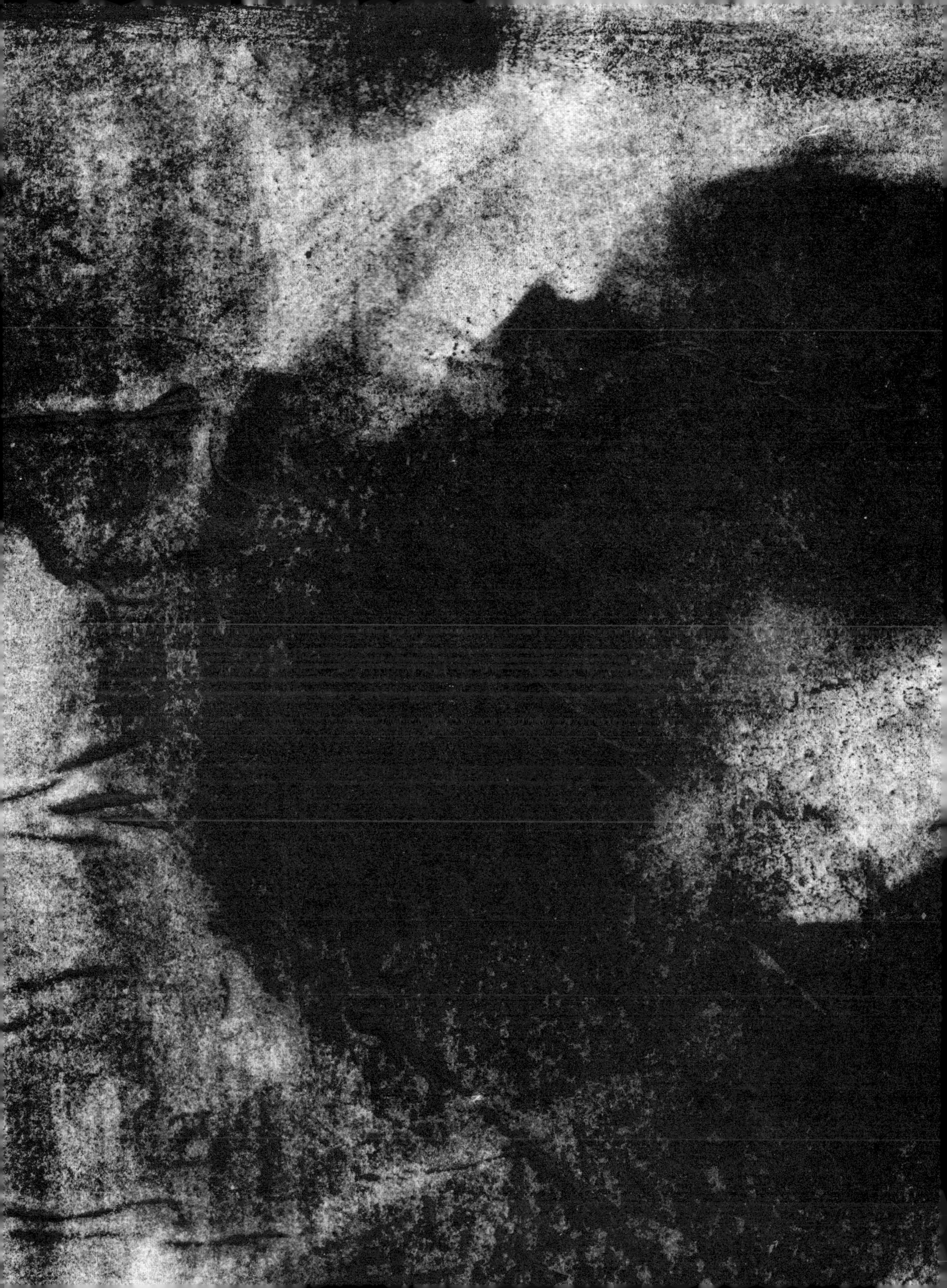

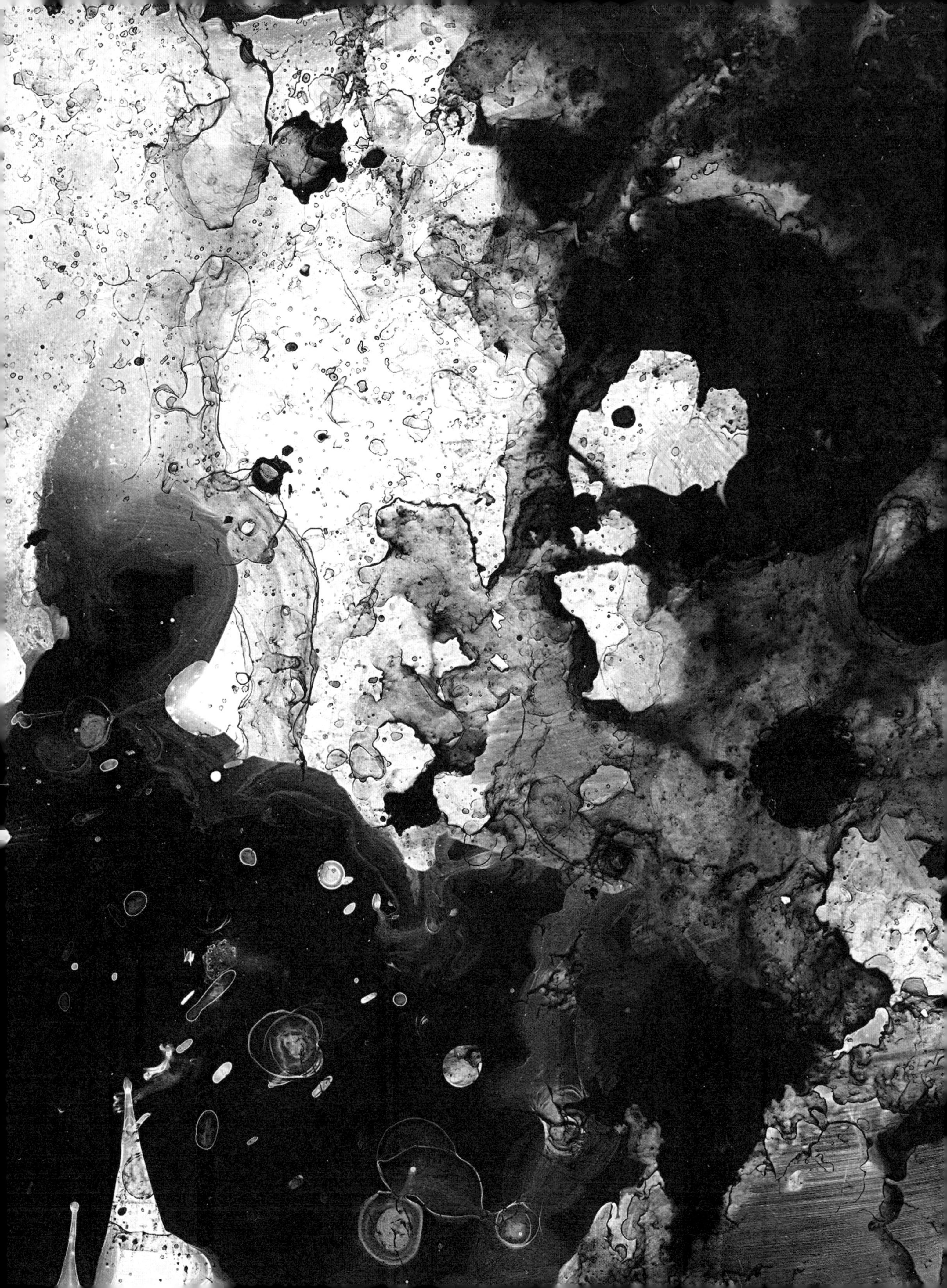

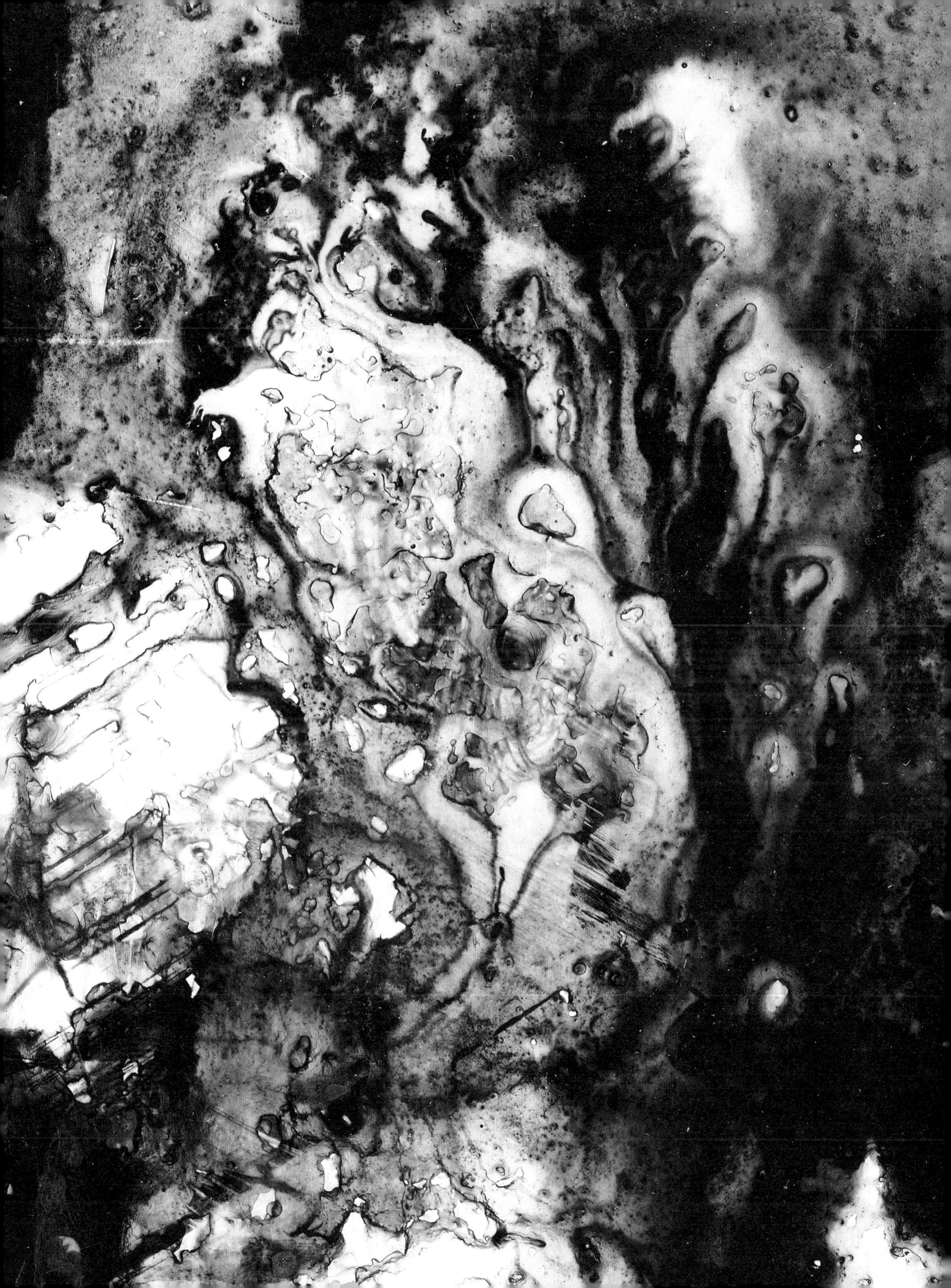

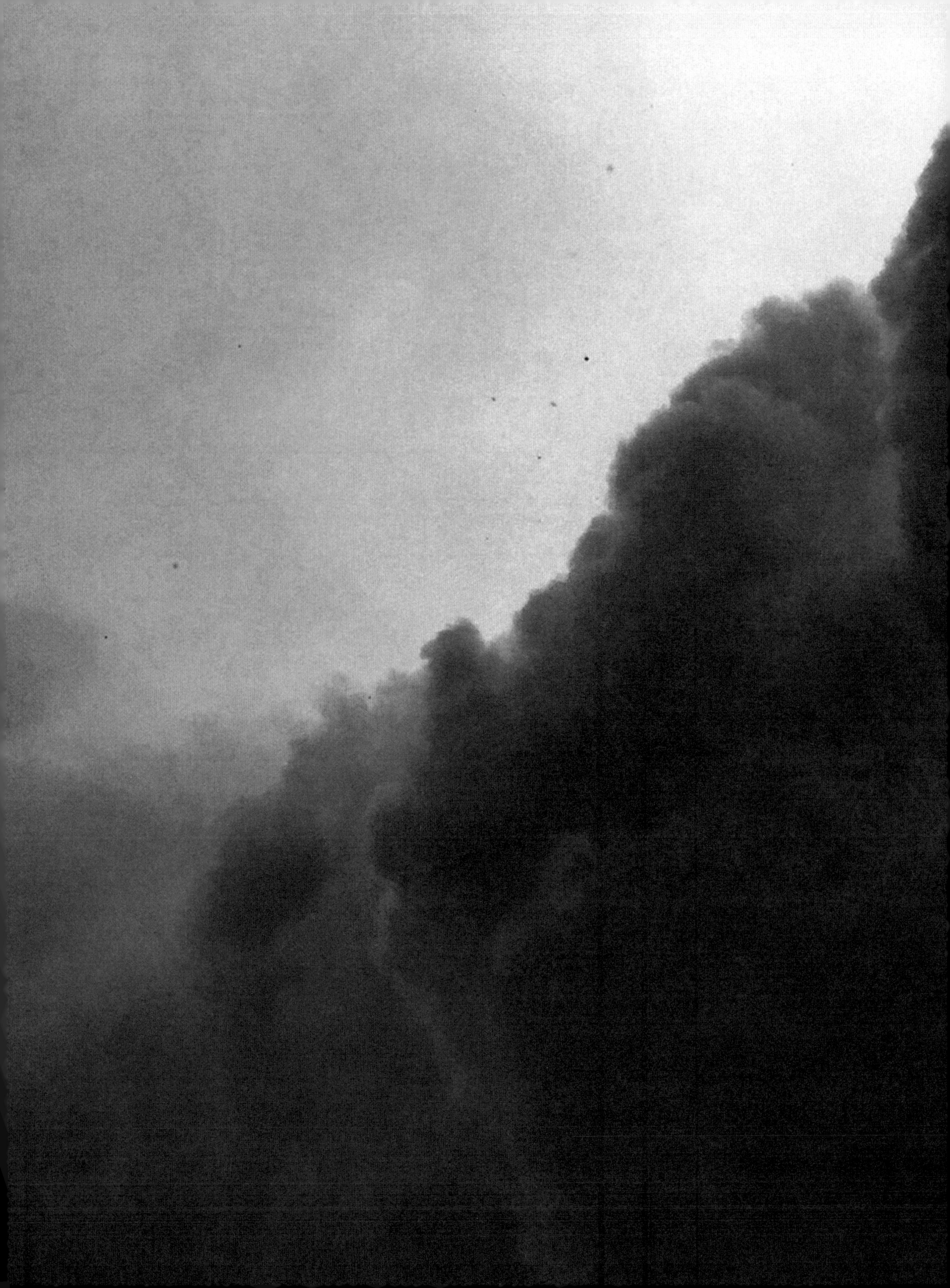

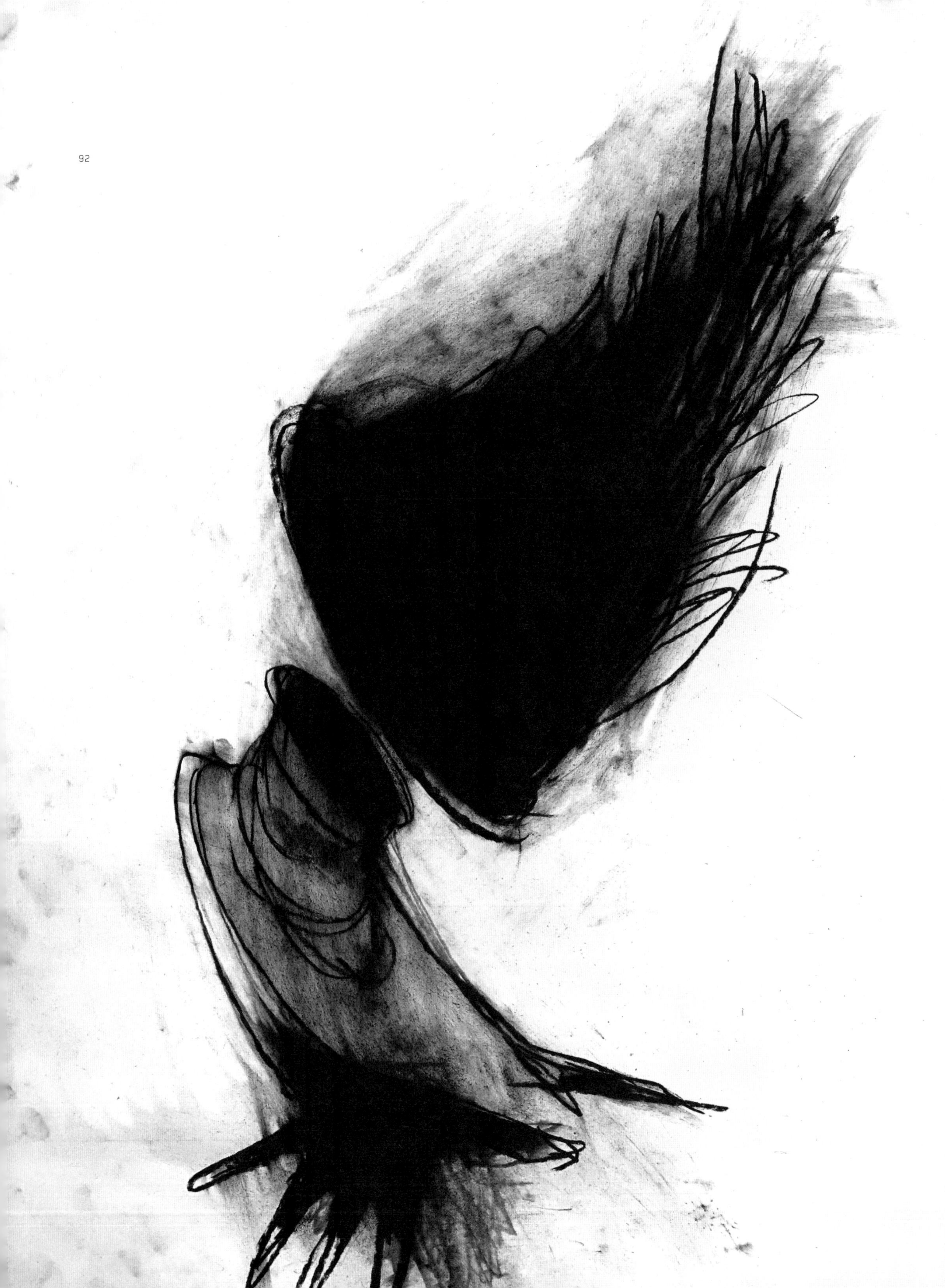

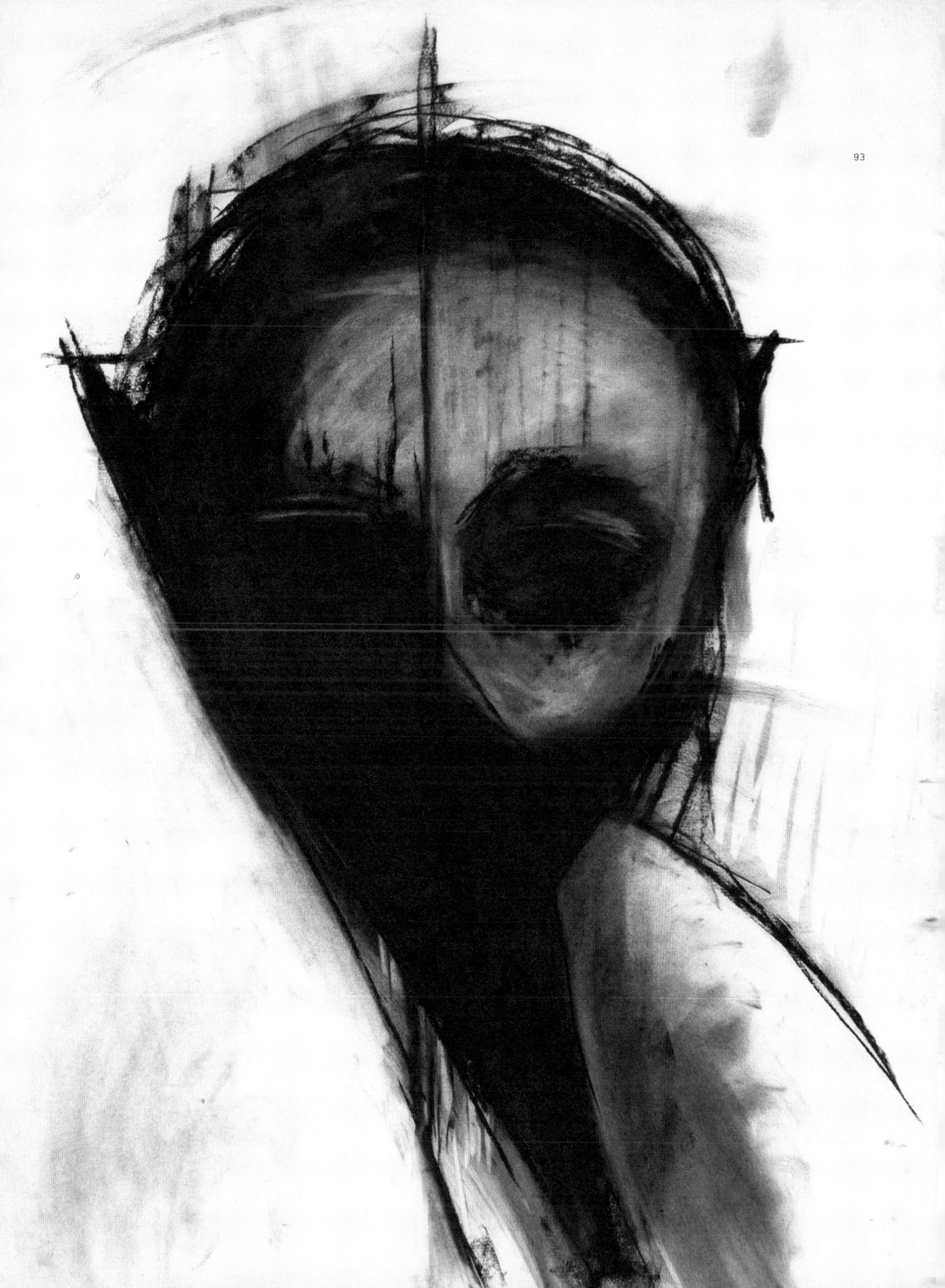

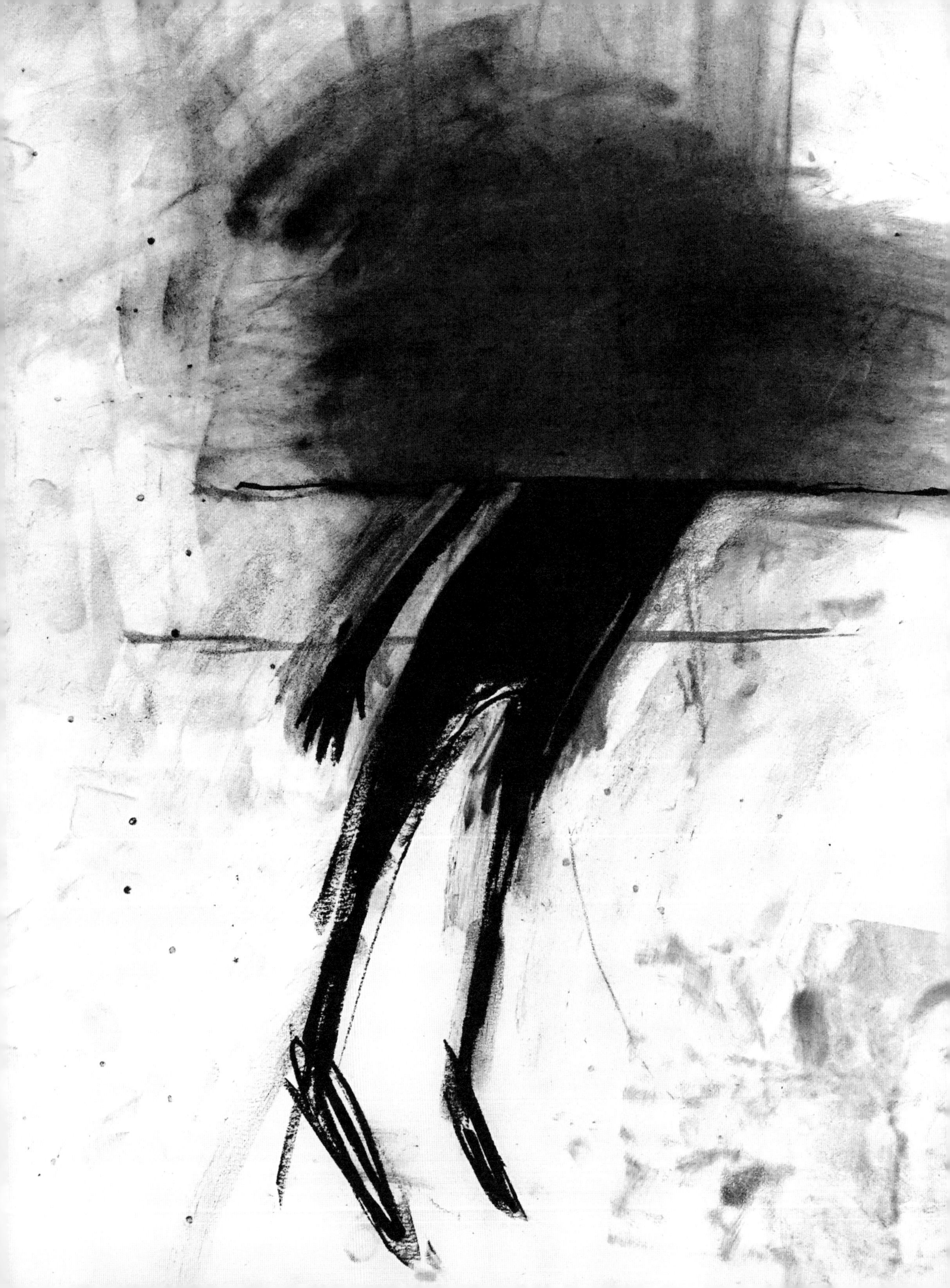

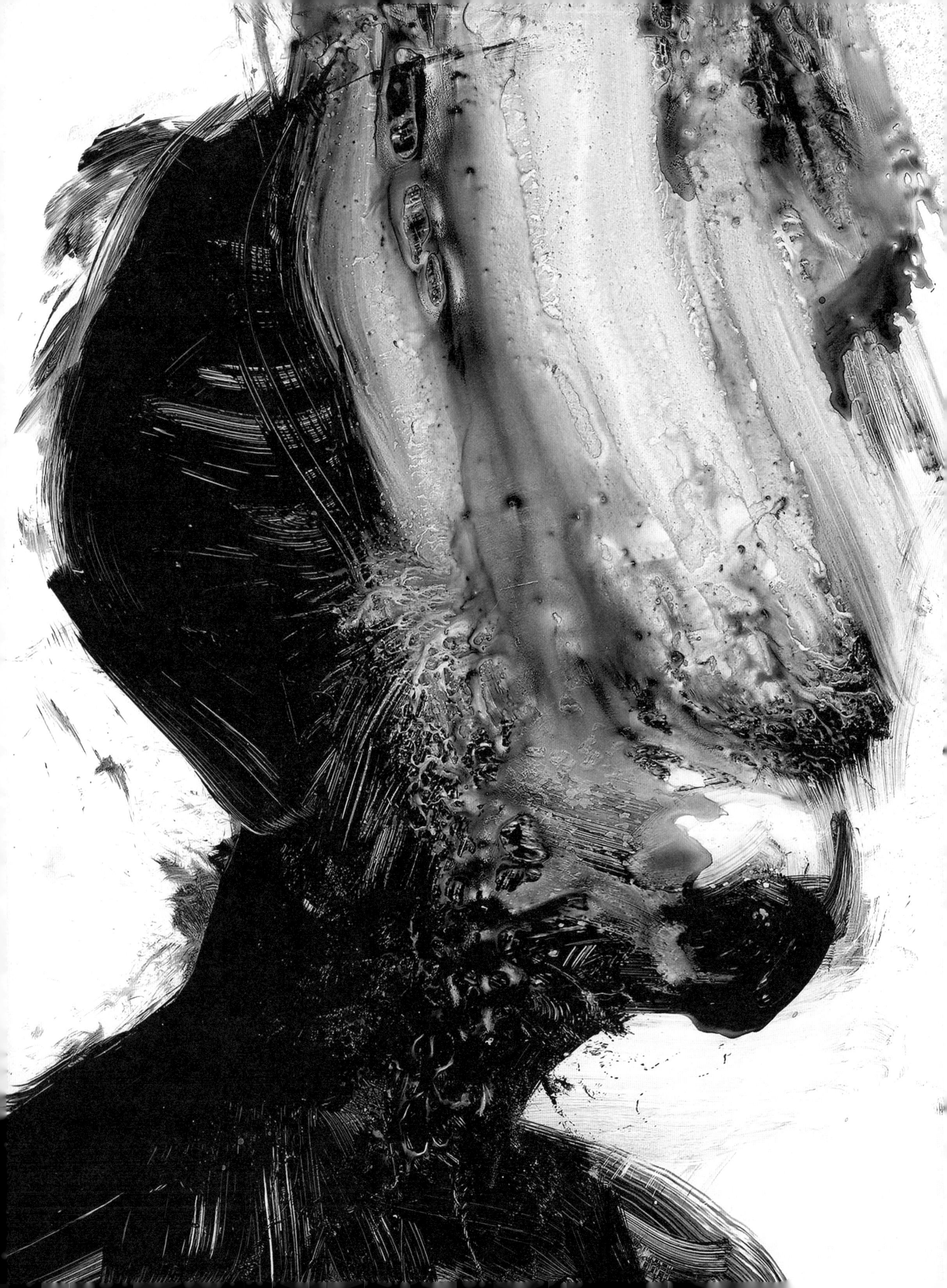

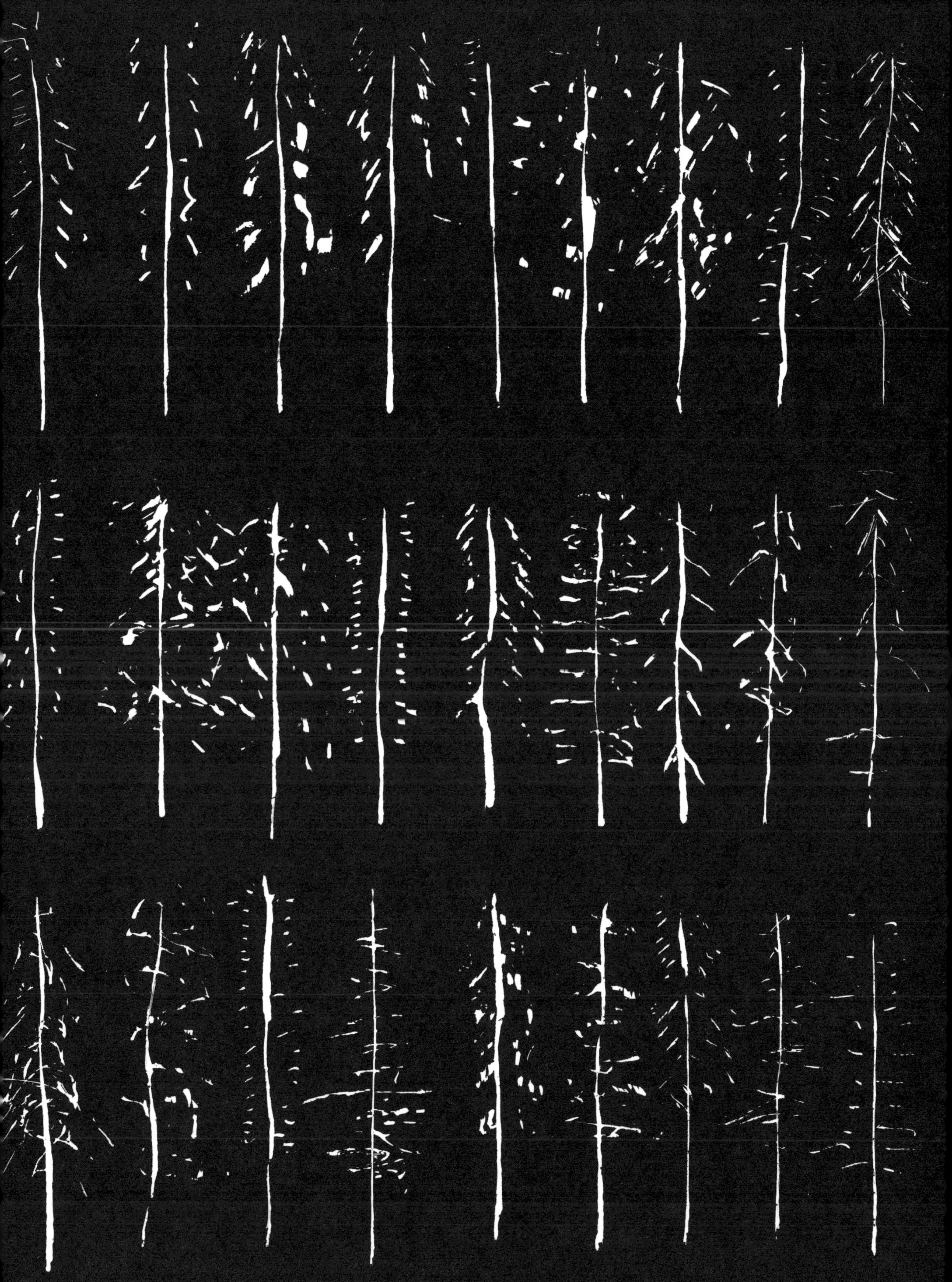

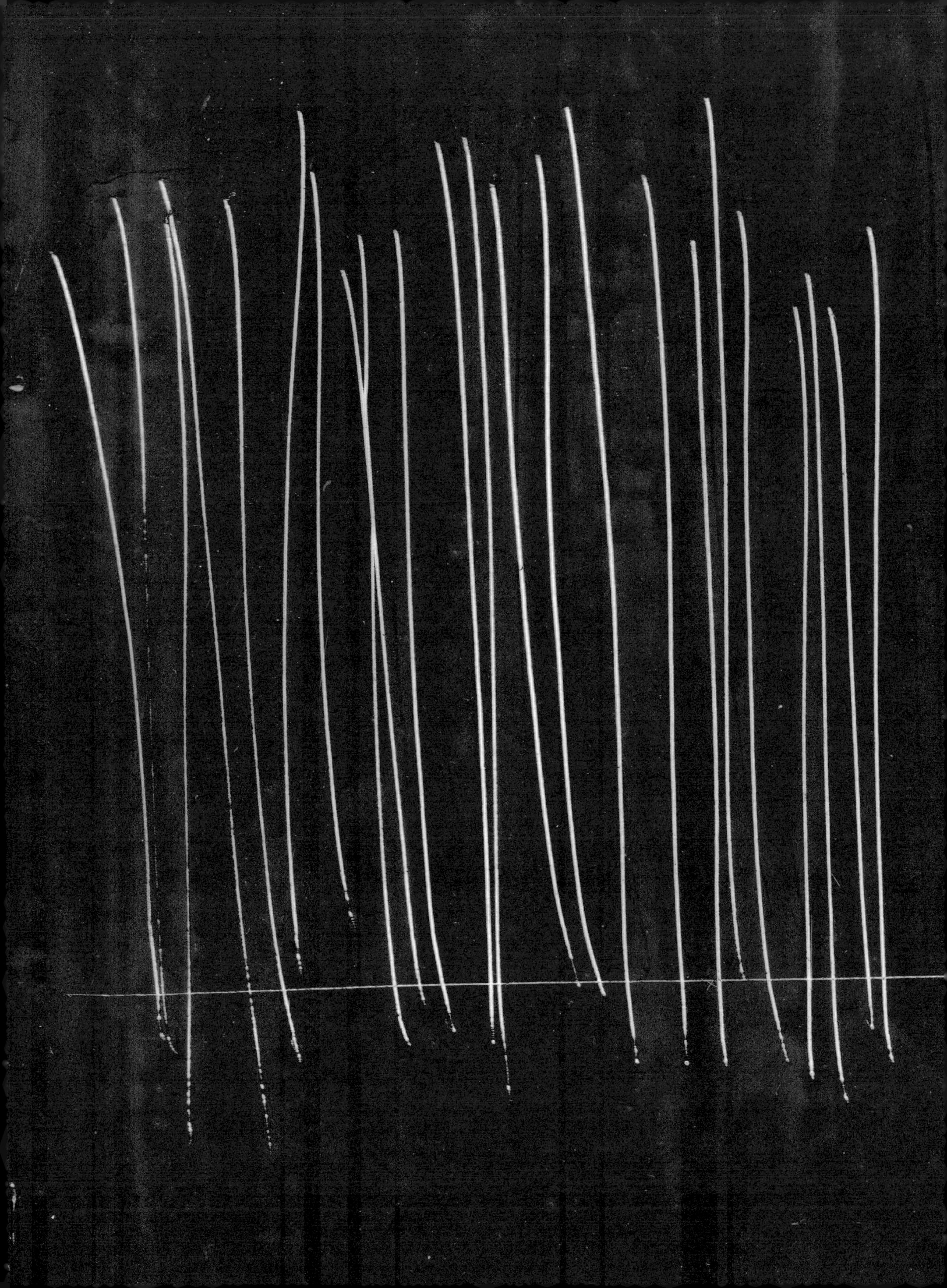

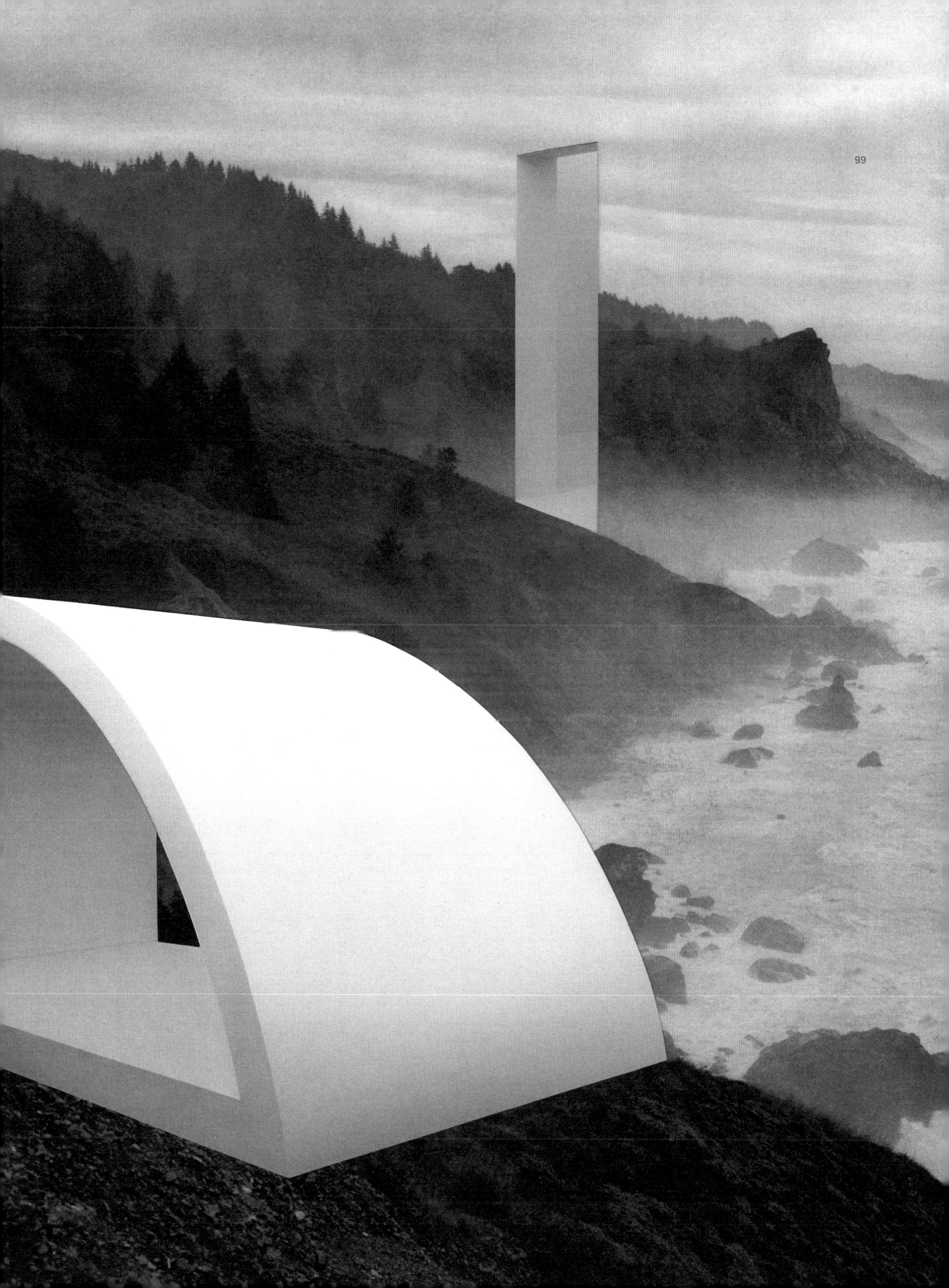

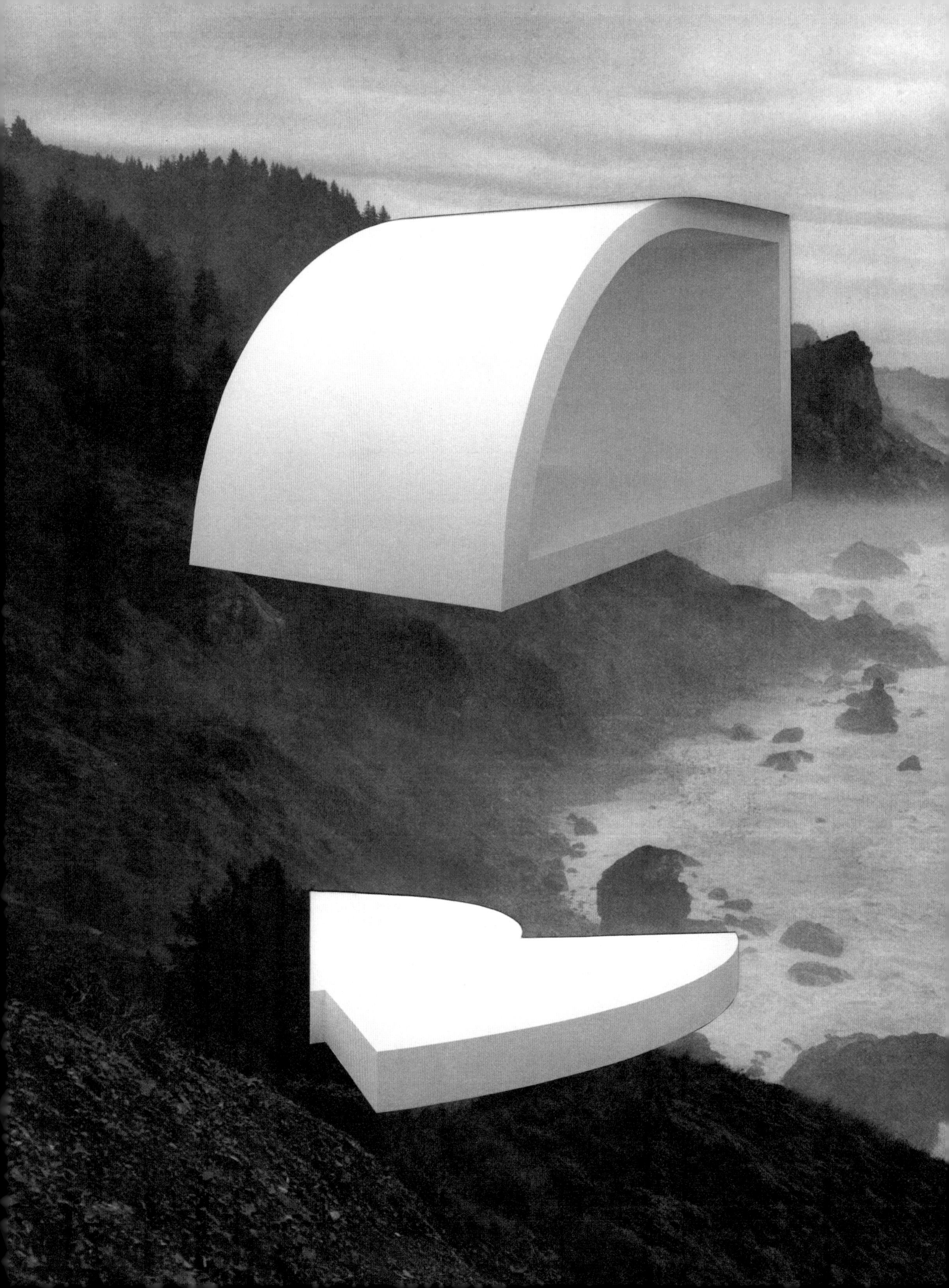

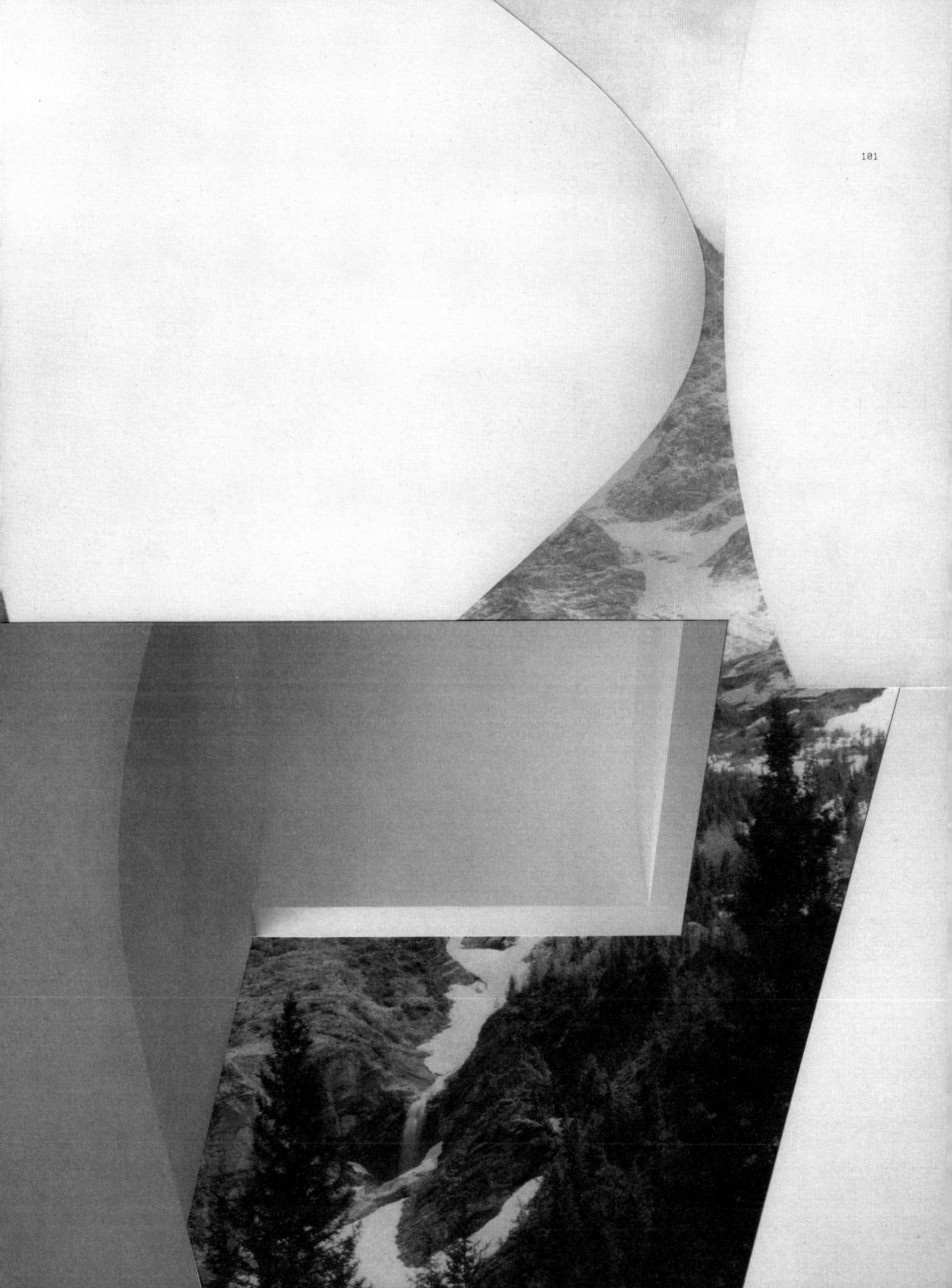

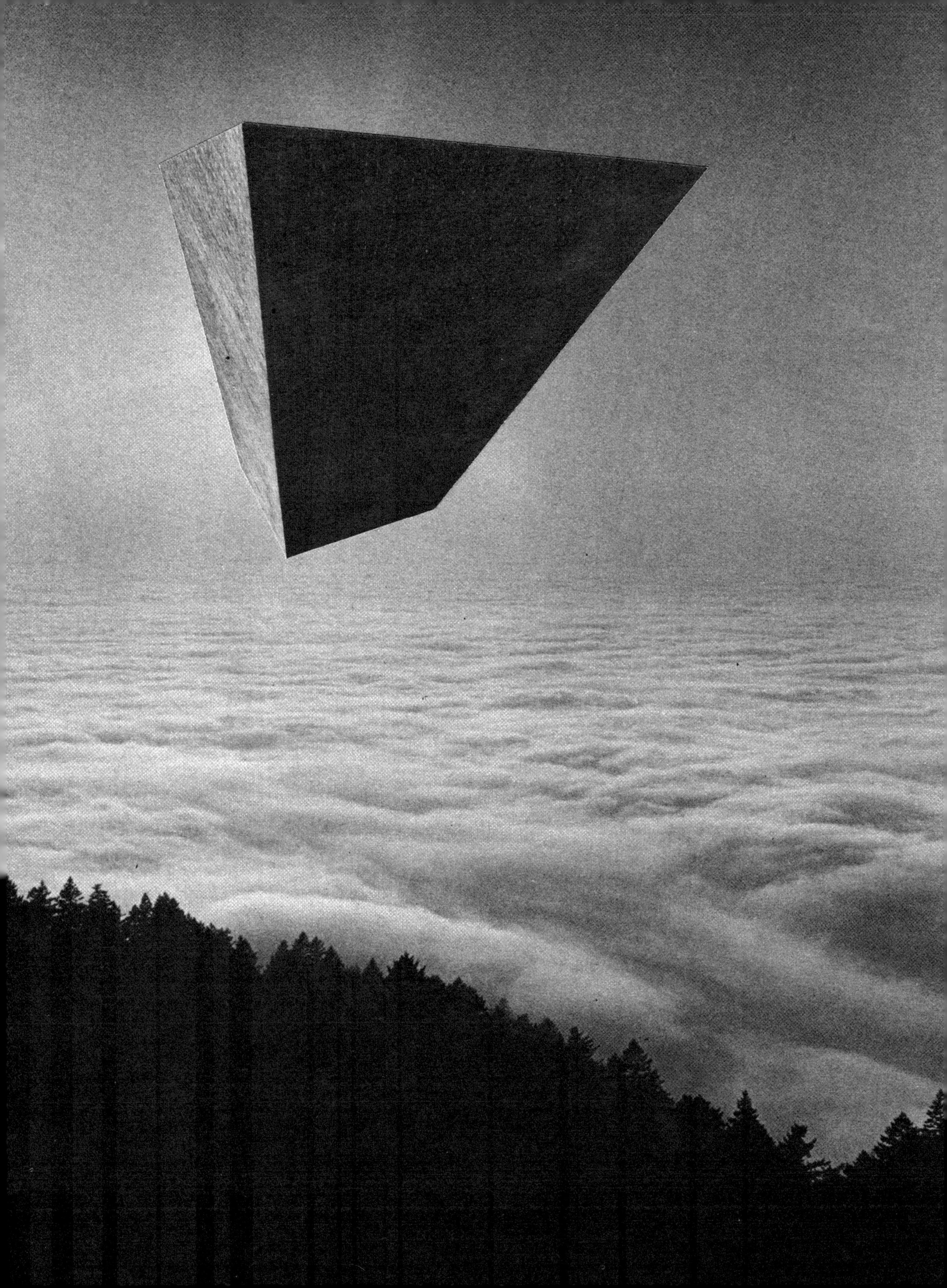

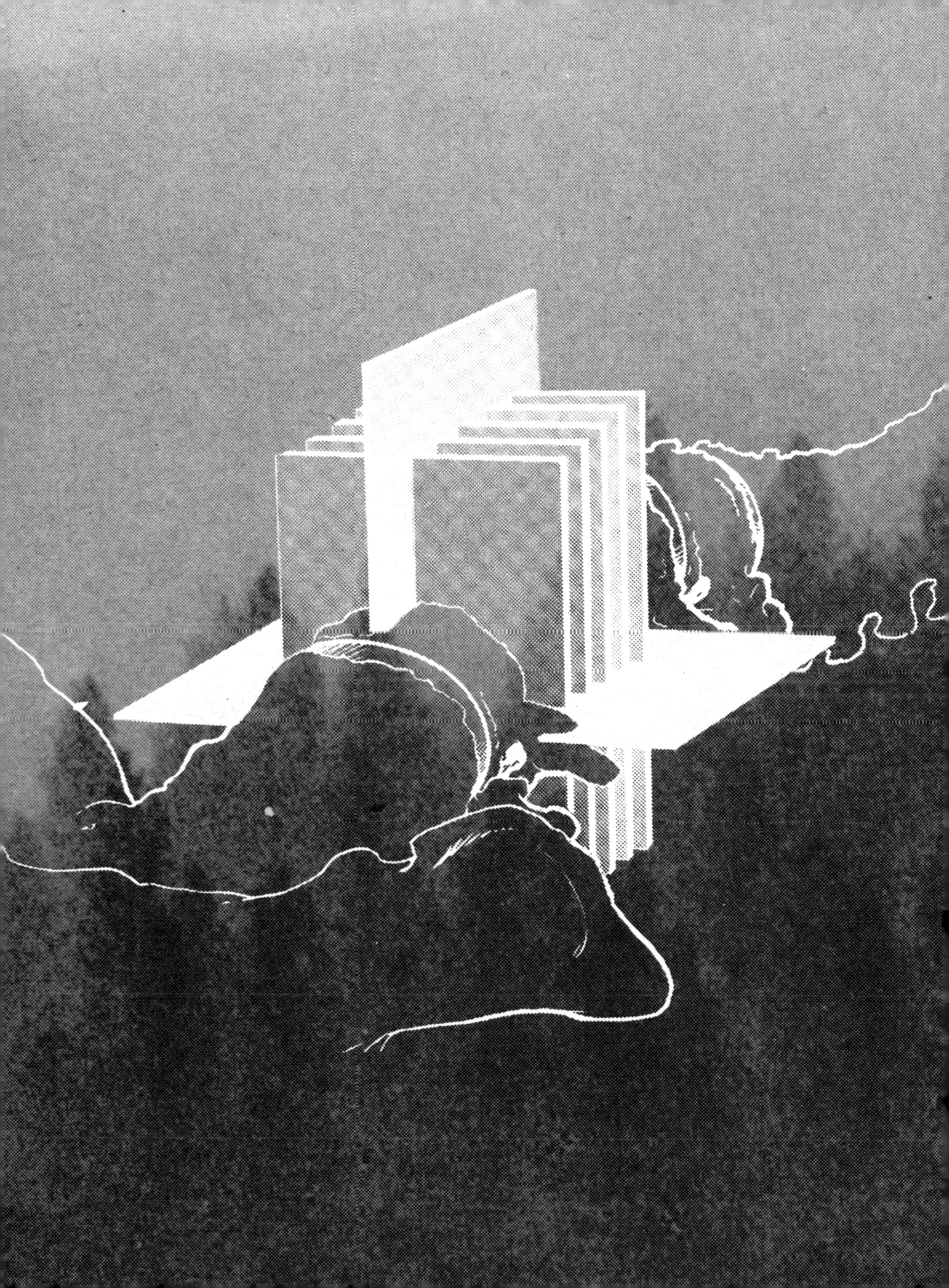

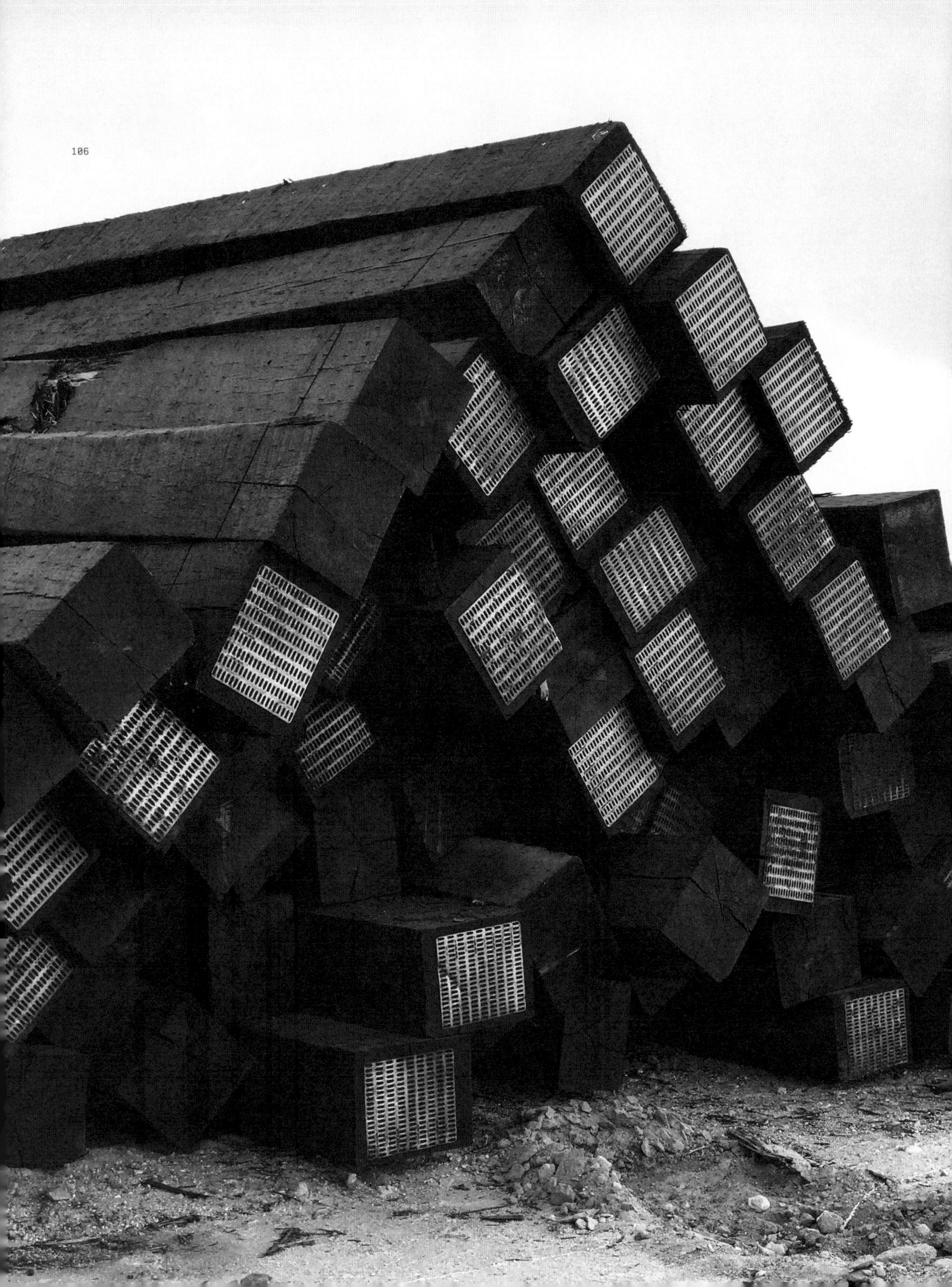

Remote viewing

Remote viewing

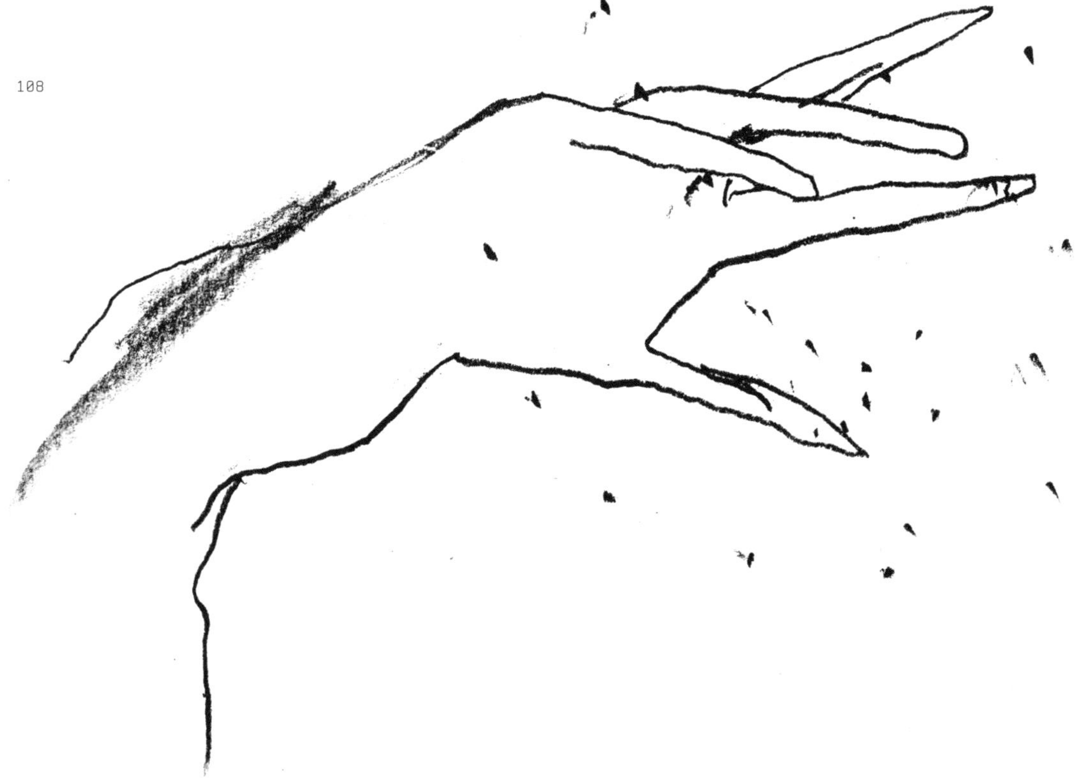

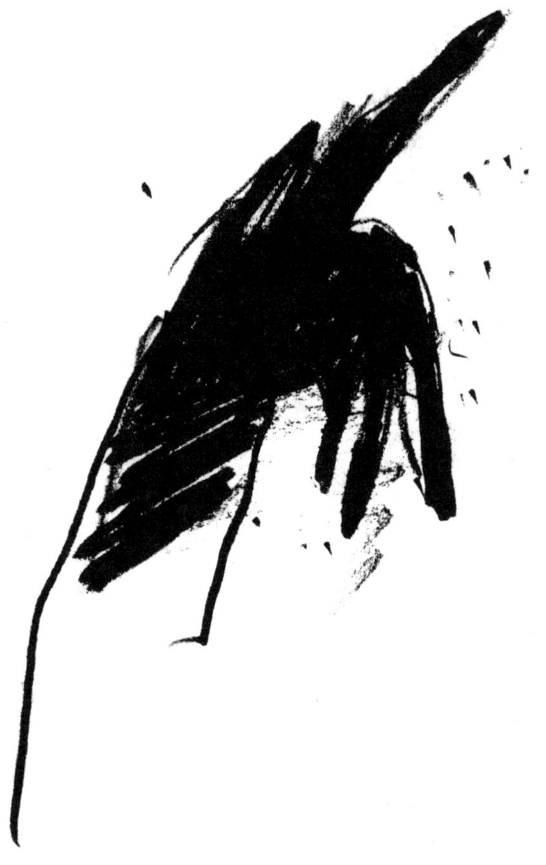

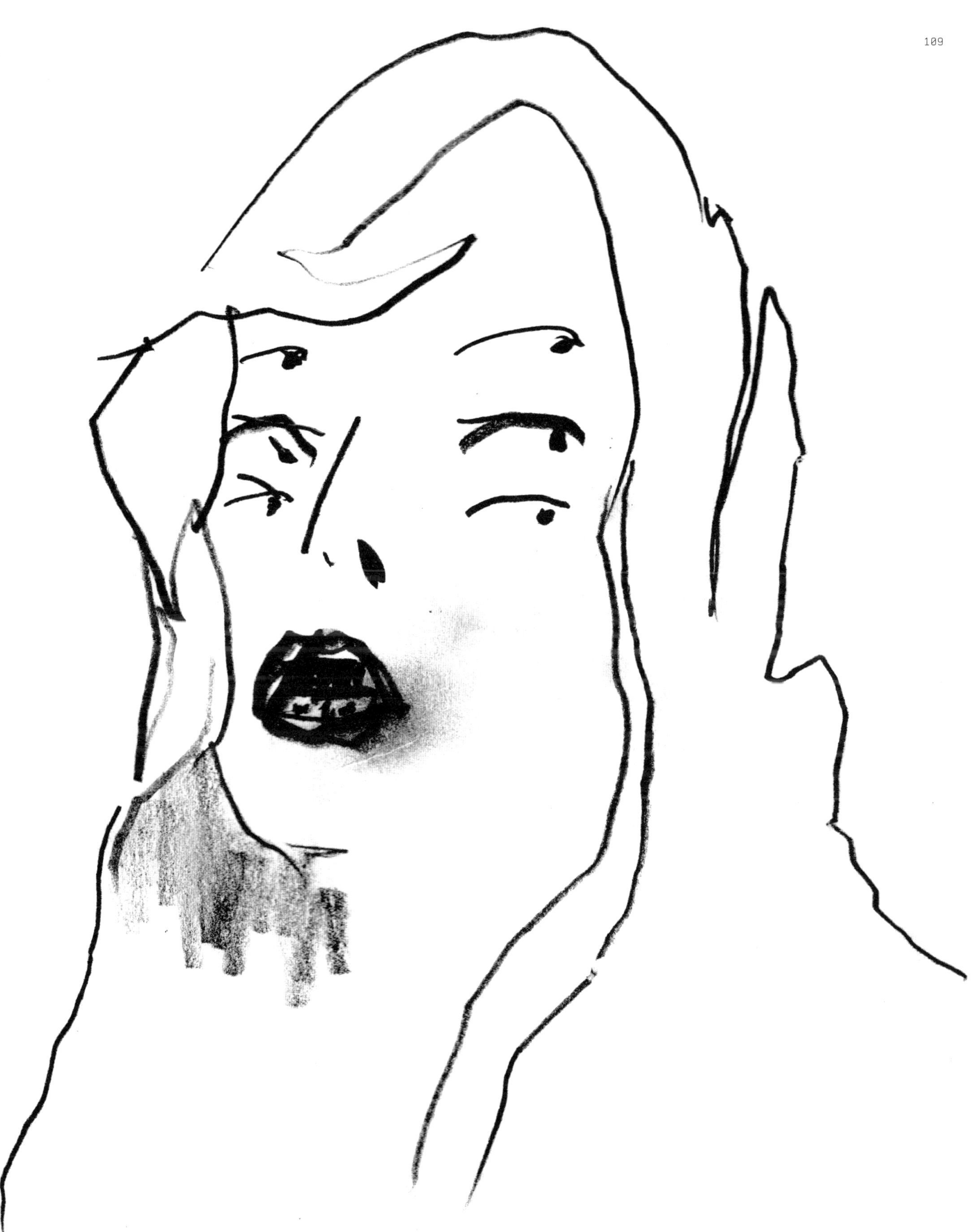

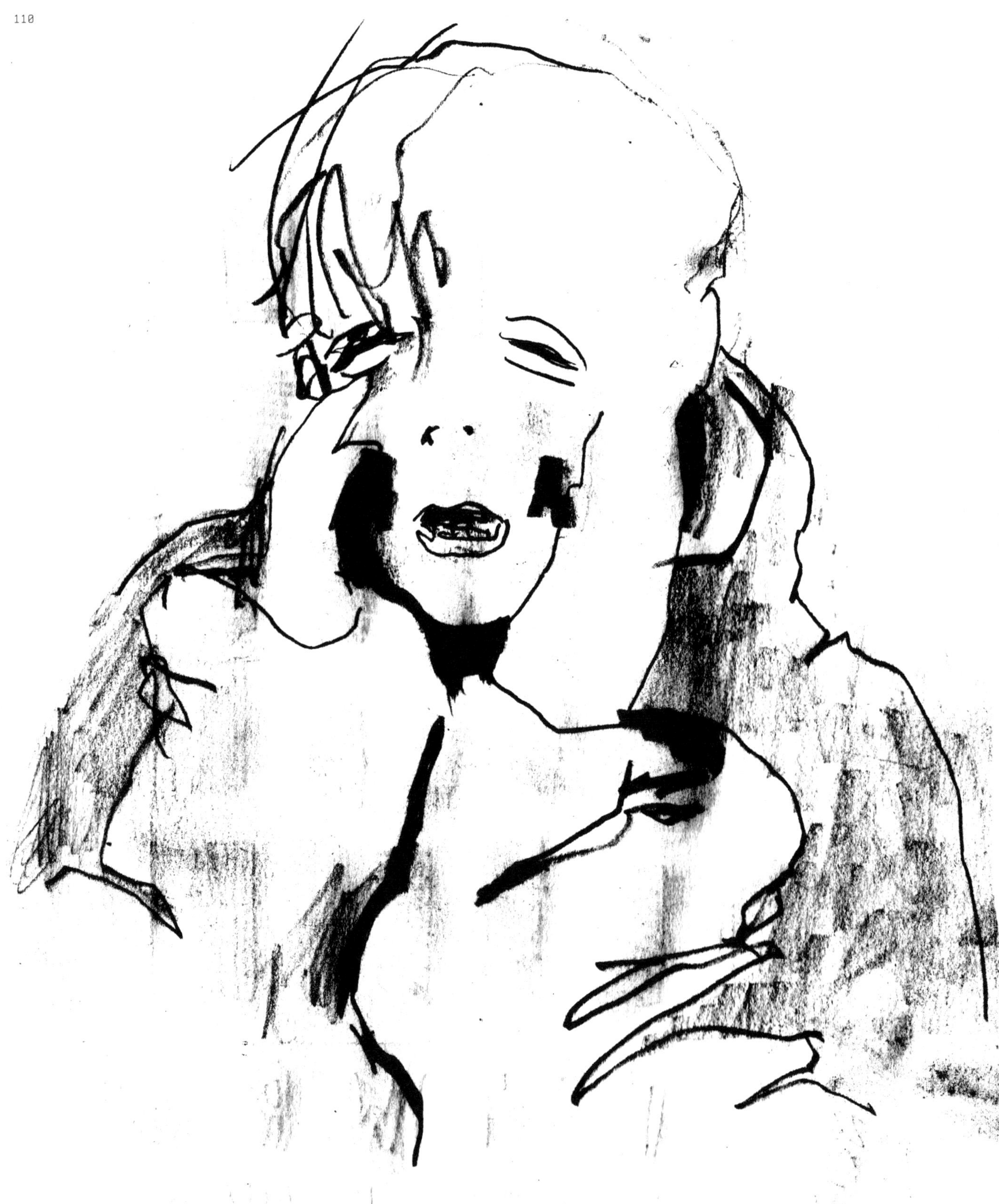

THE ONLY
PORTAL
PORTAL IS
ONLY
ONLY
IS
PORTAL
PORTAL IS
INWARD
INWARD

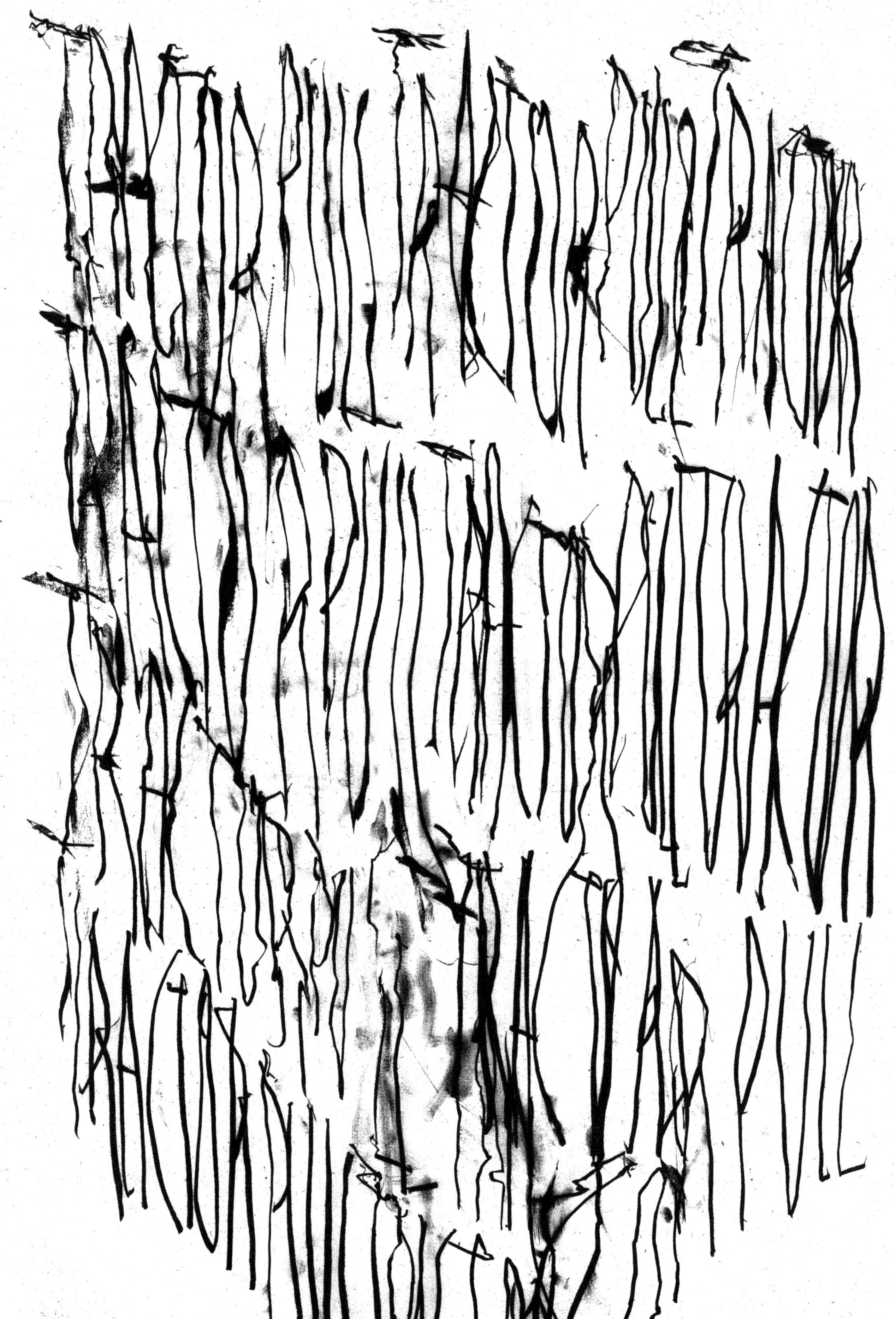

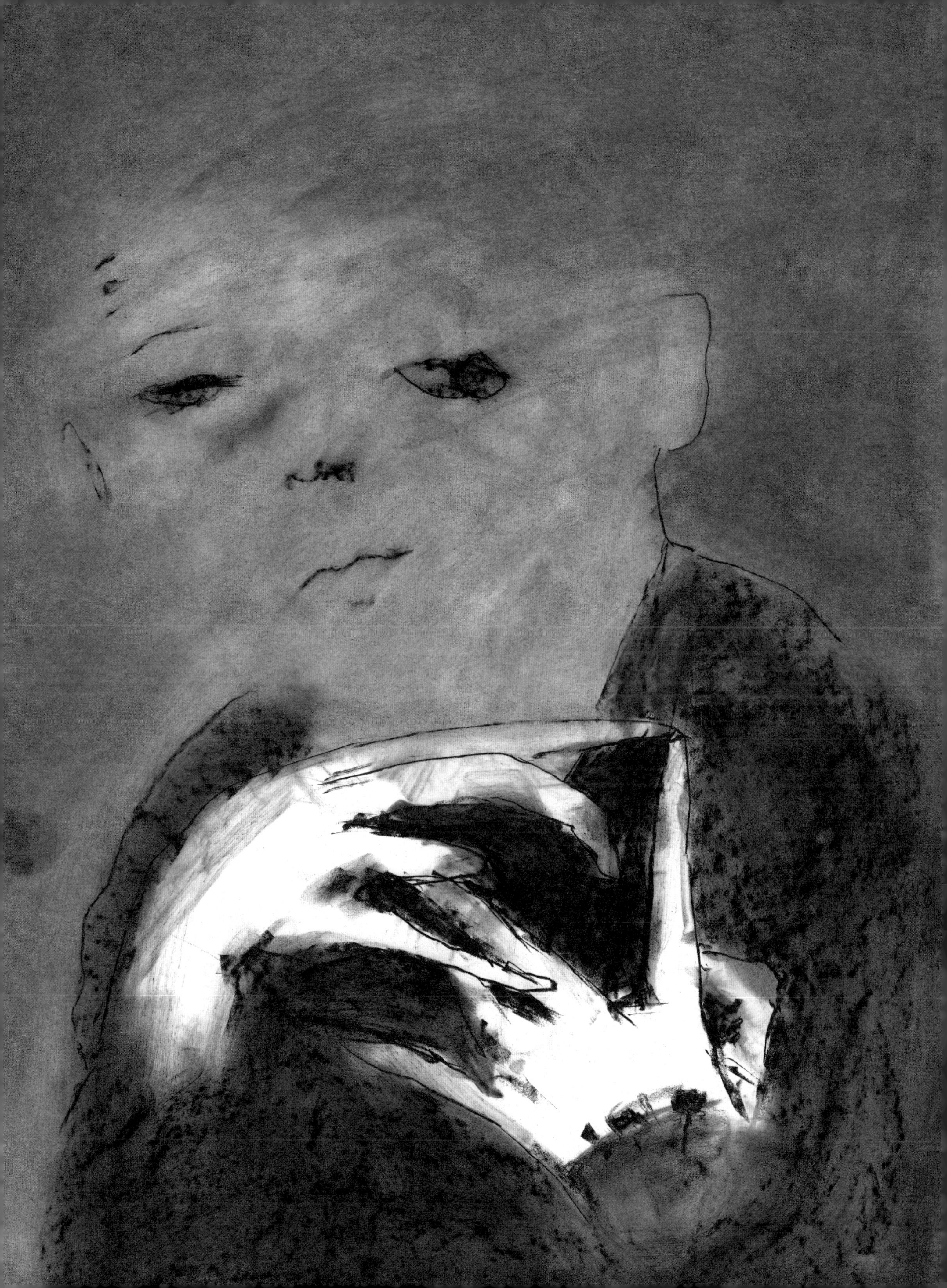

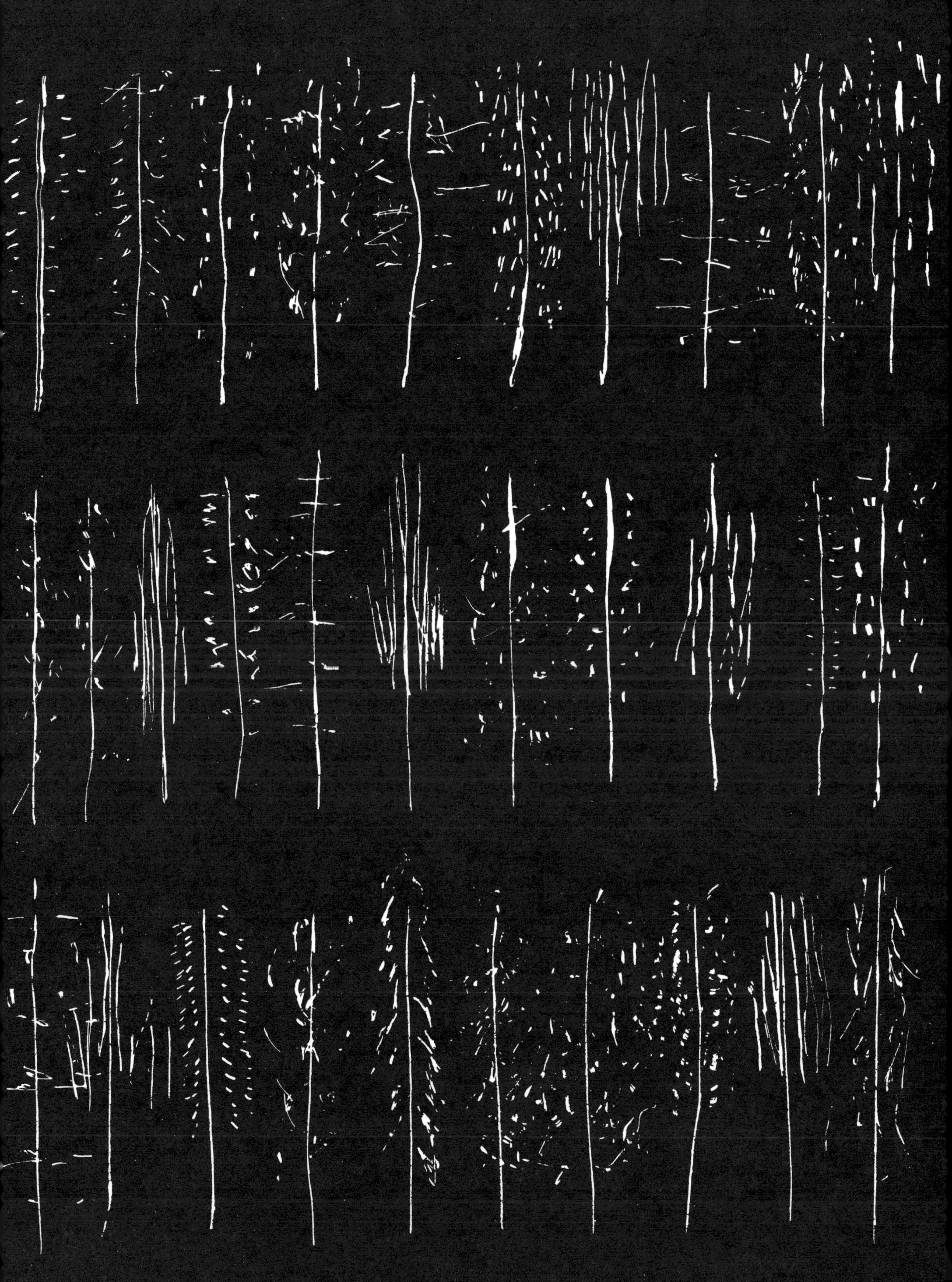

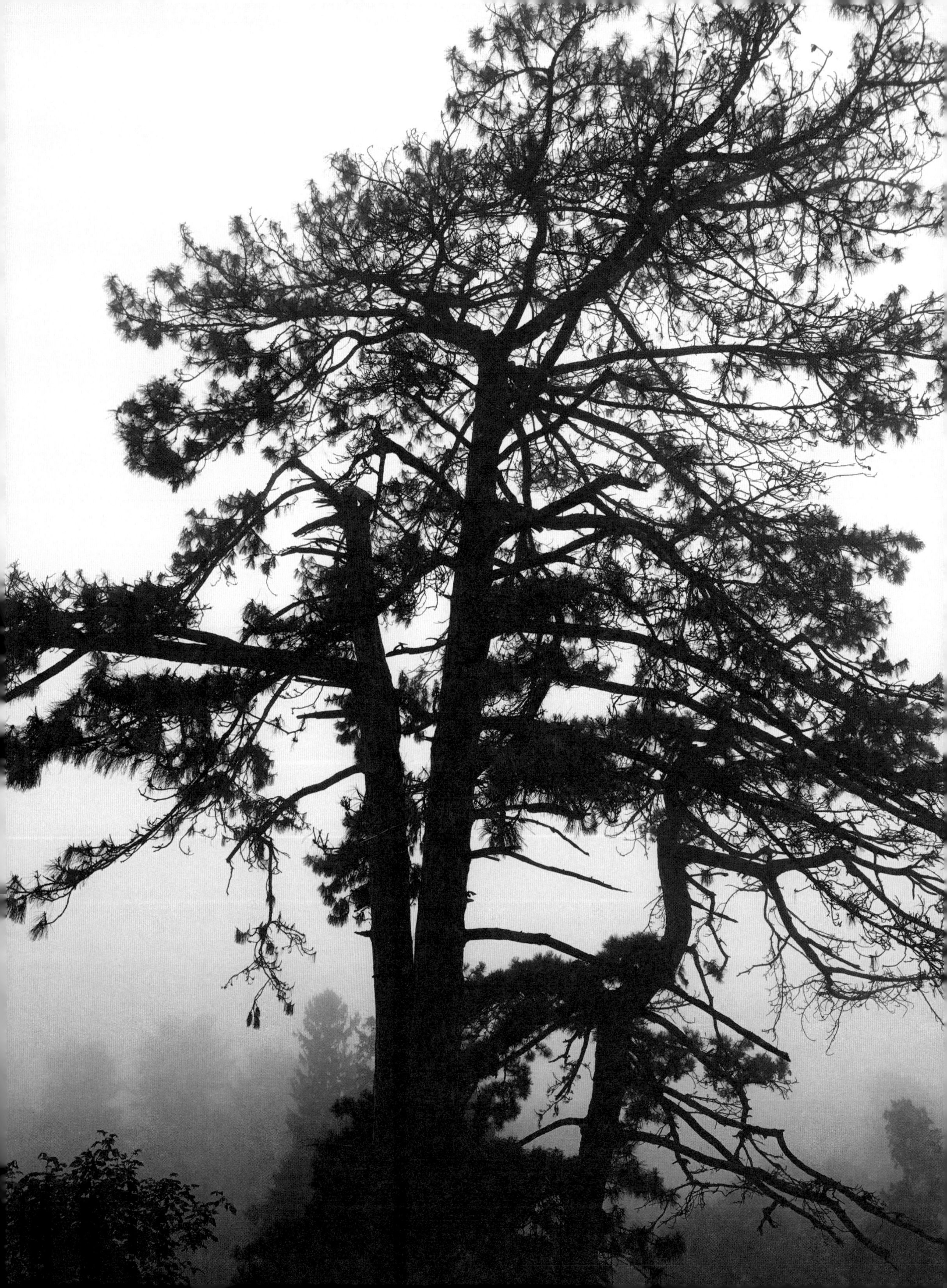

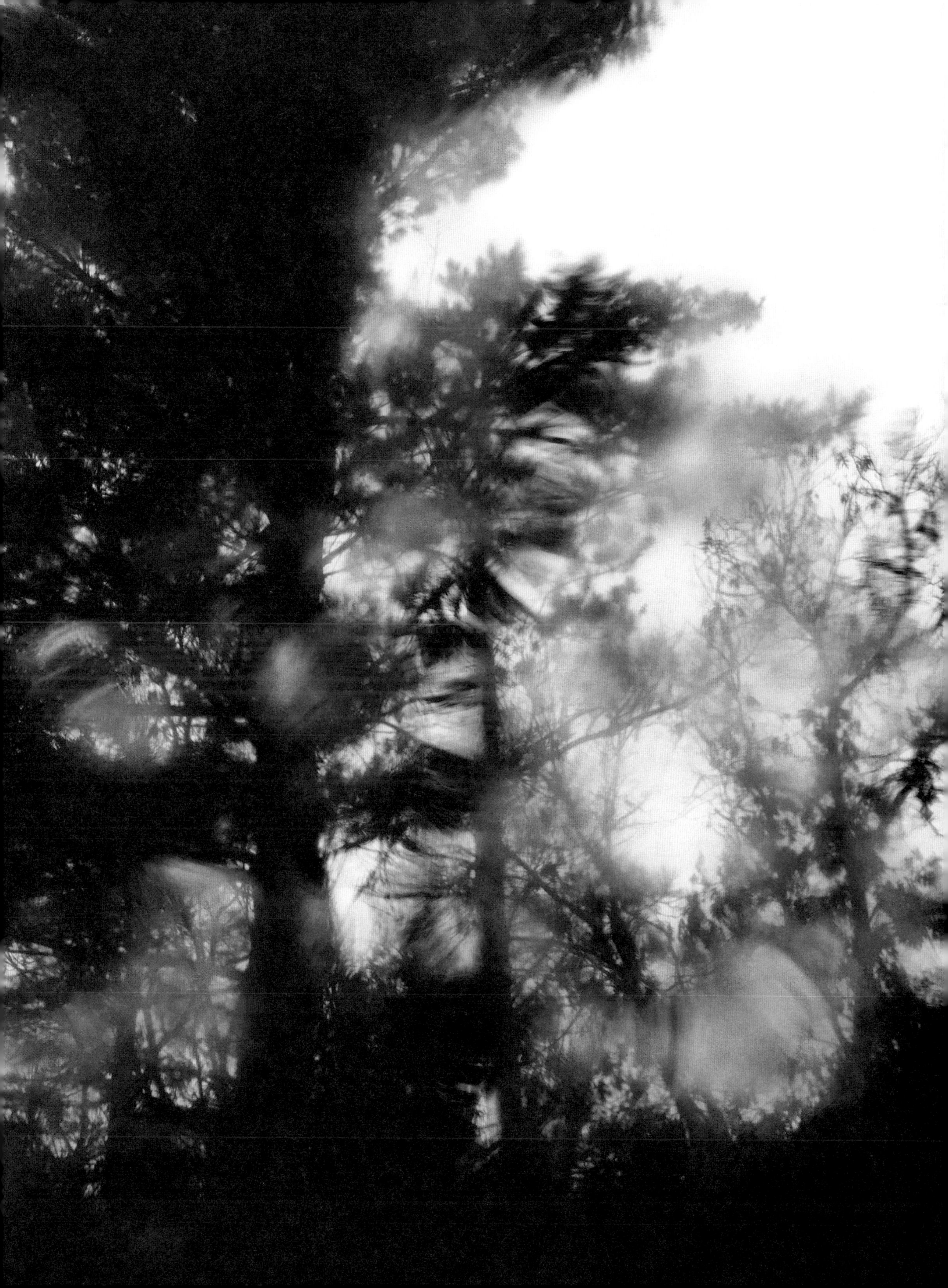

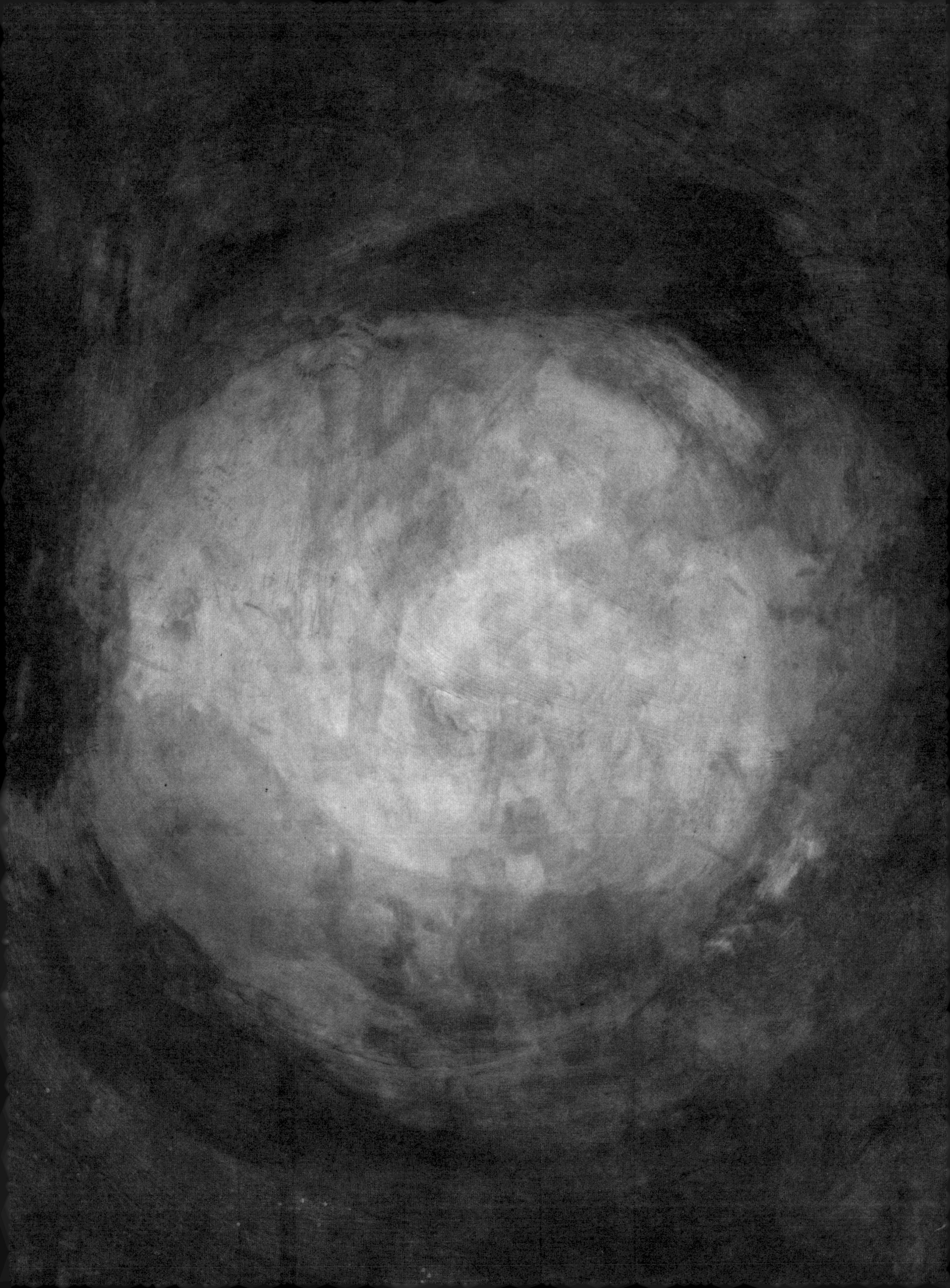

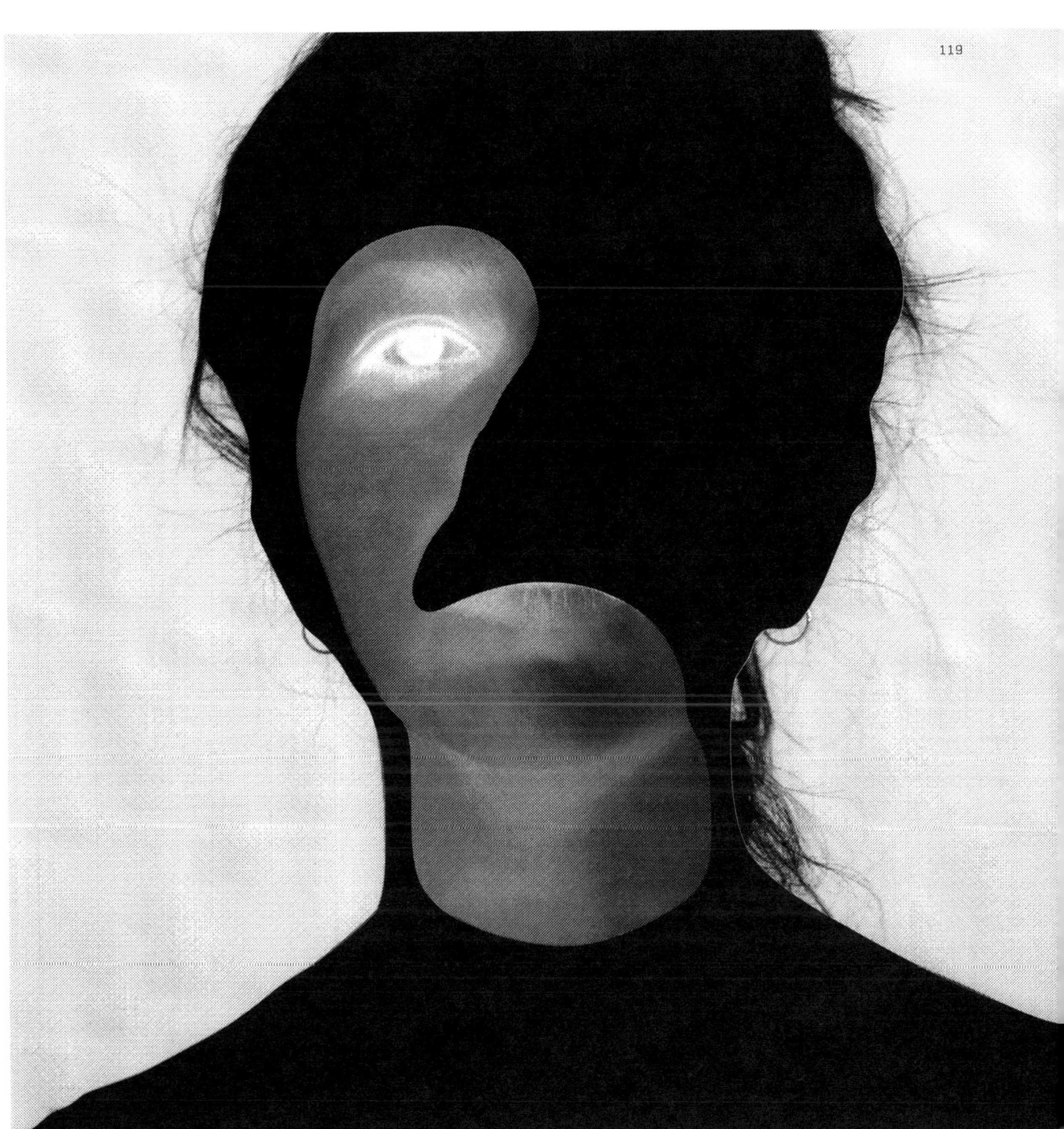

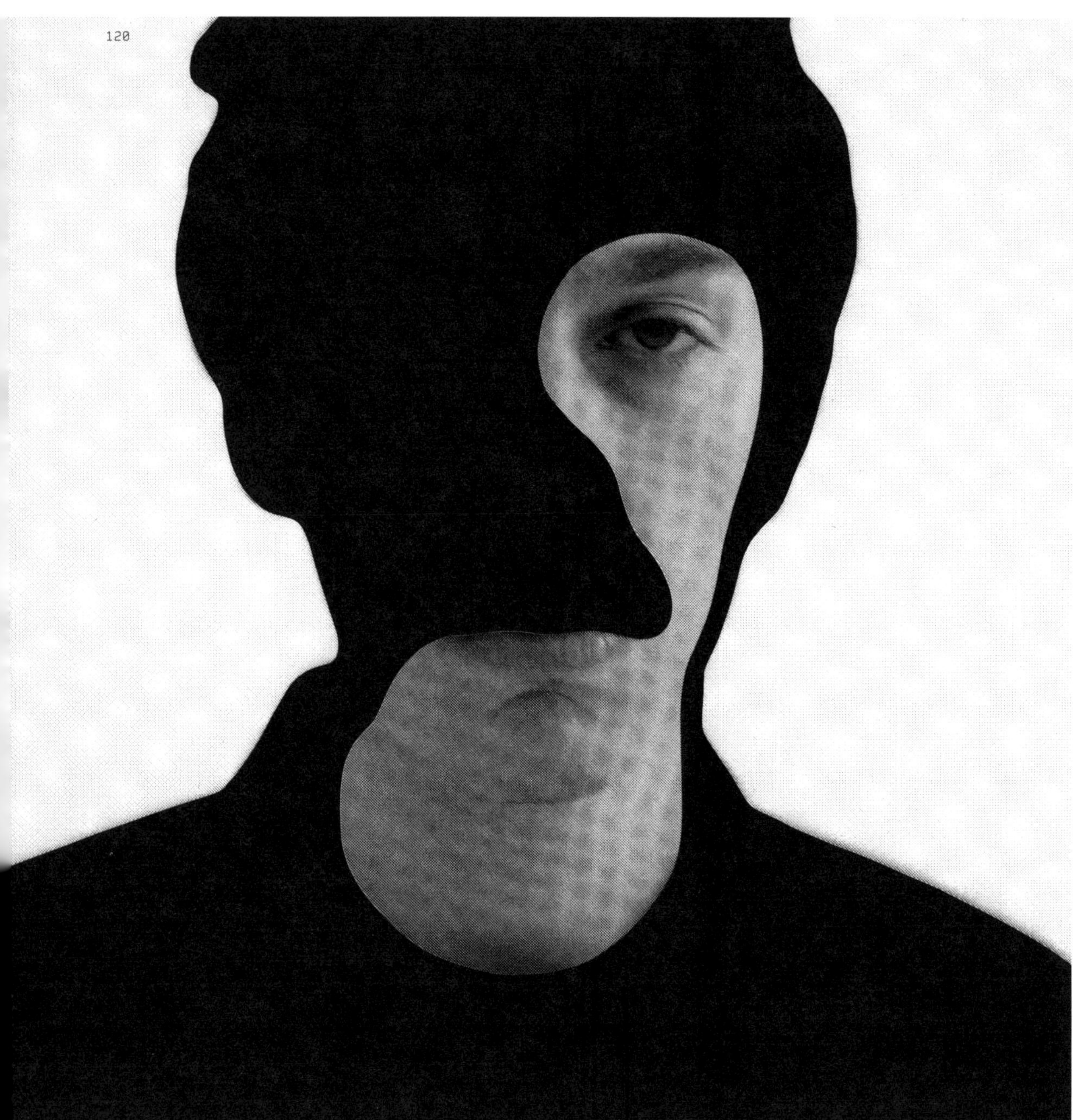

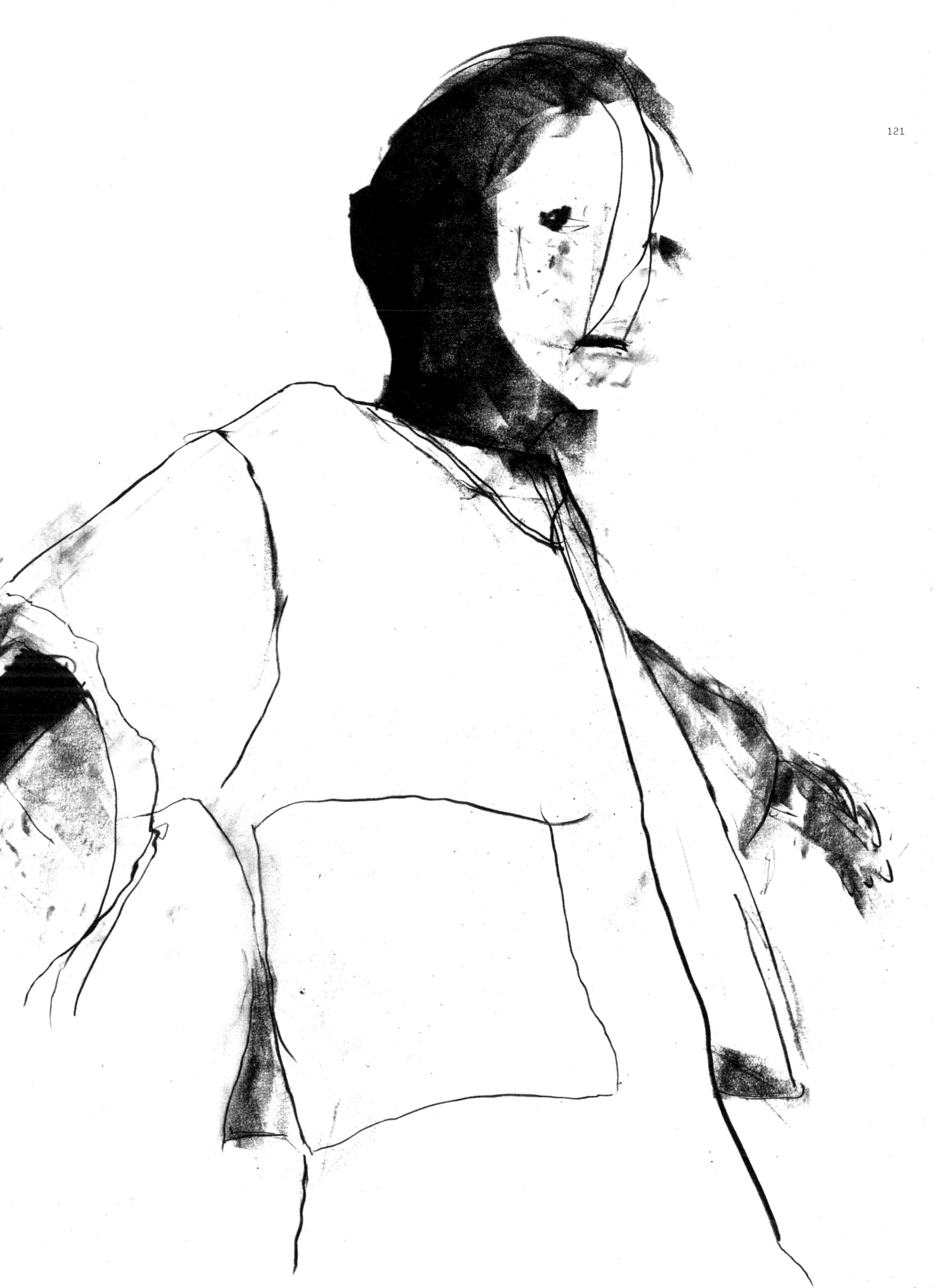

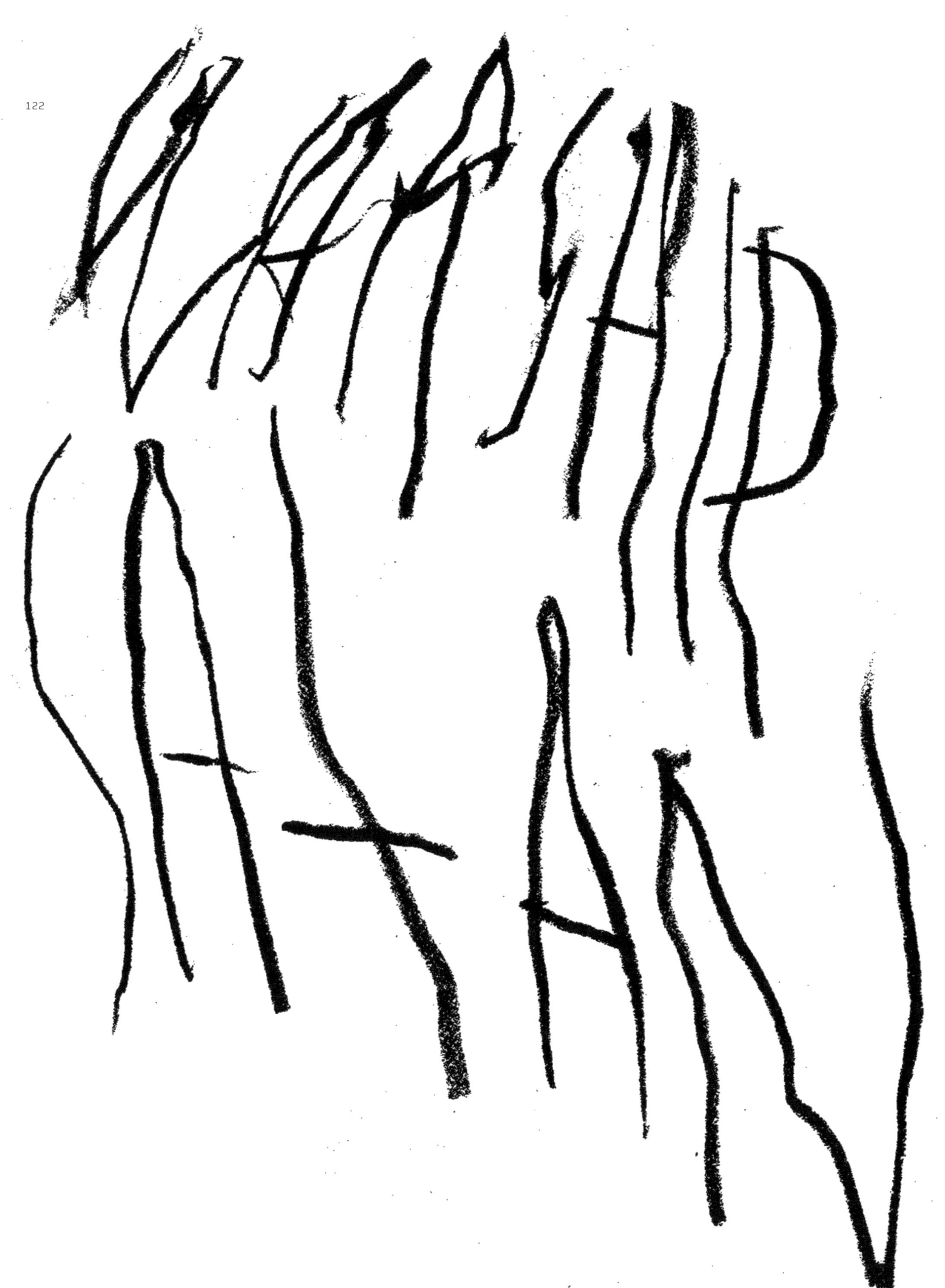

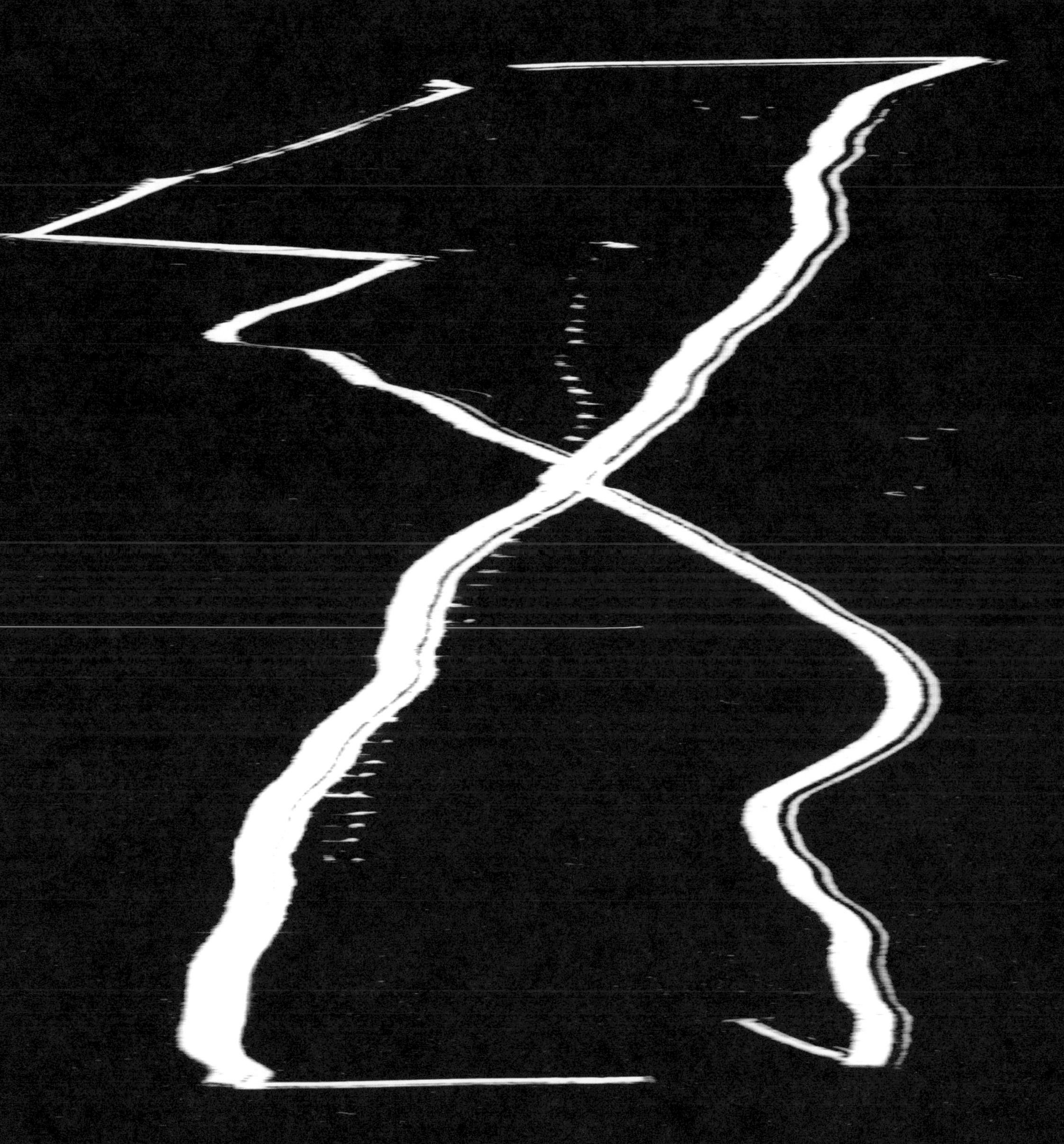

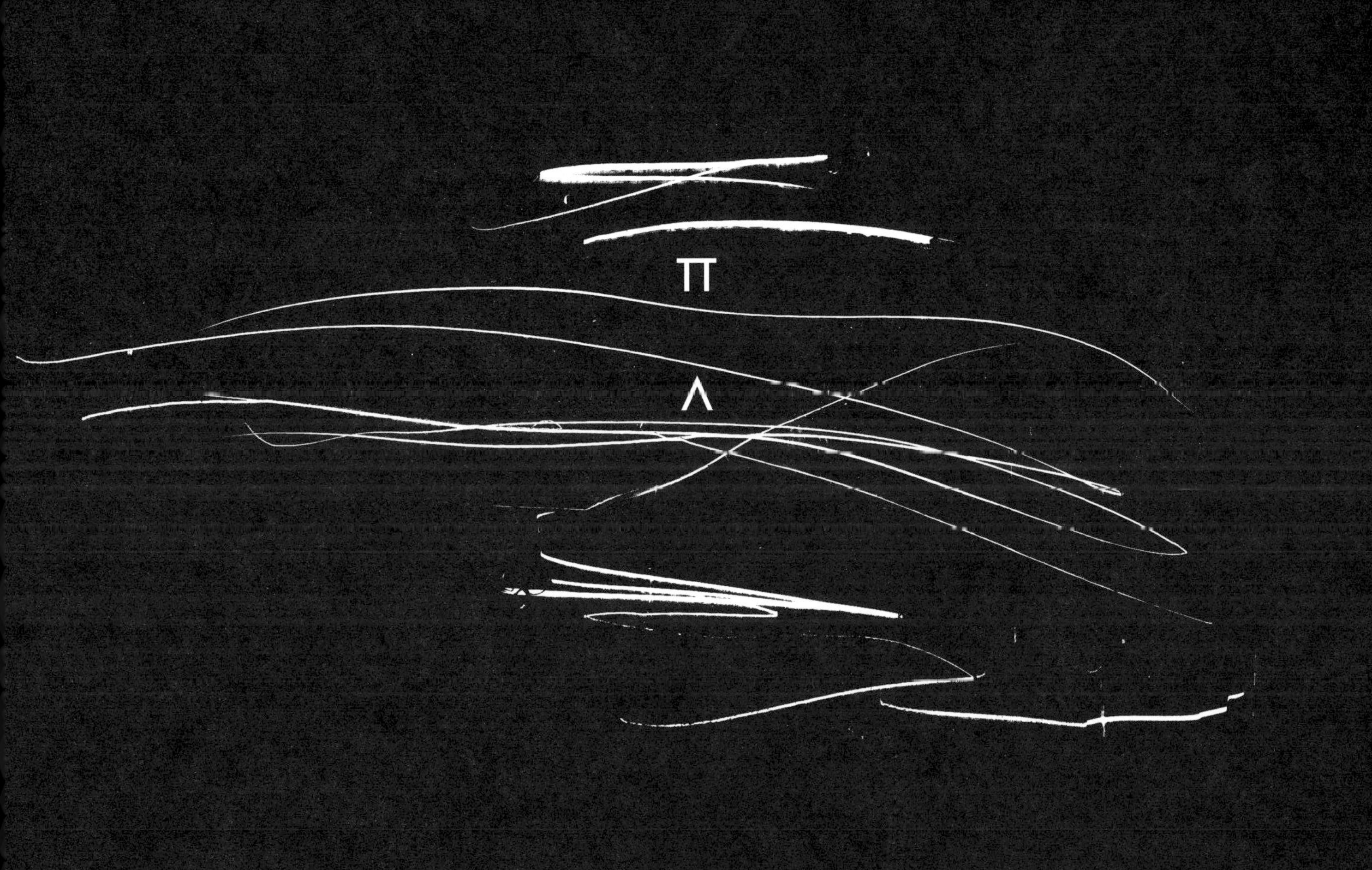

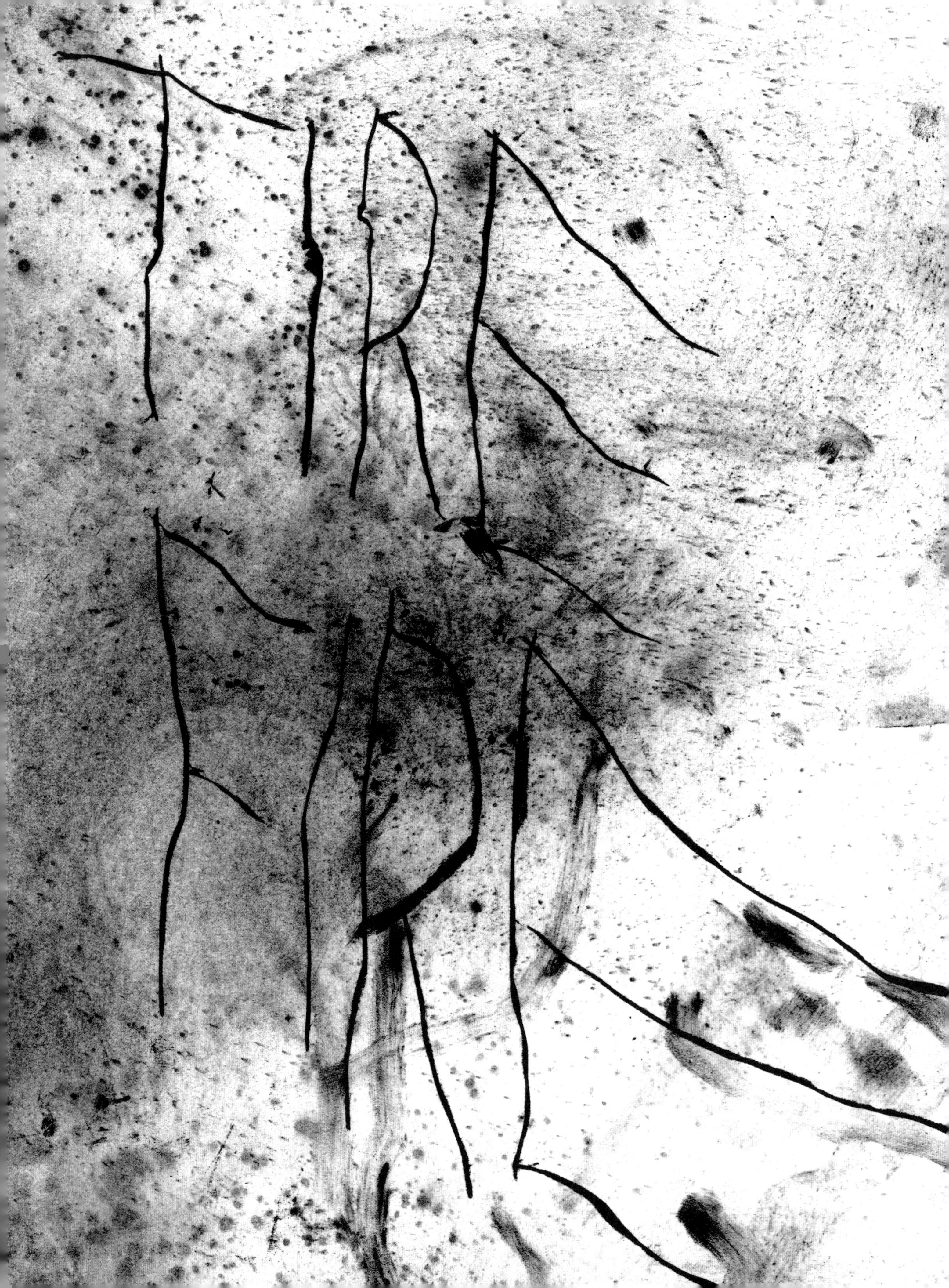

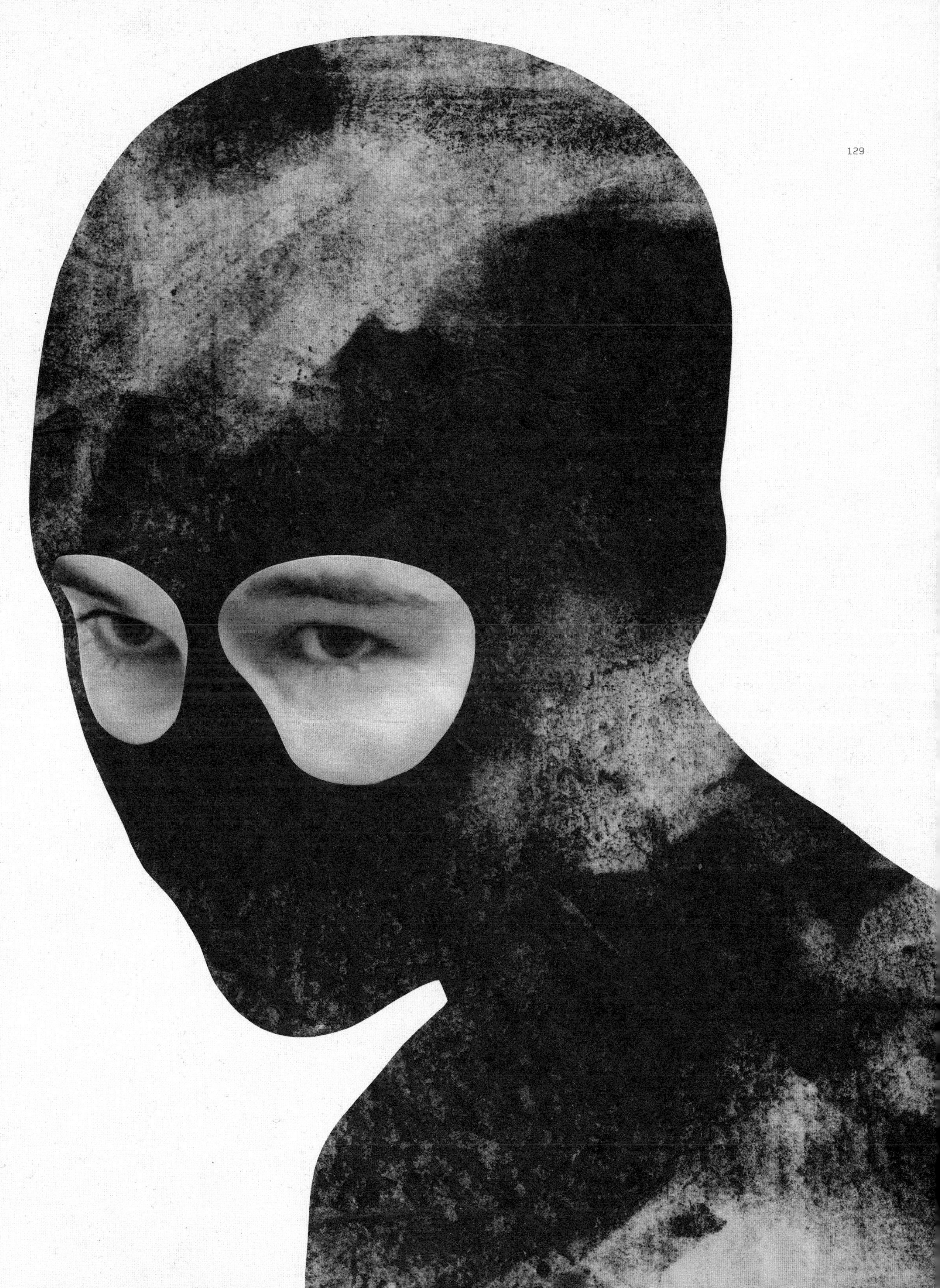

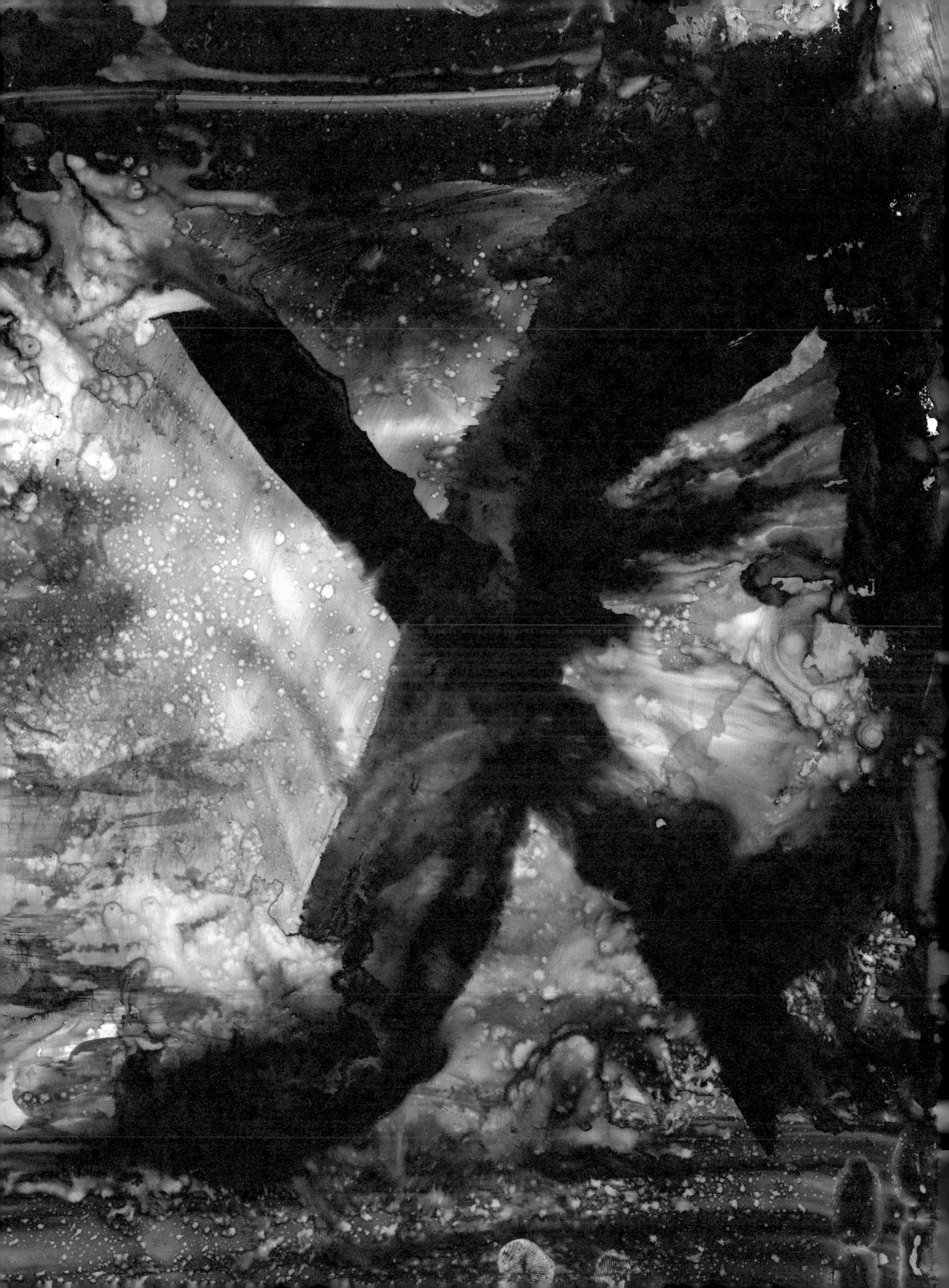

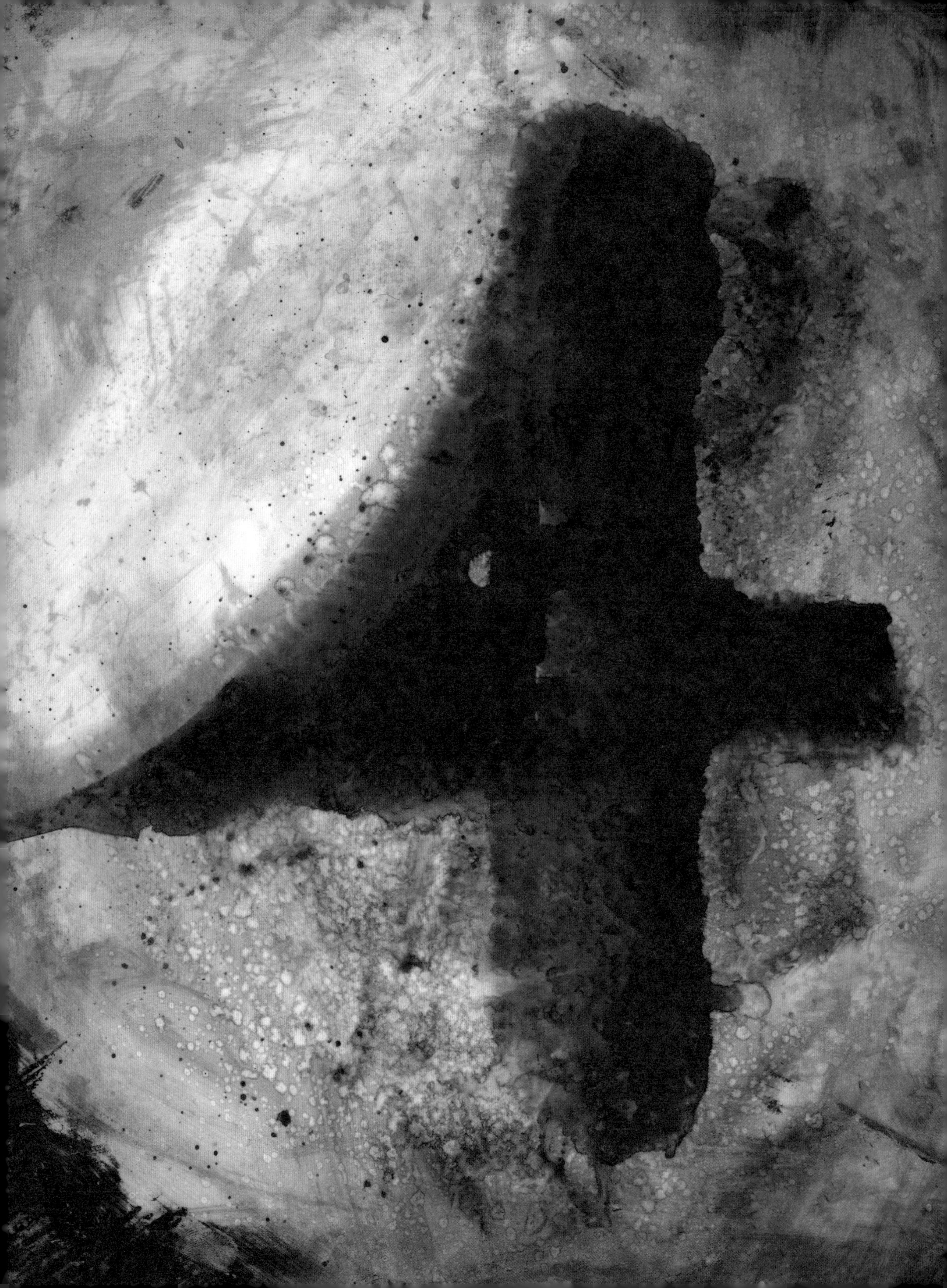

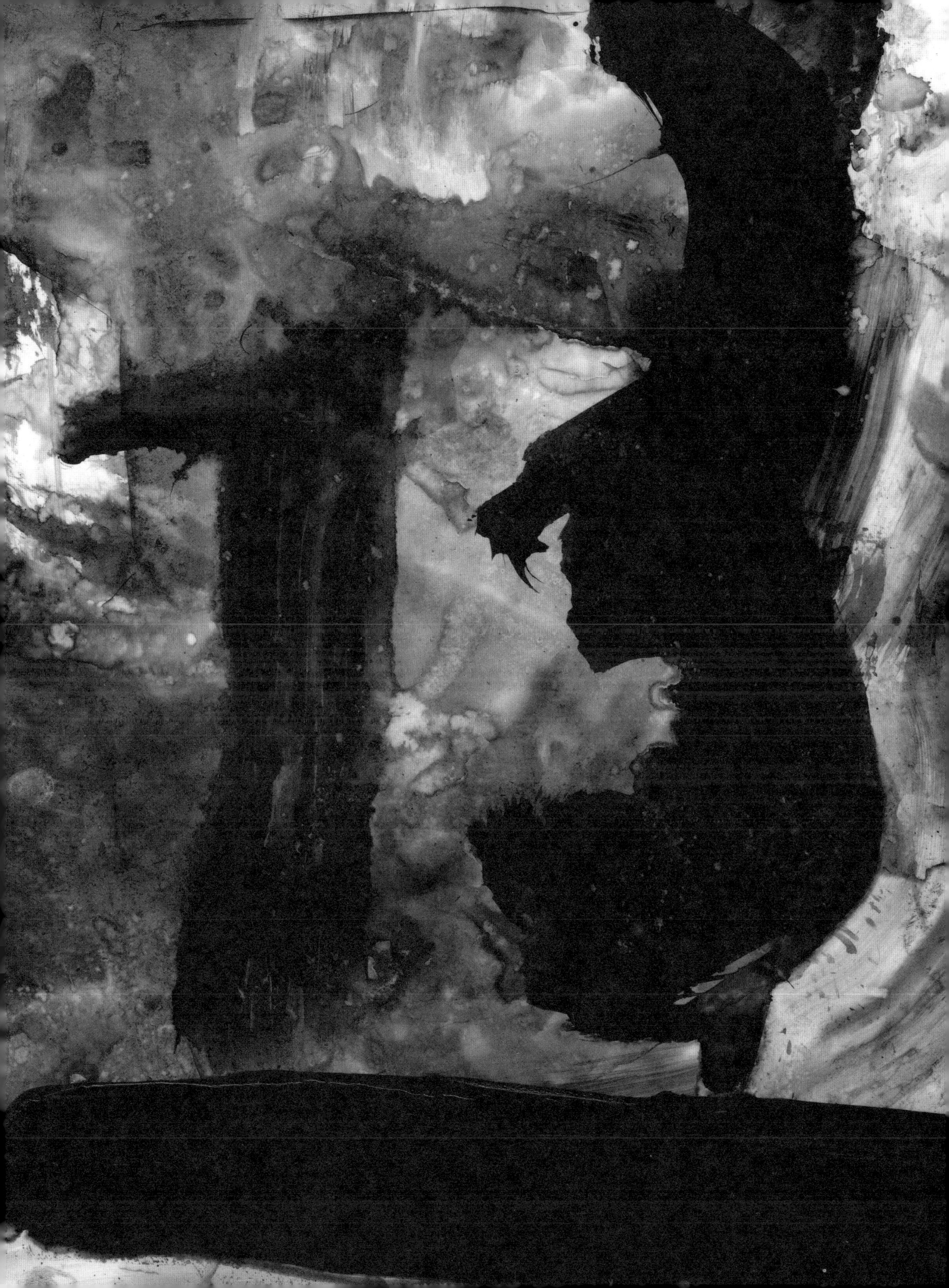

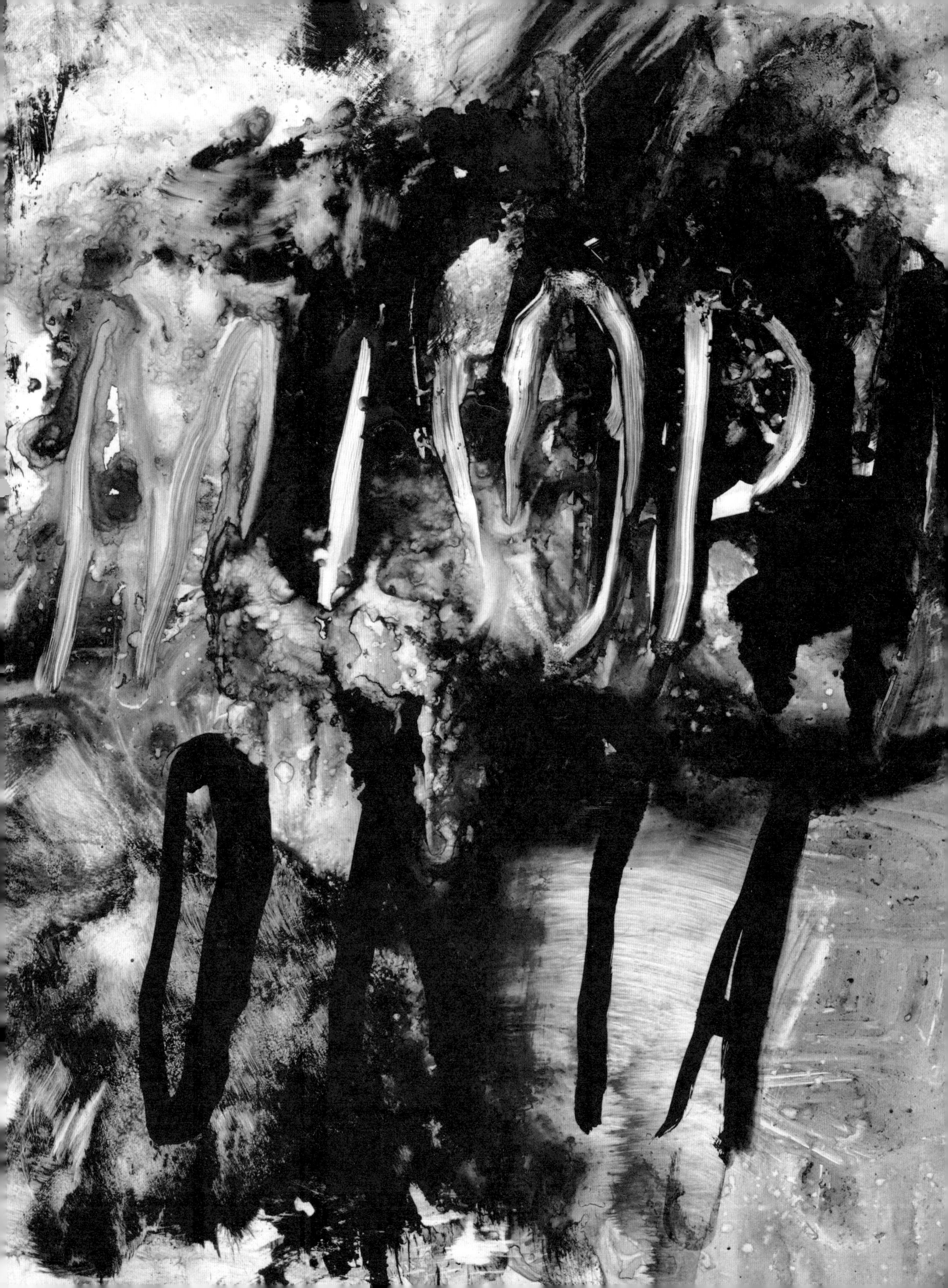

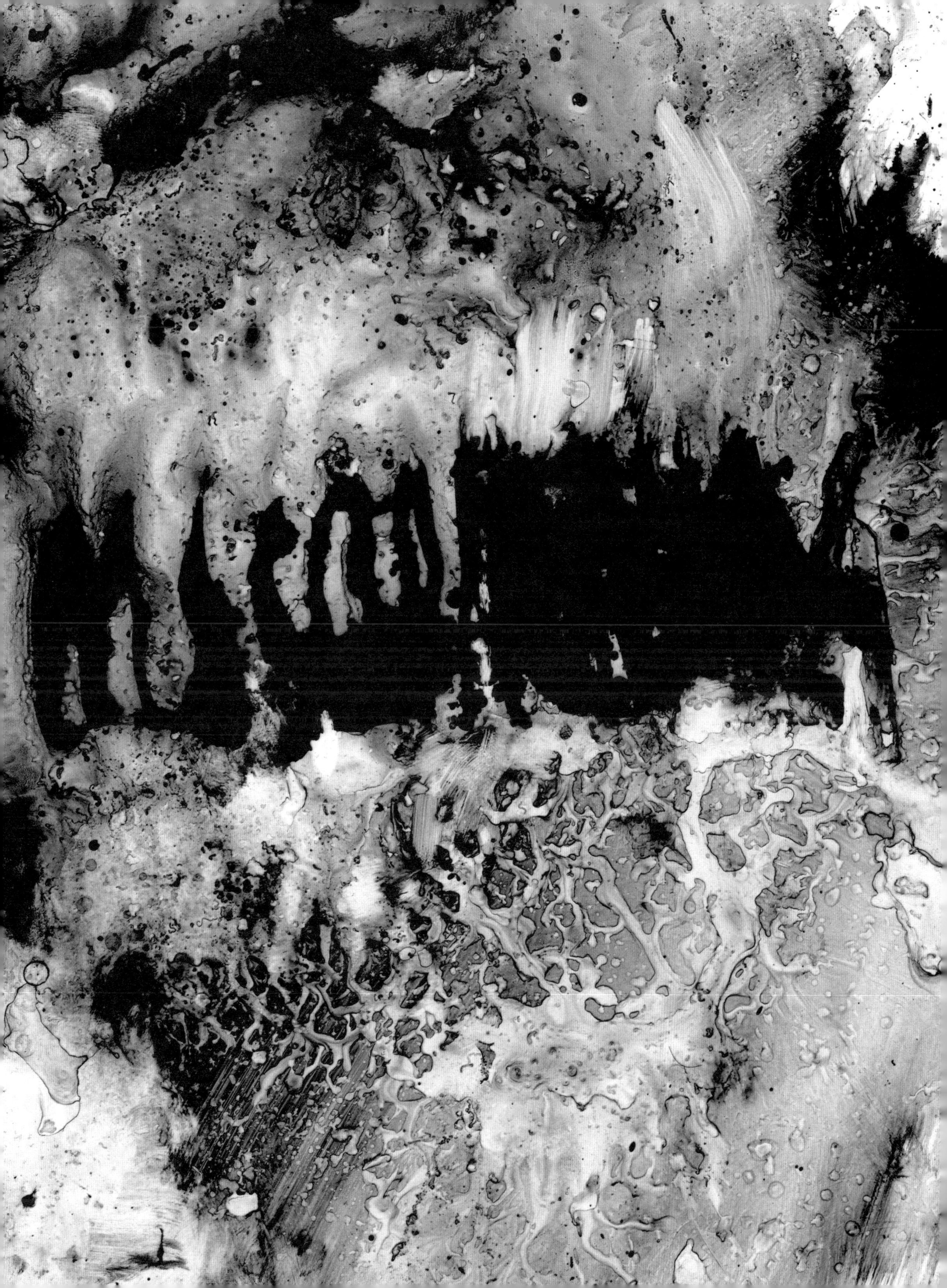

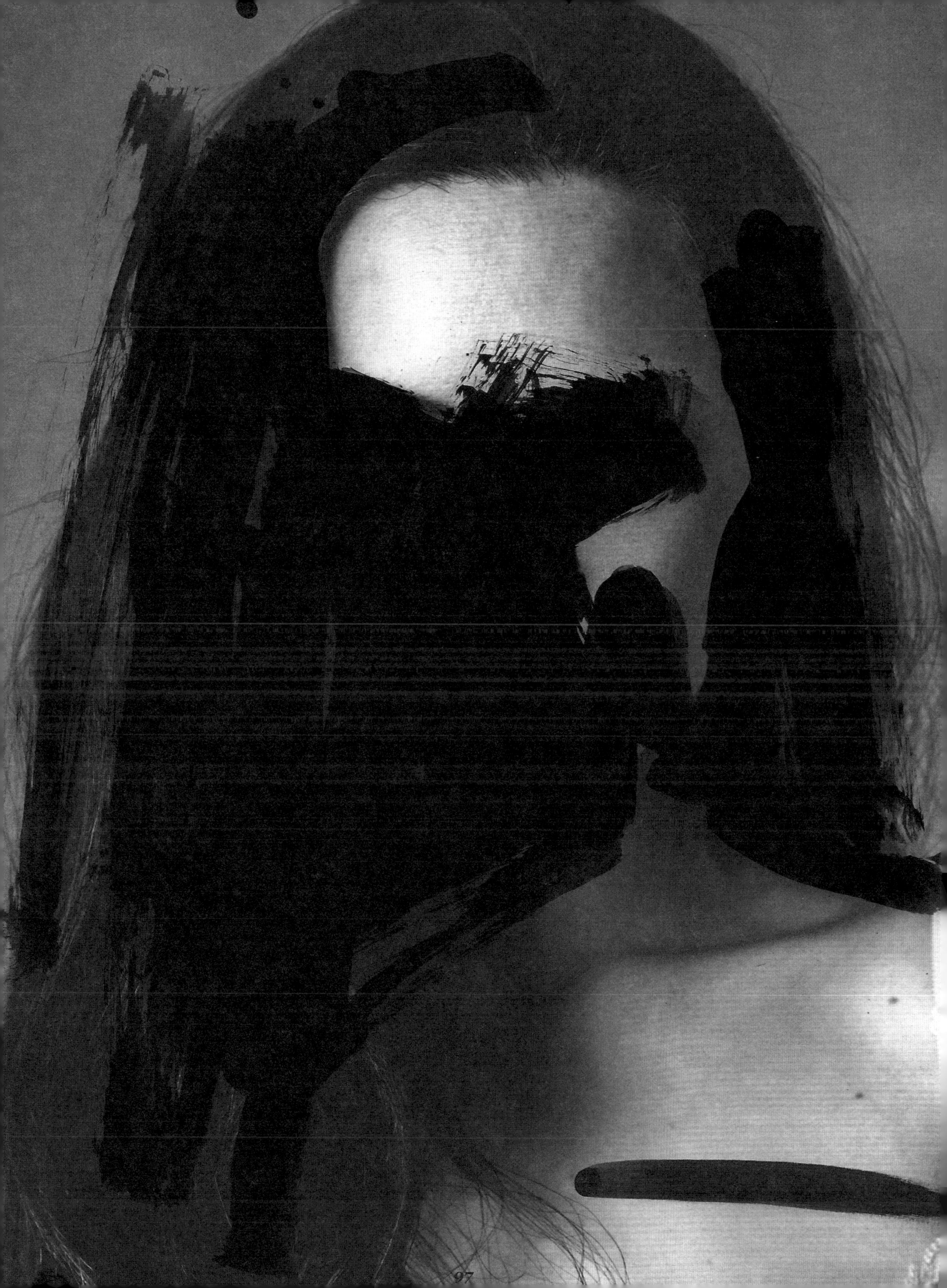

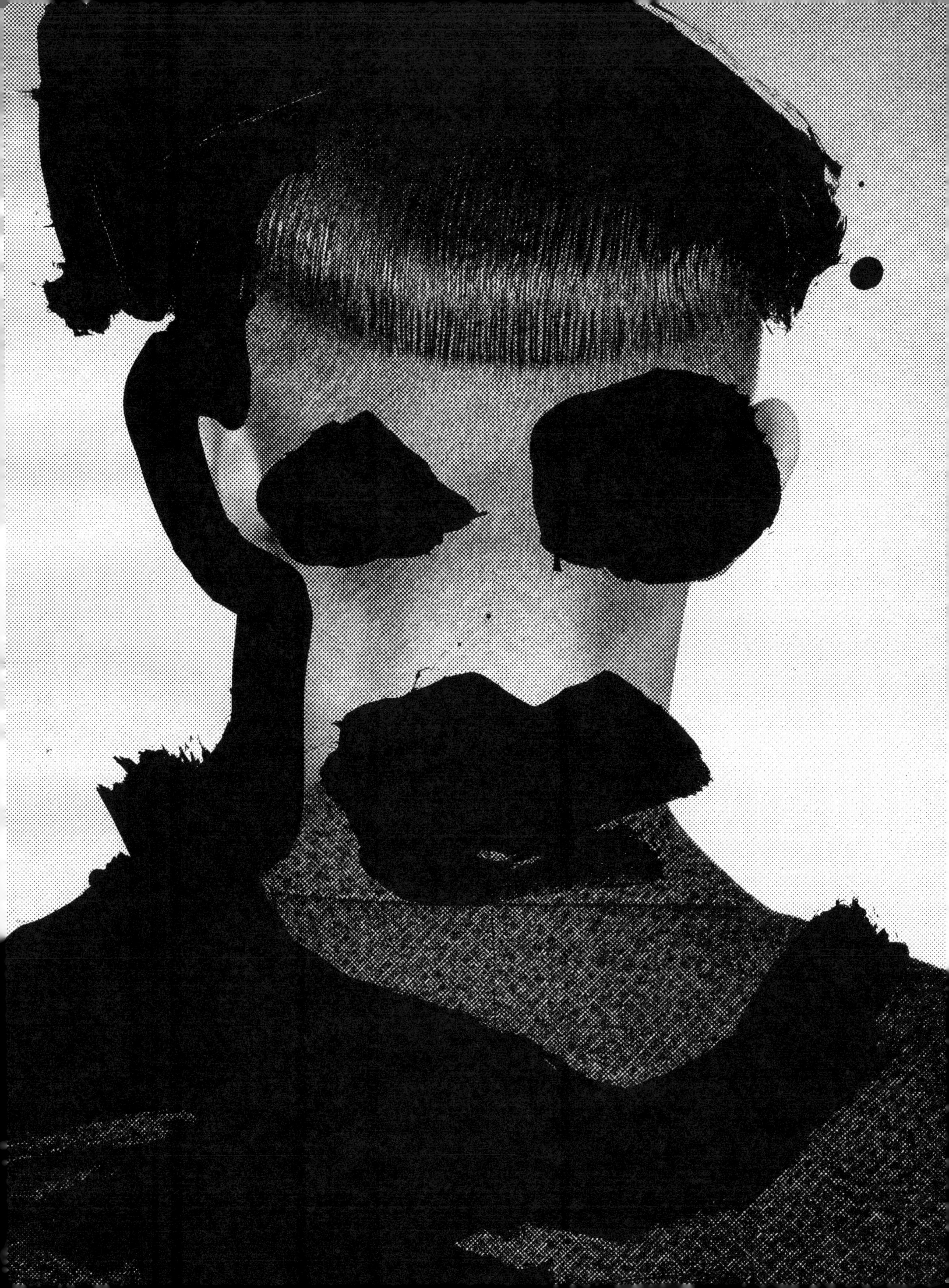

NA
photography — WINTER VANDENBRINK
LONDON, ENGLAND

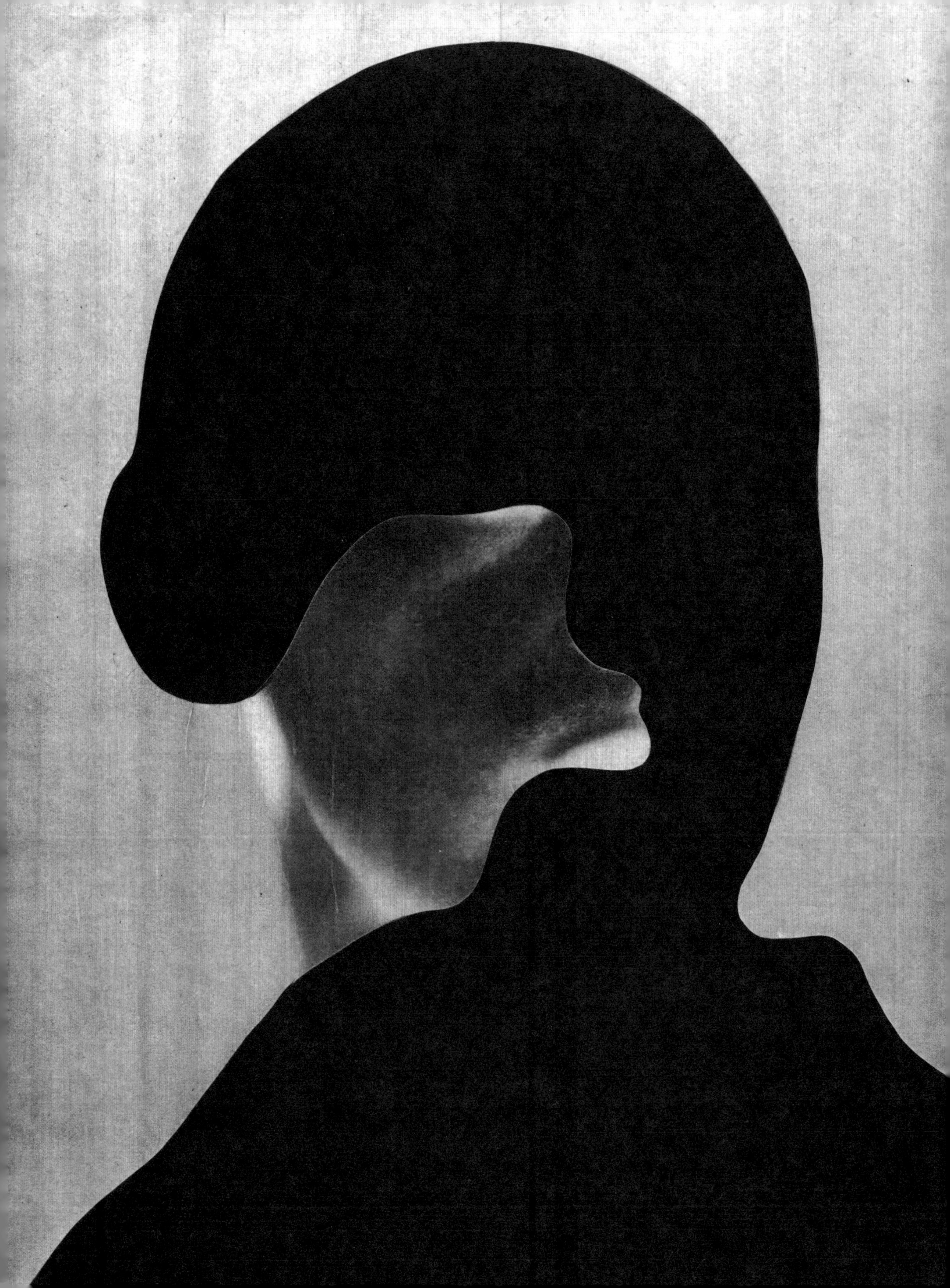

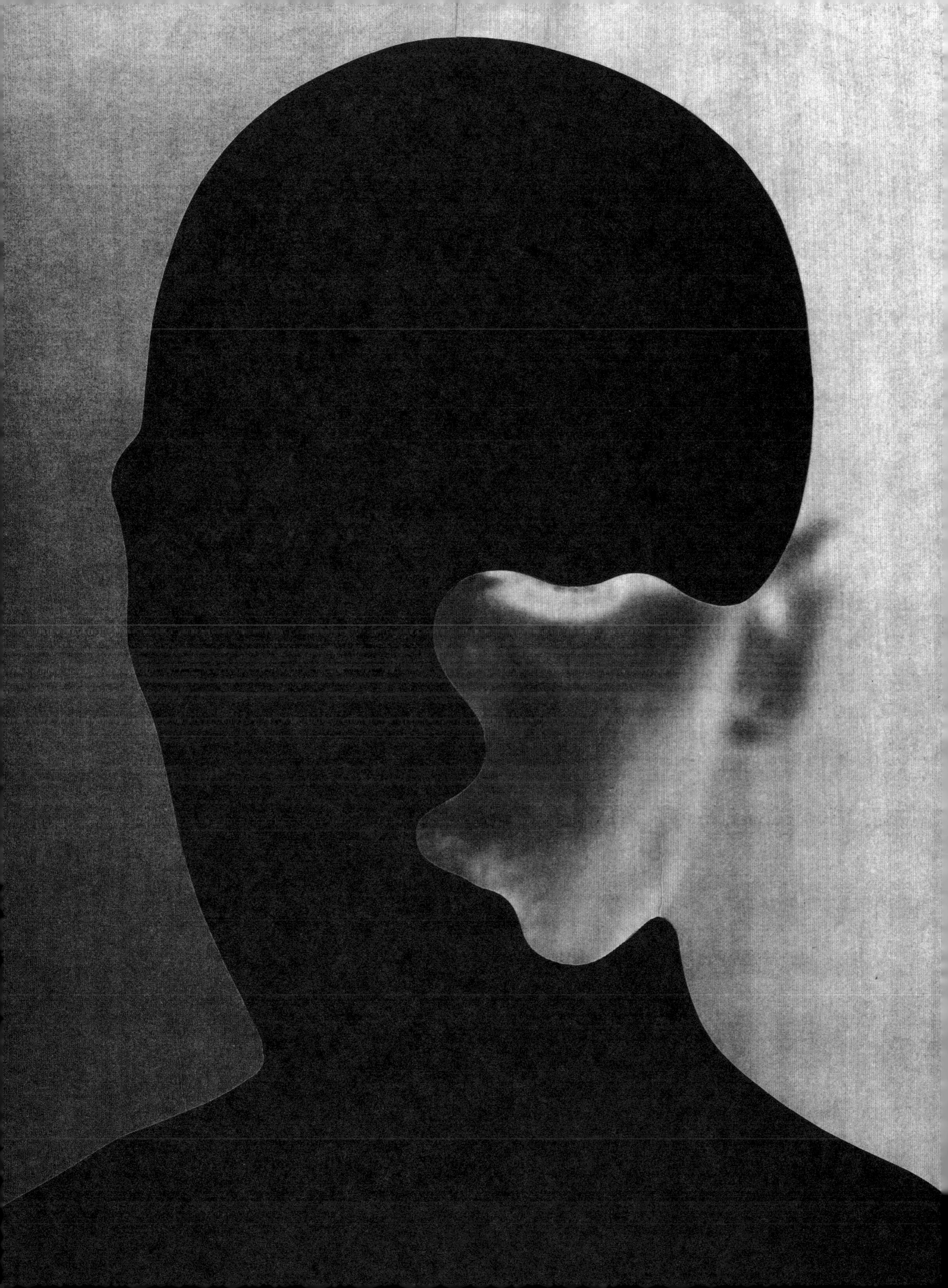

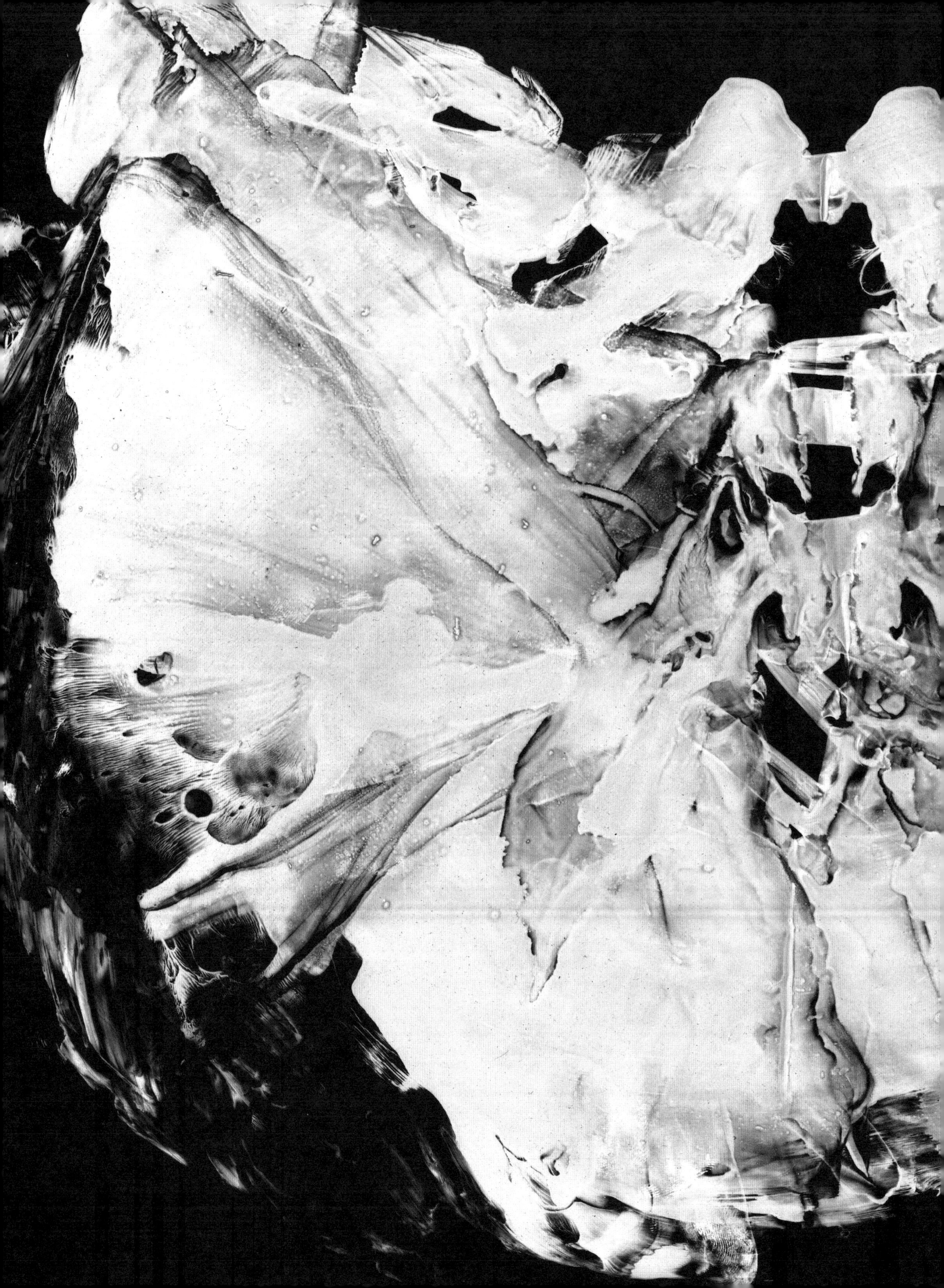

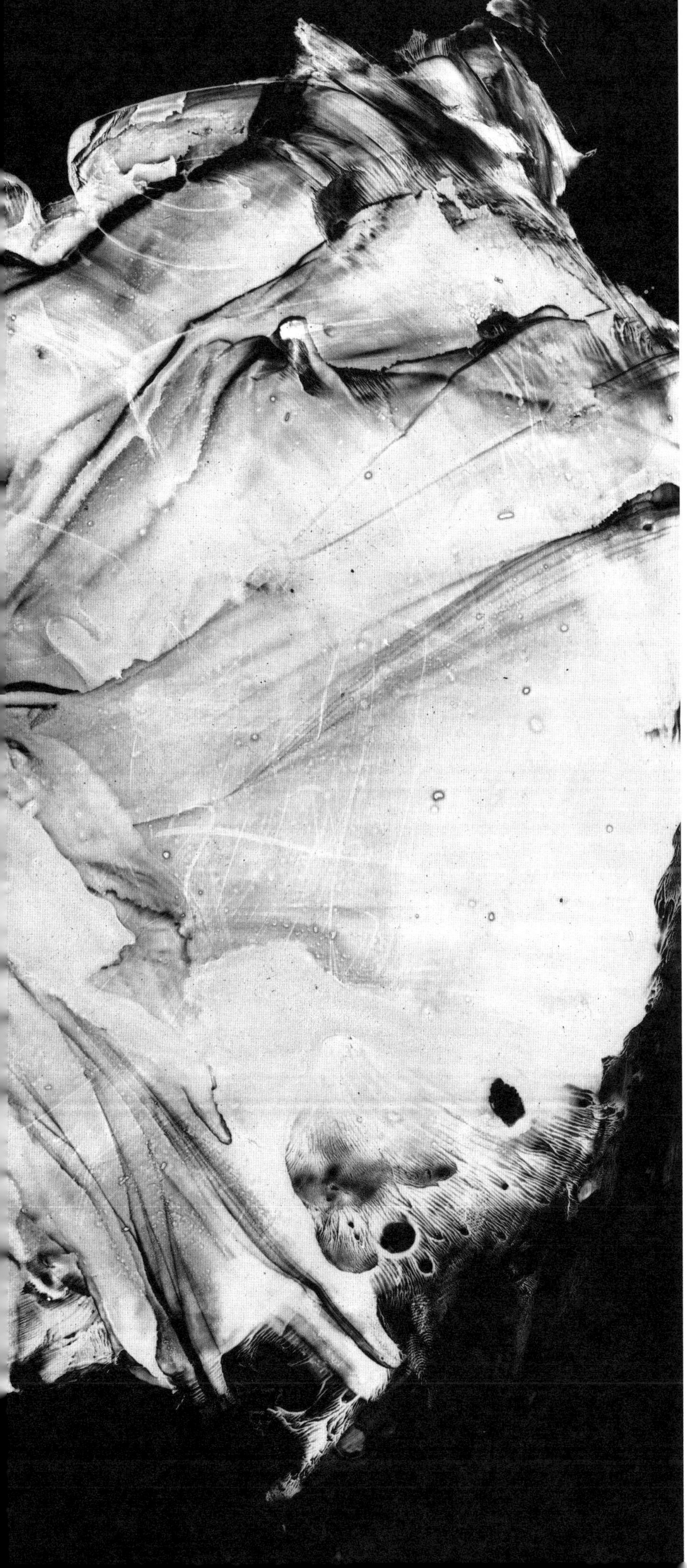

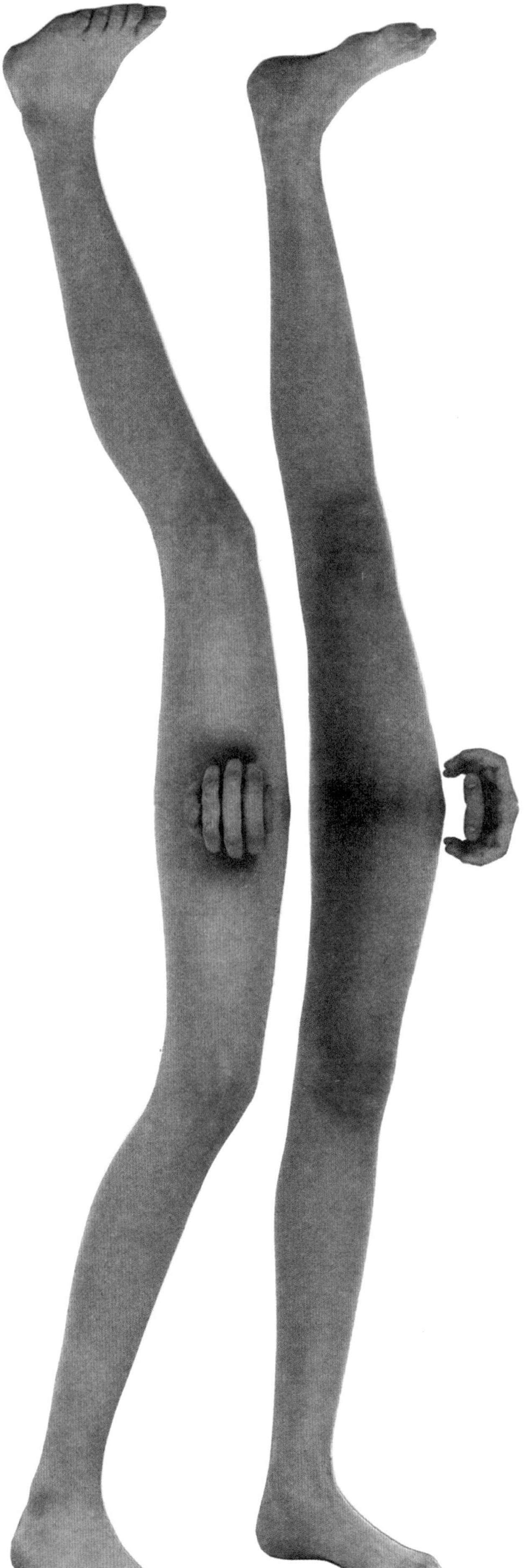

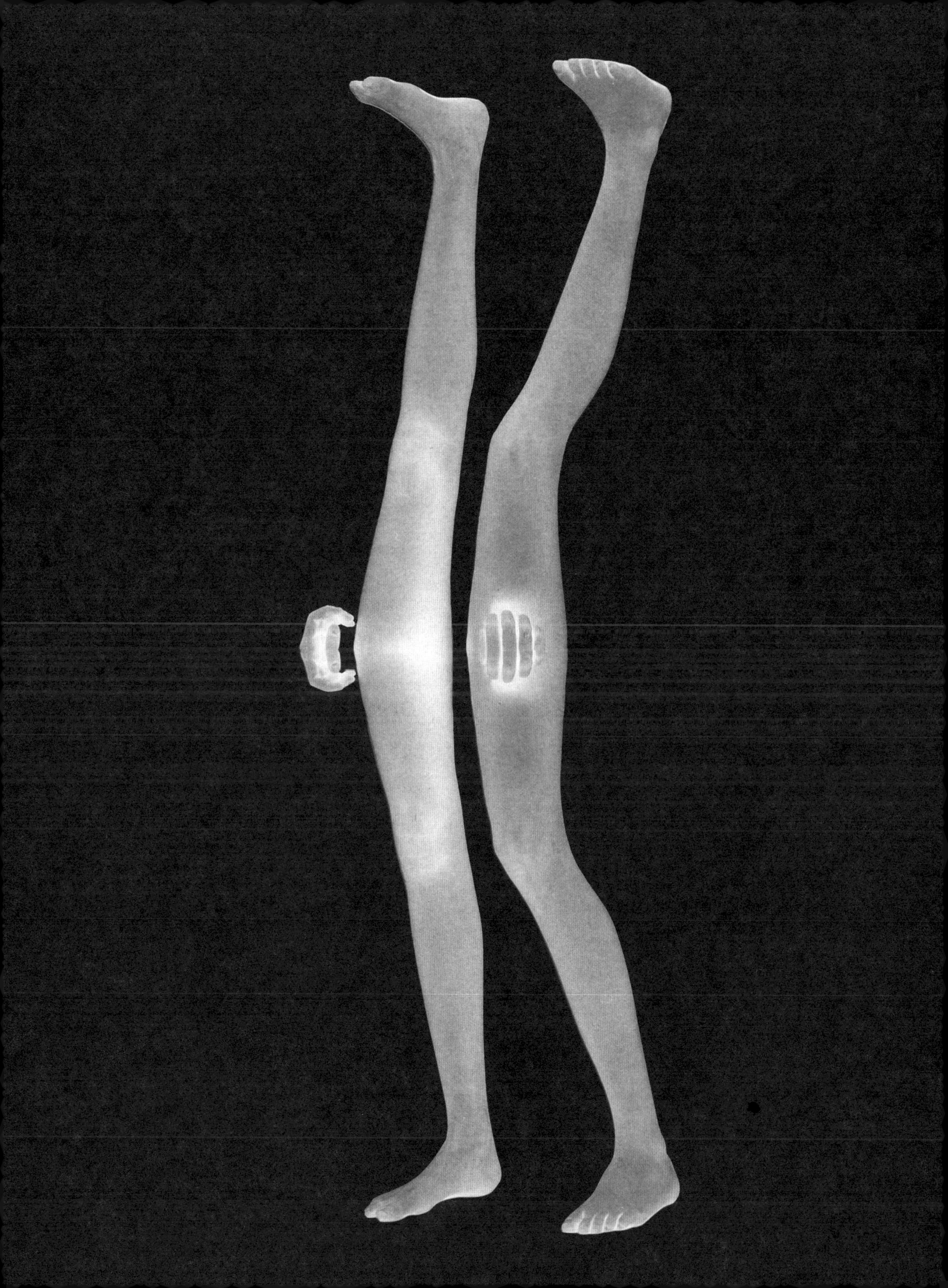

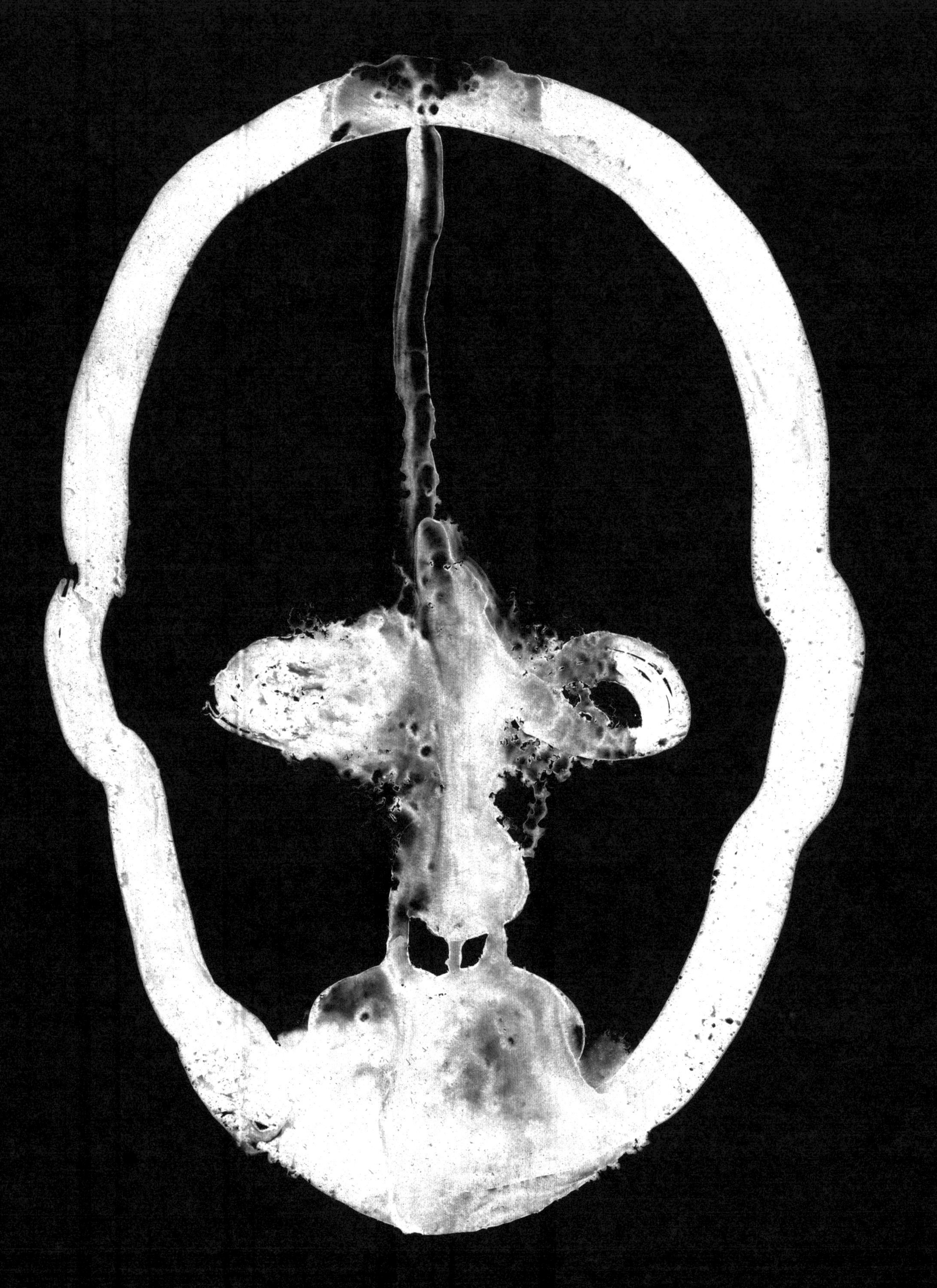

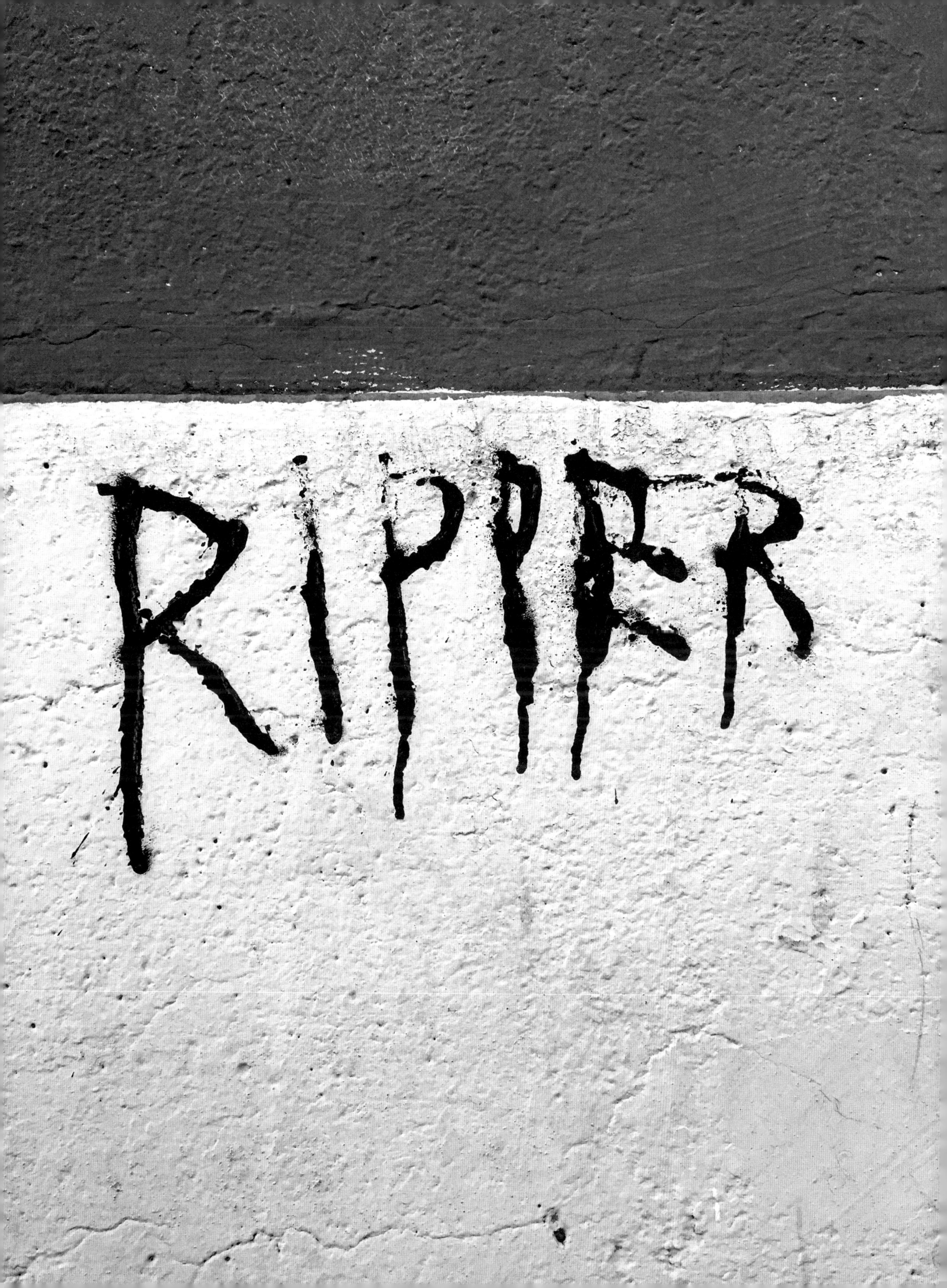
RIPPER

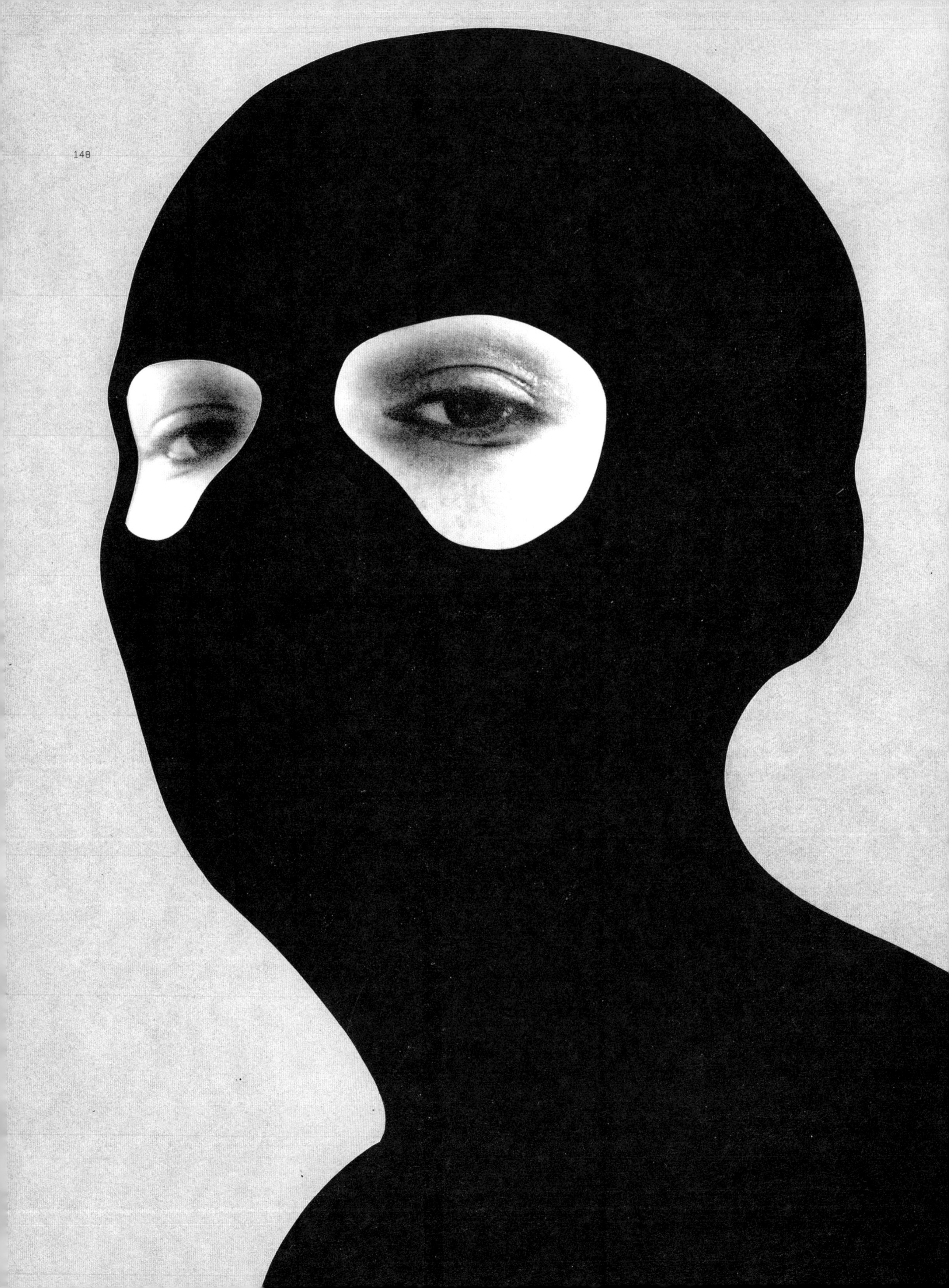

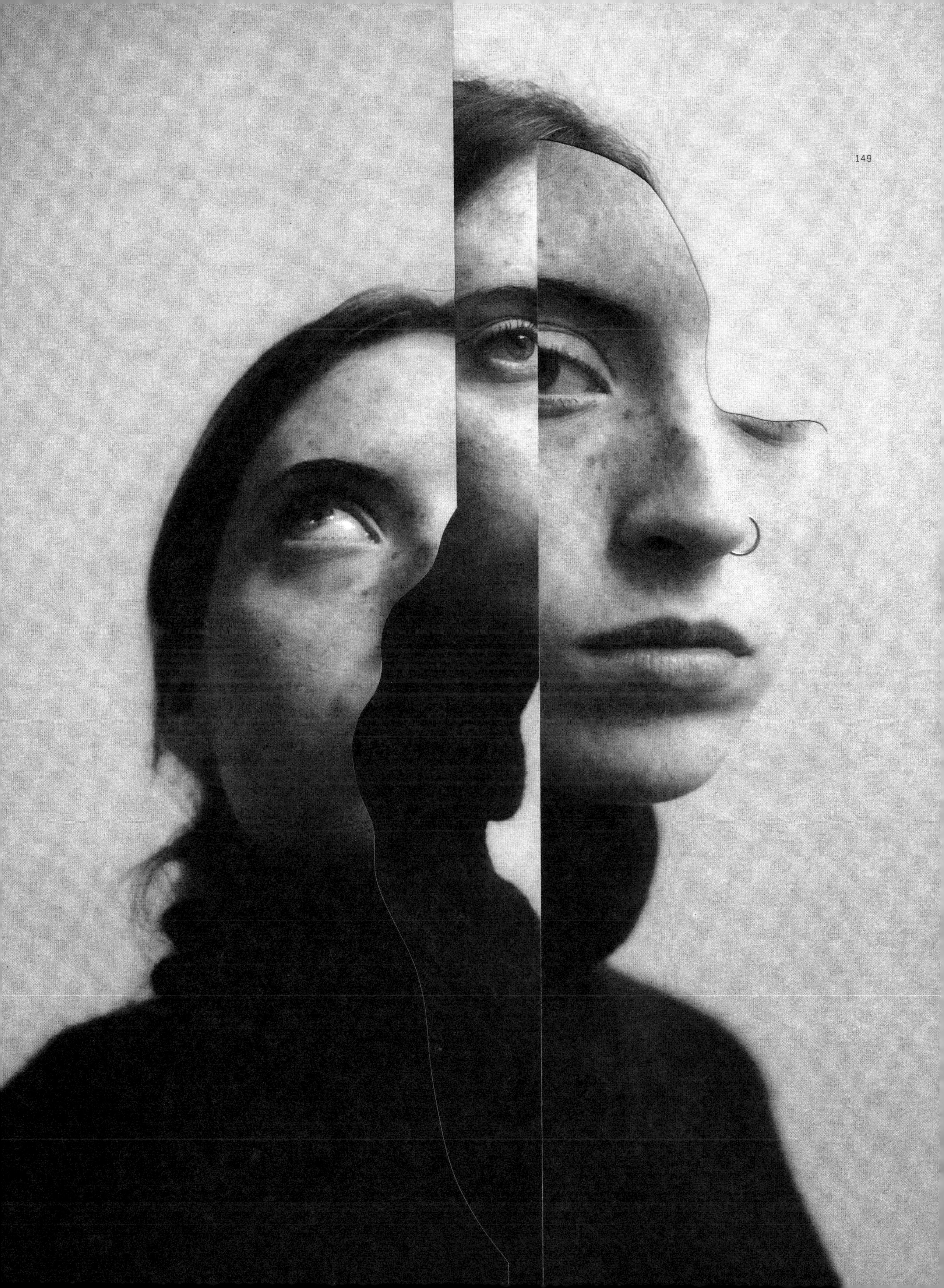

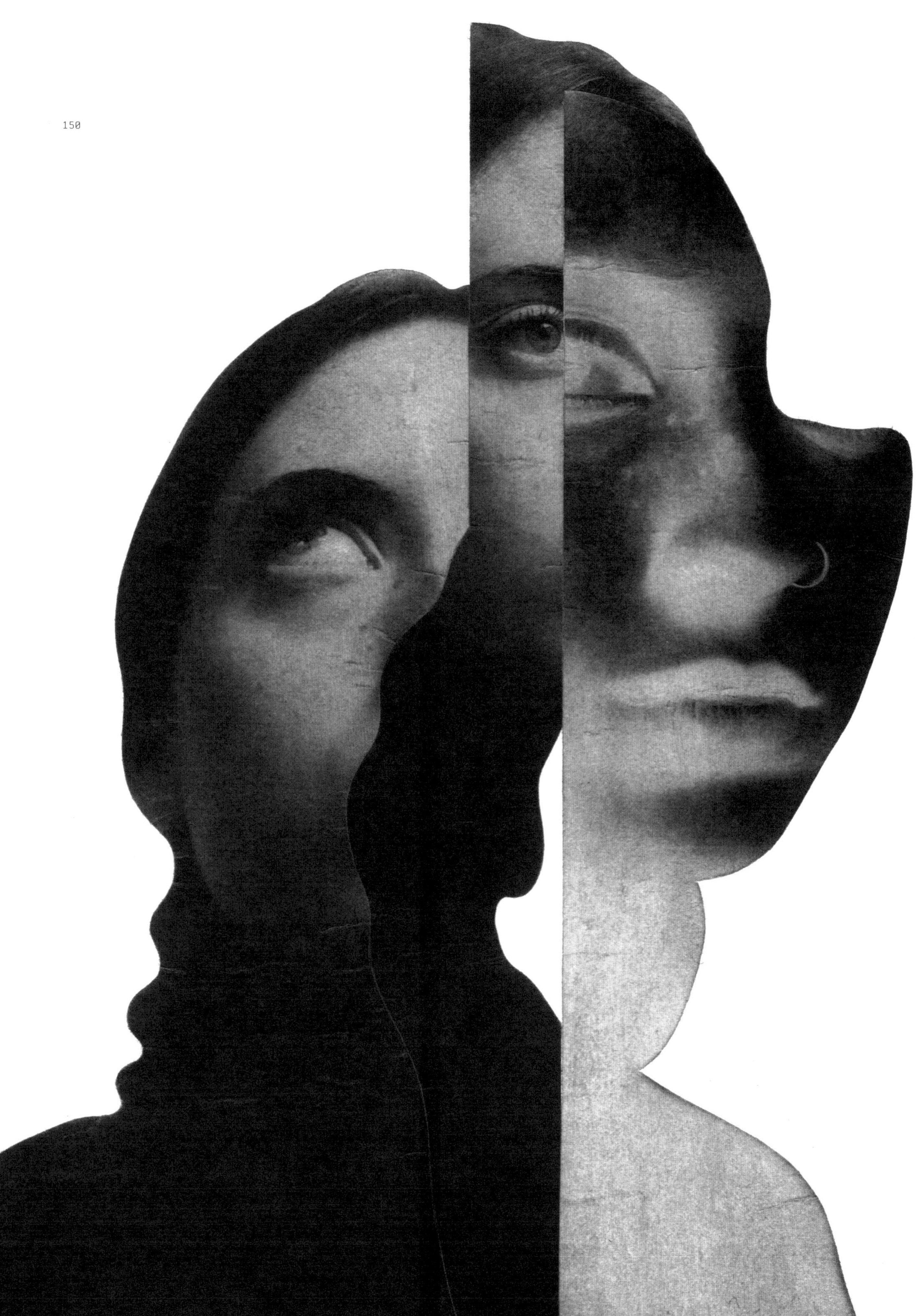

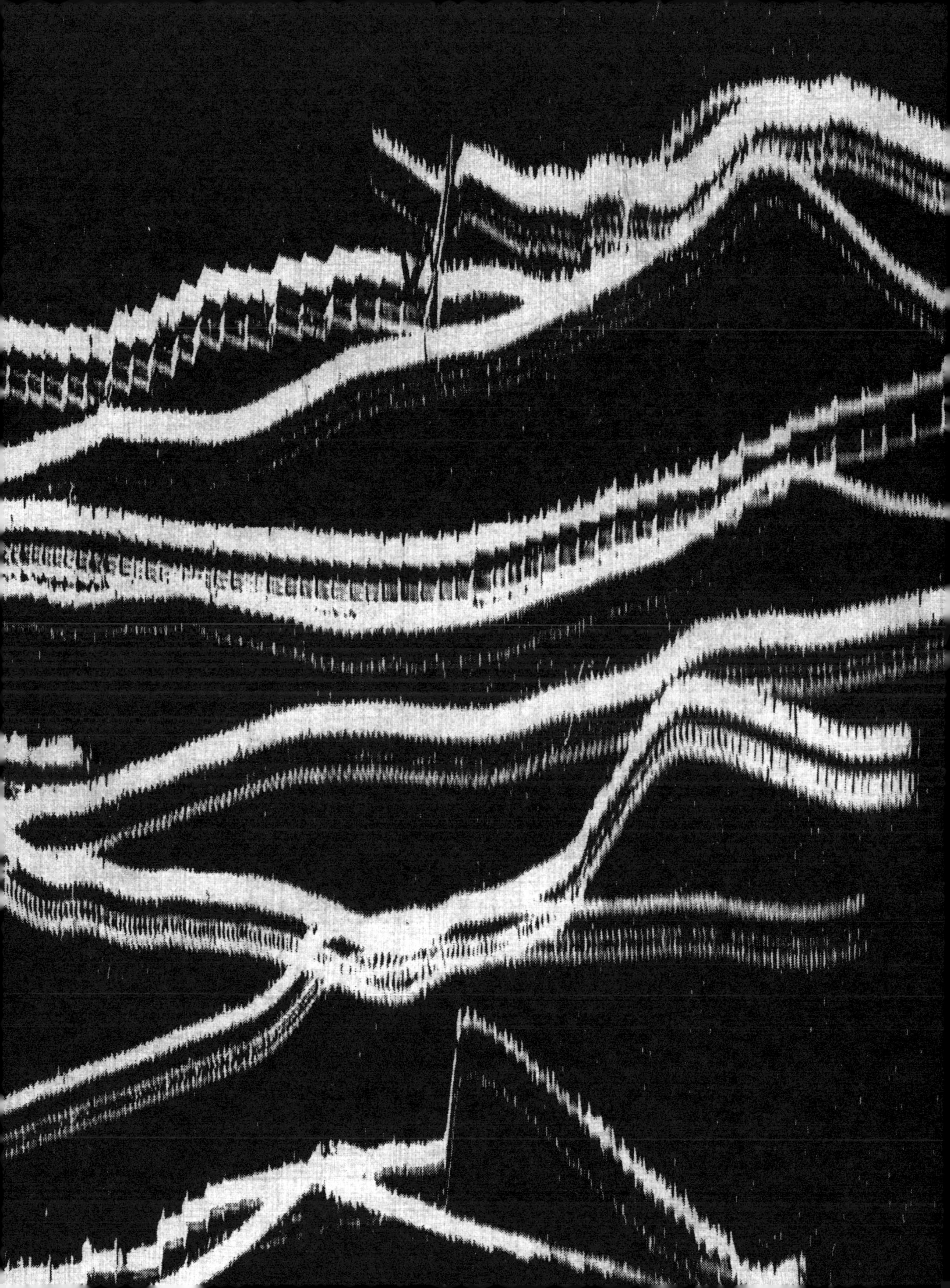

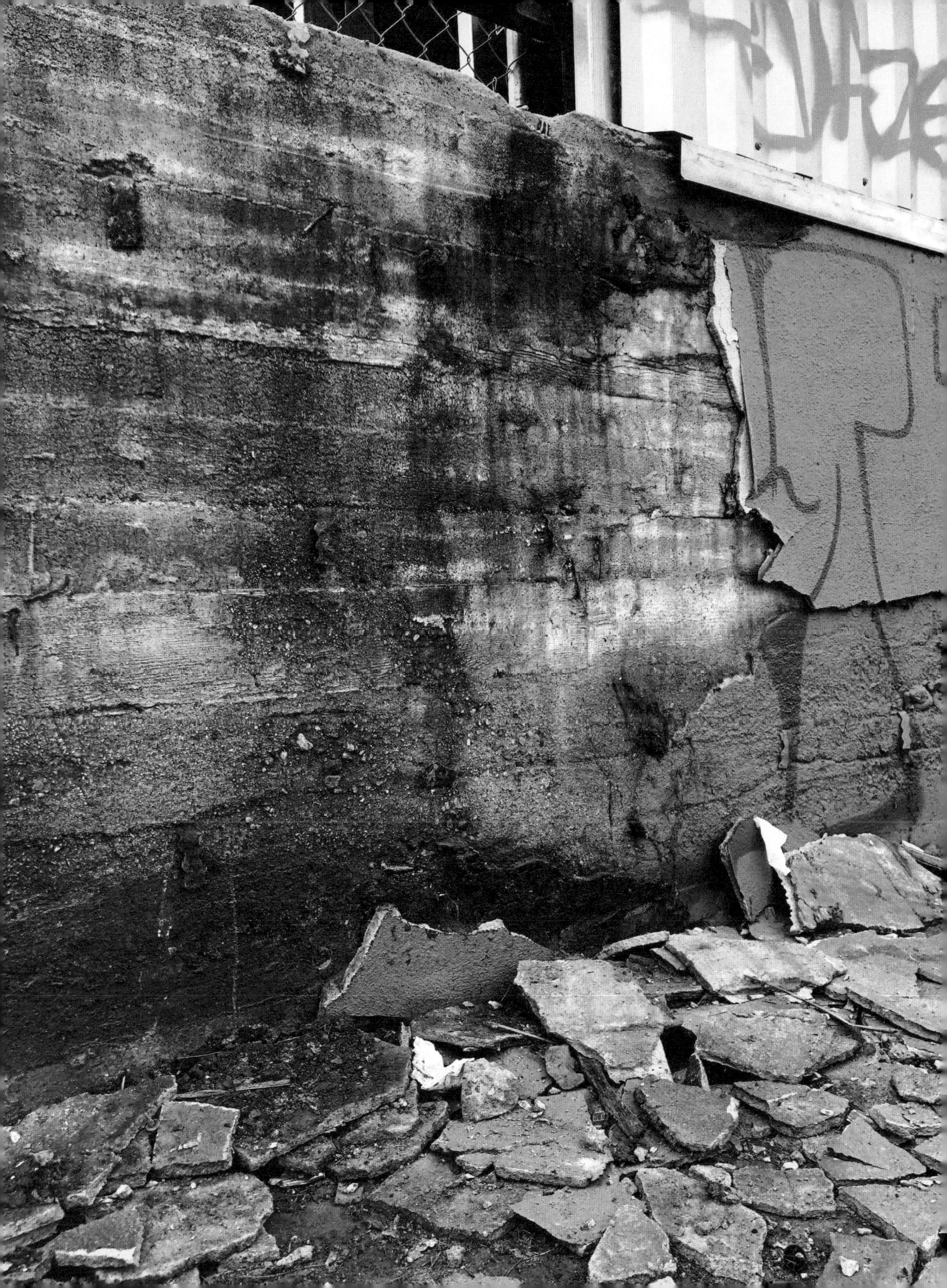

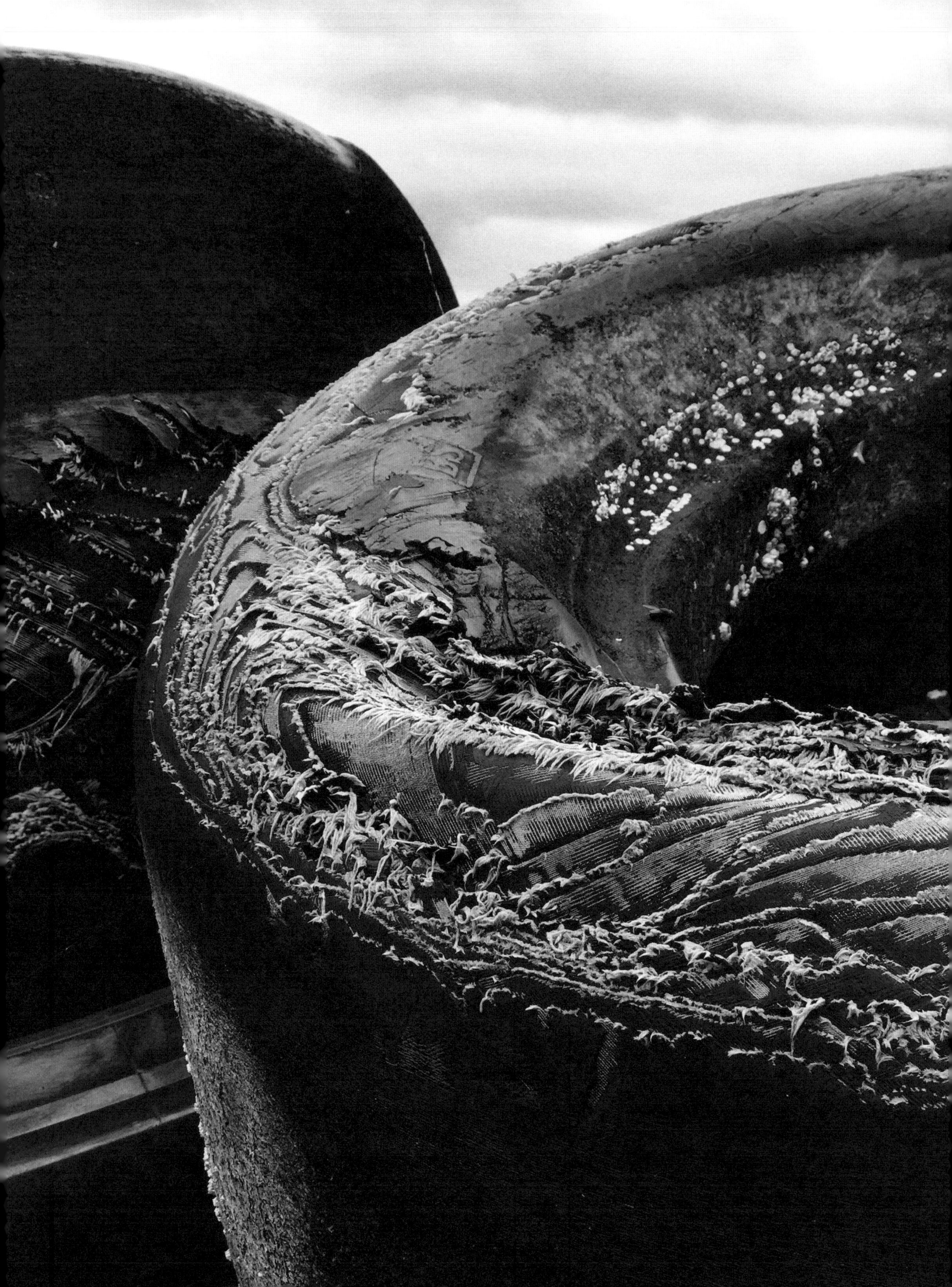

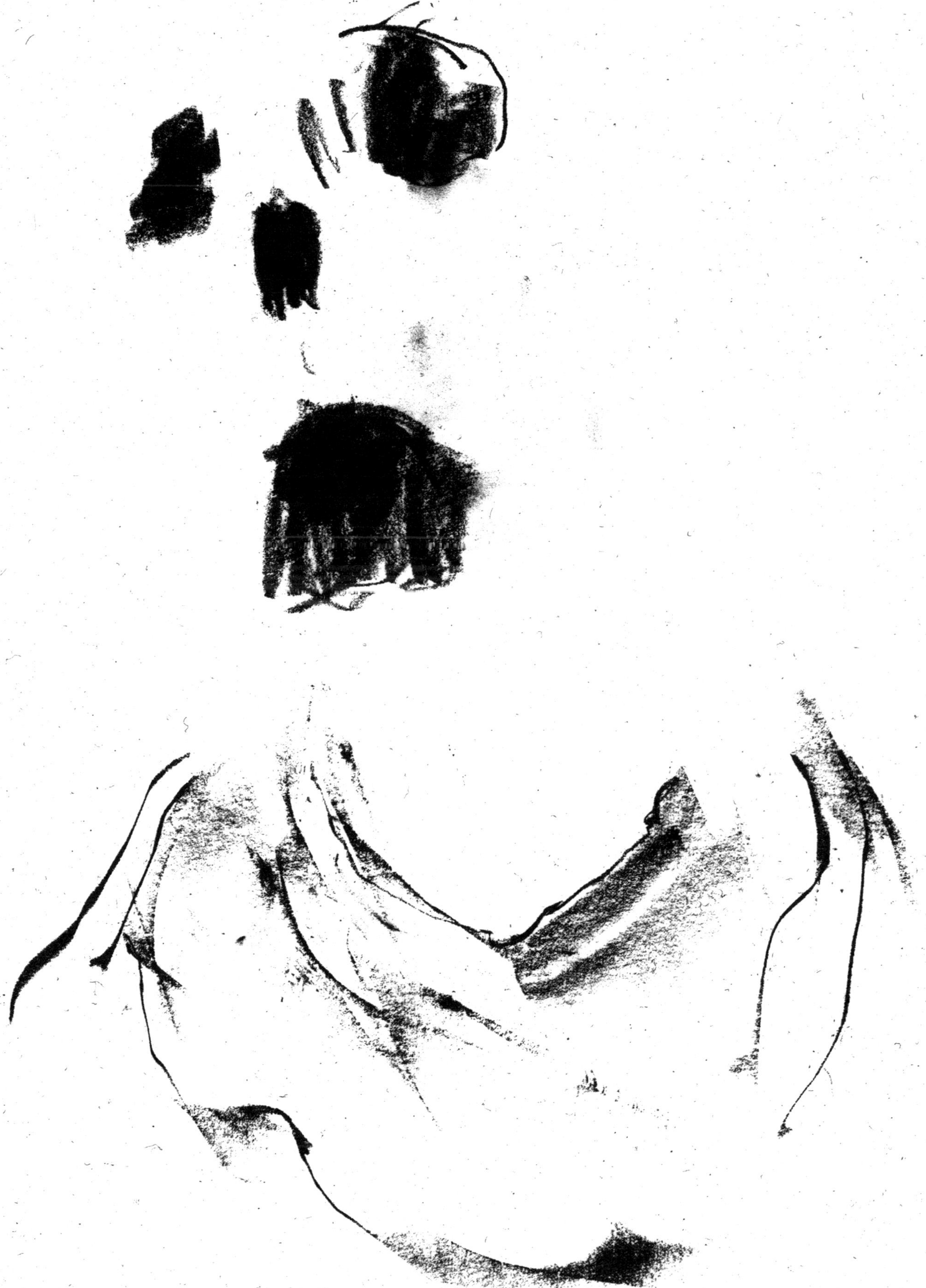

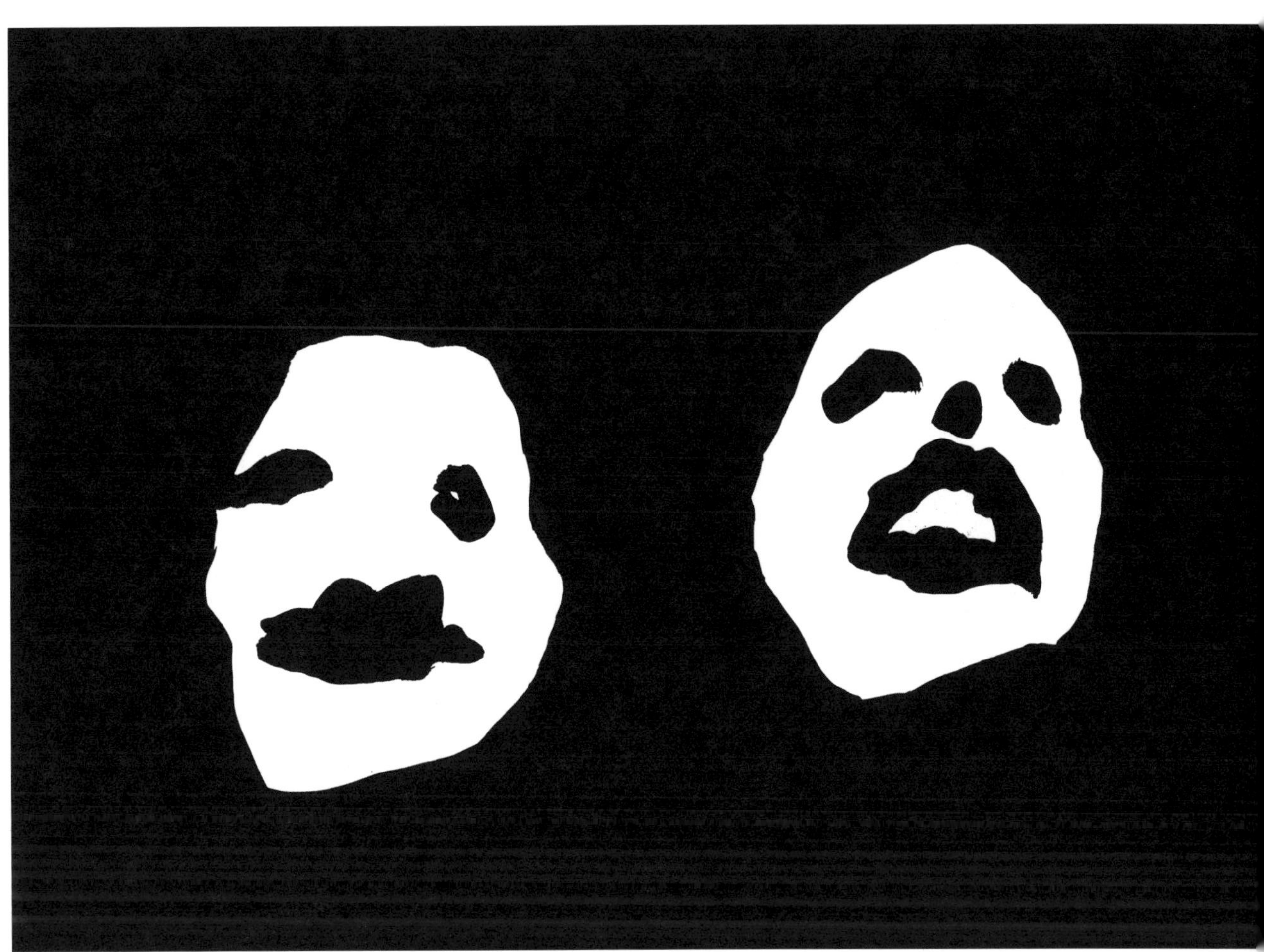

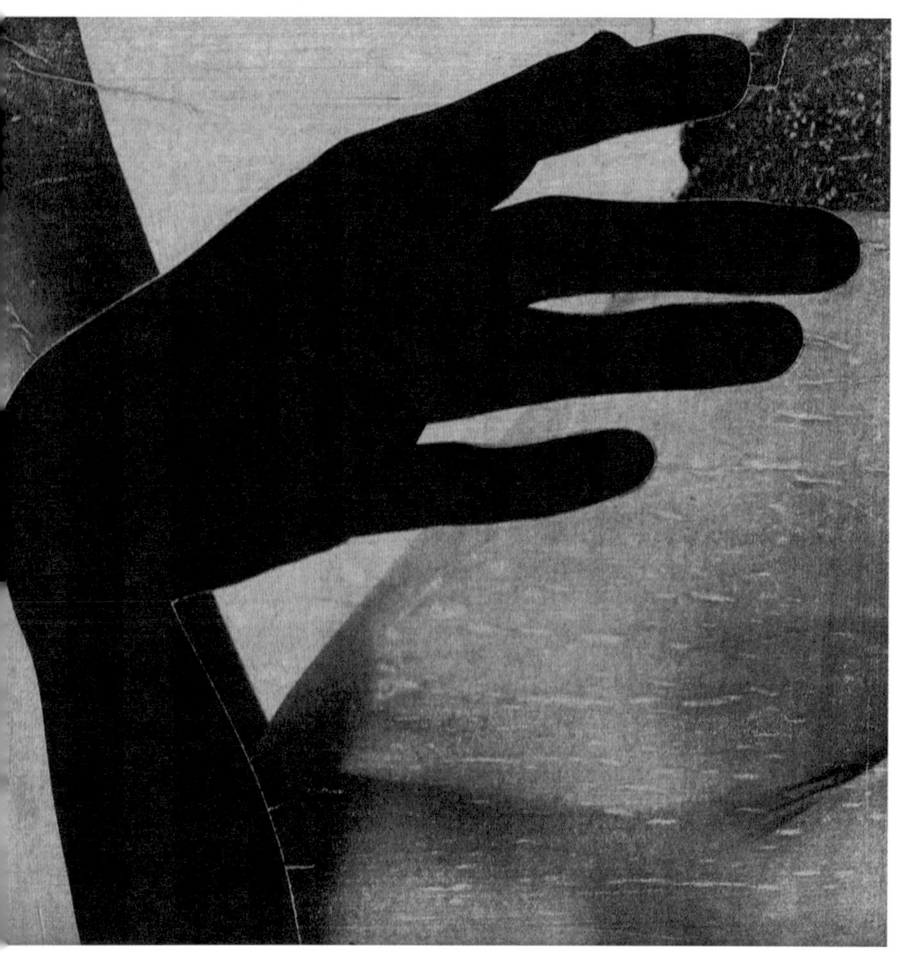

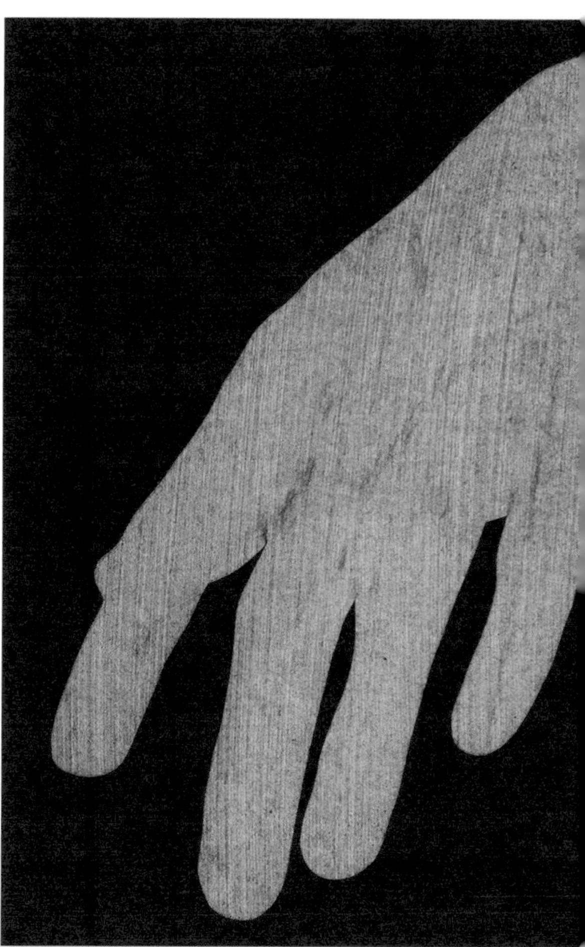

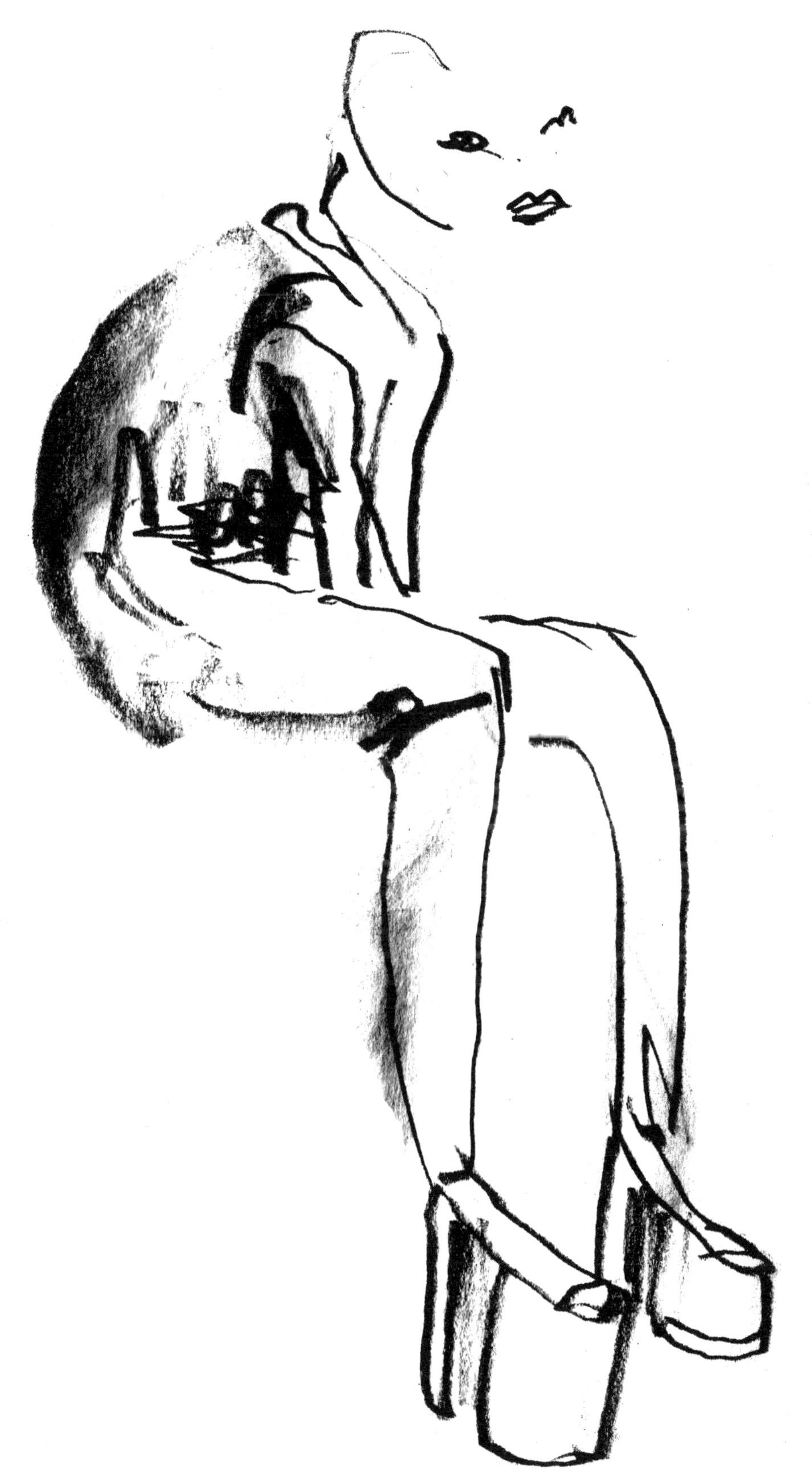

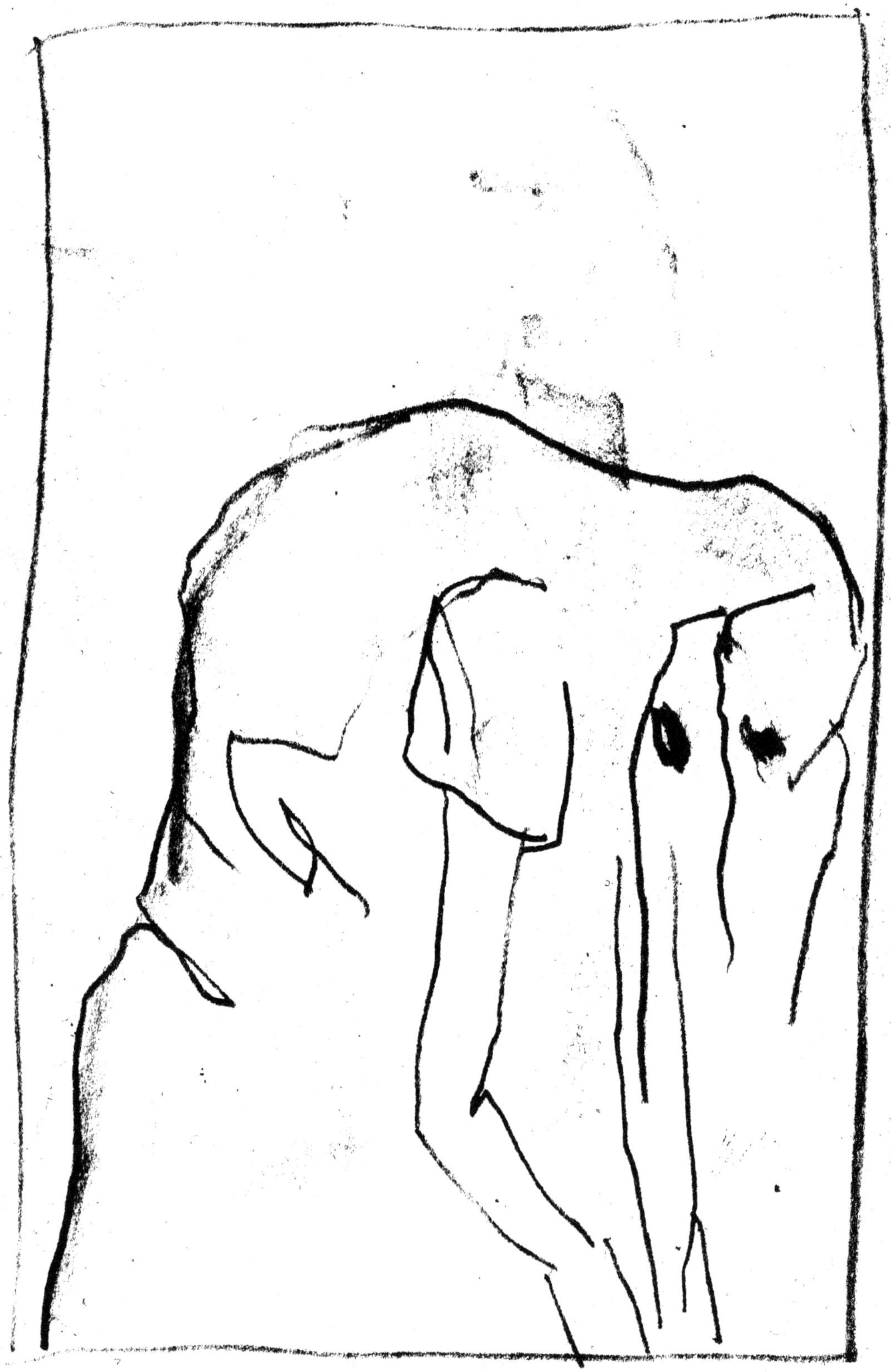

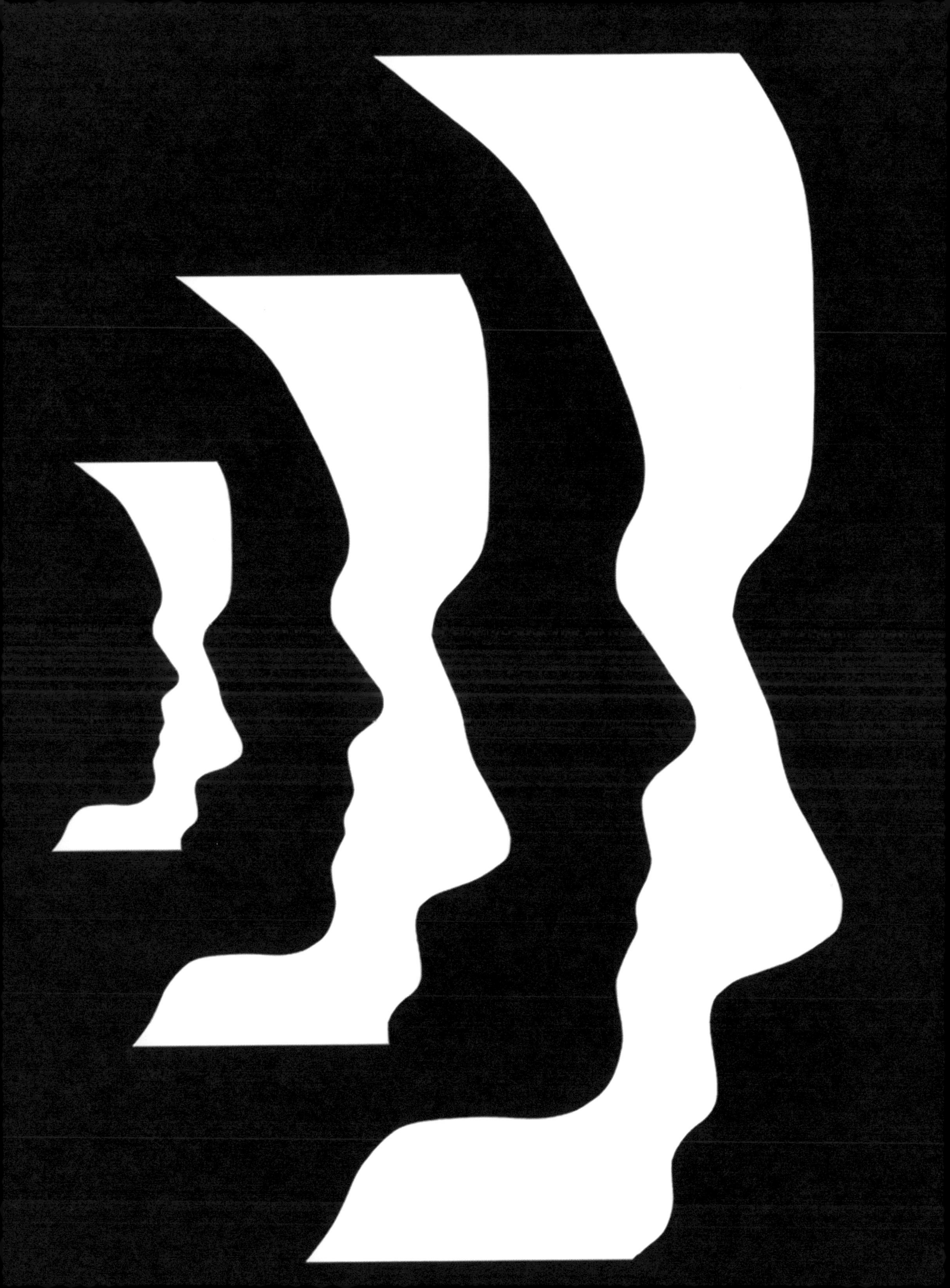

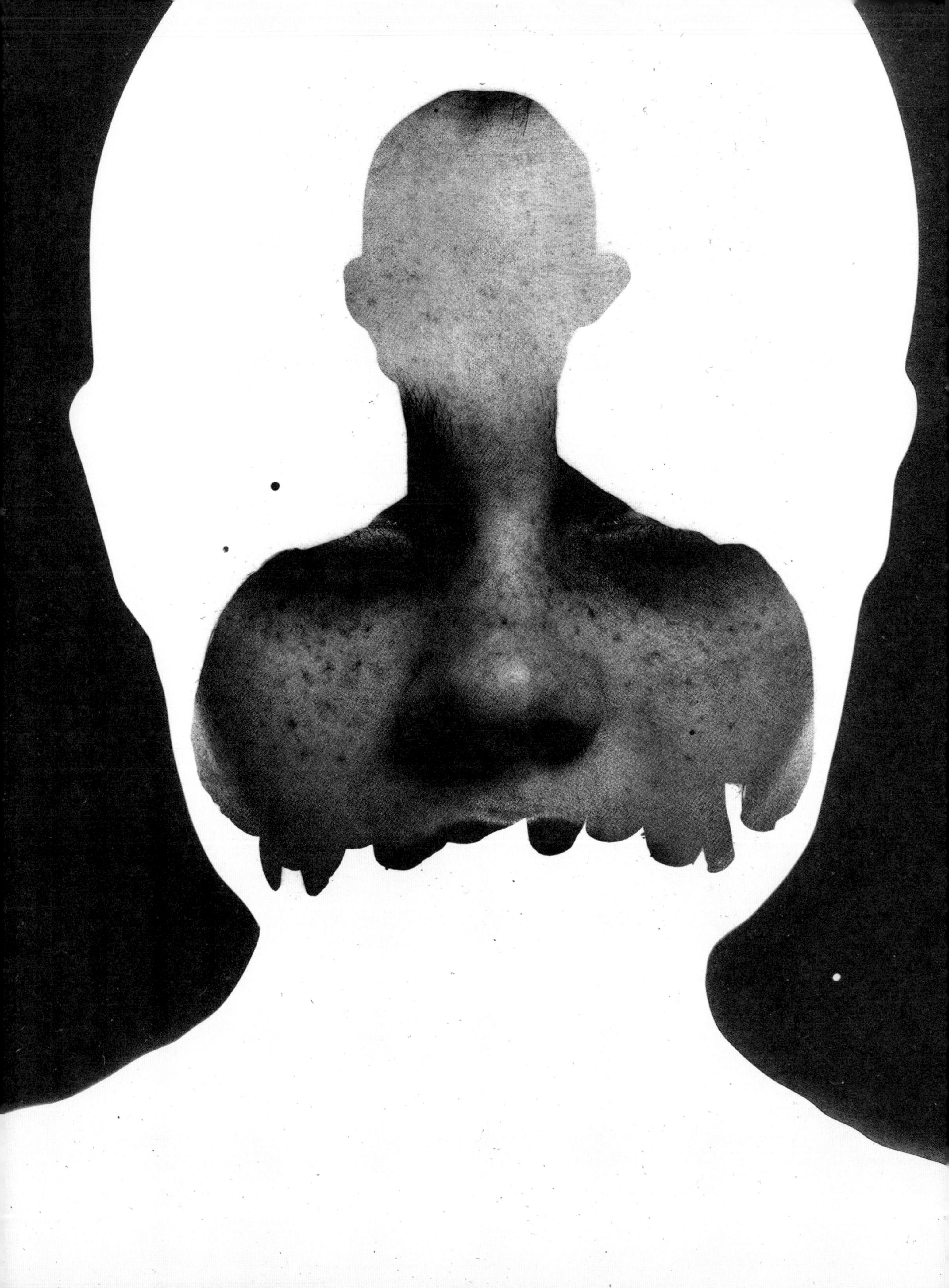

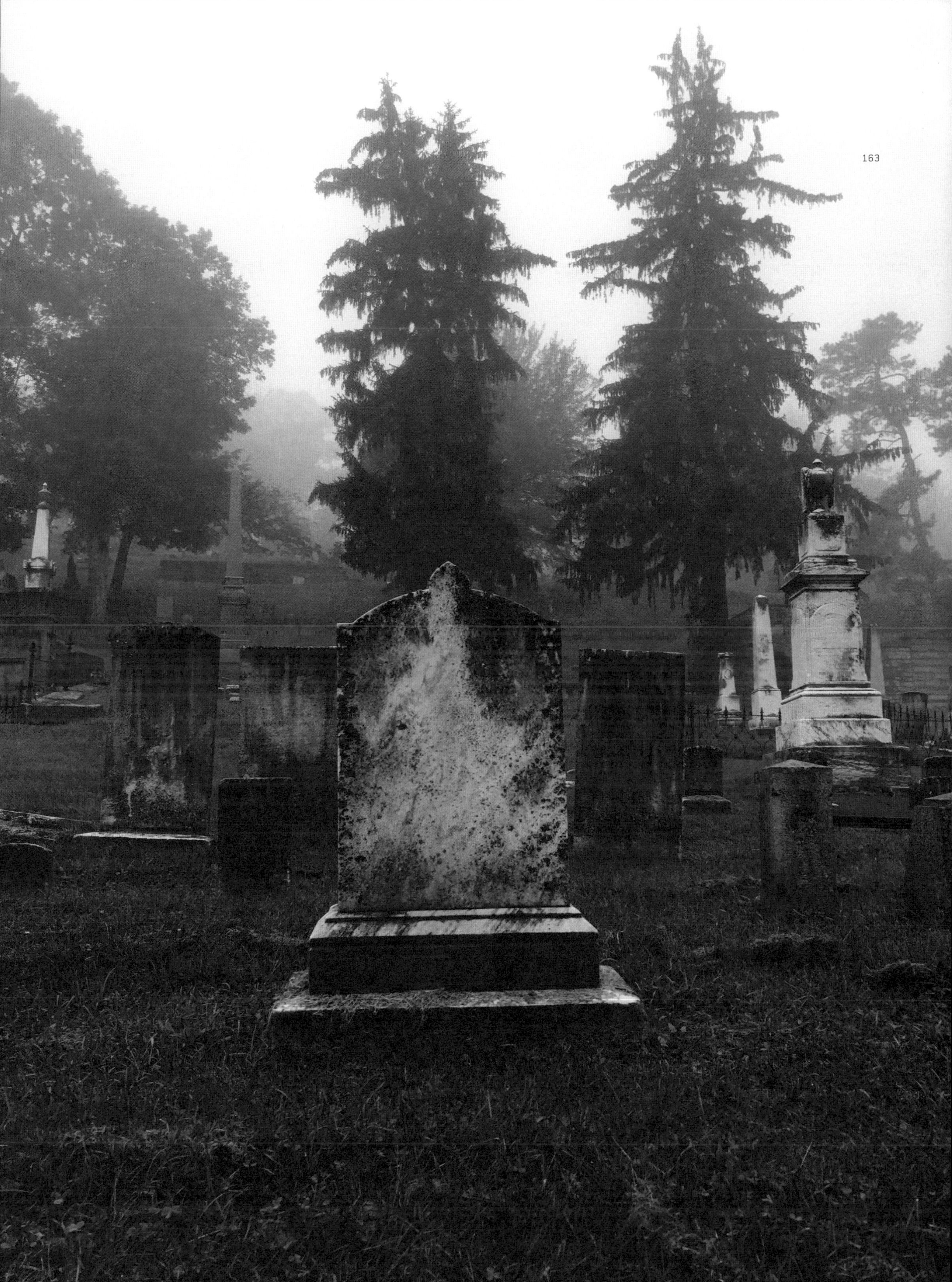

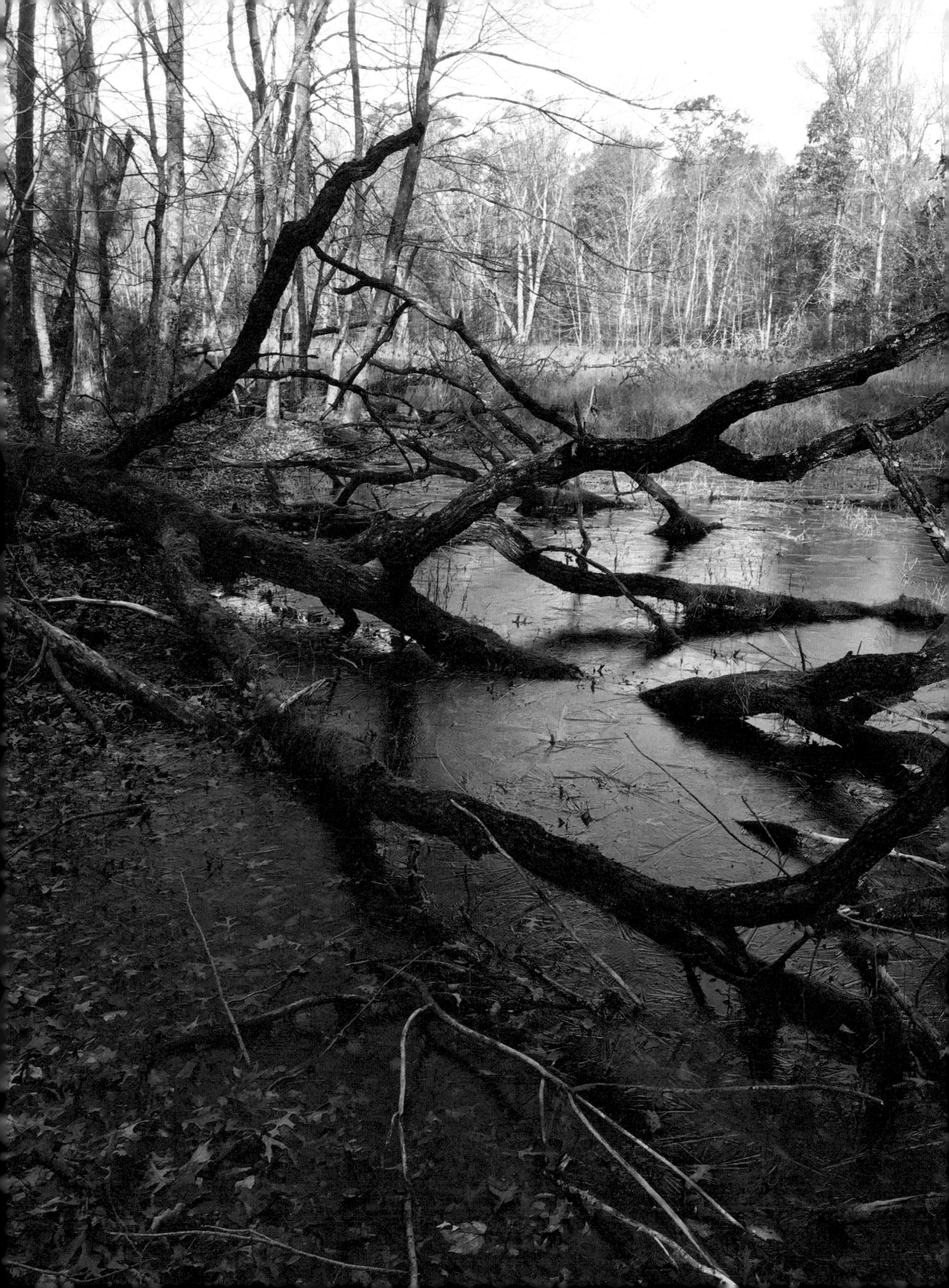

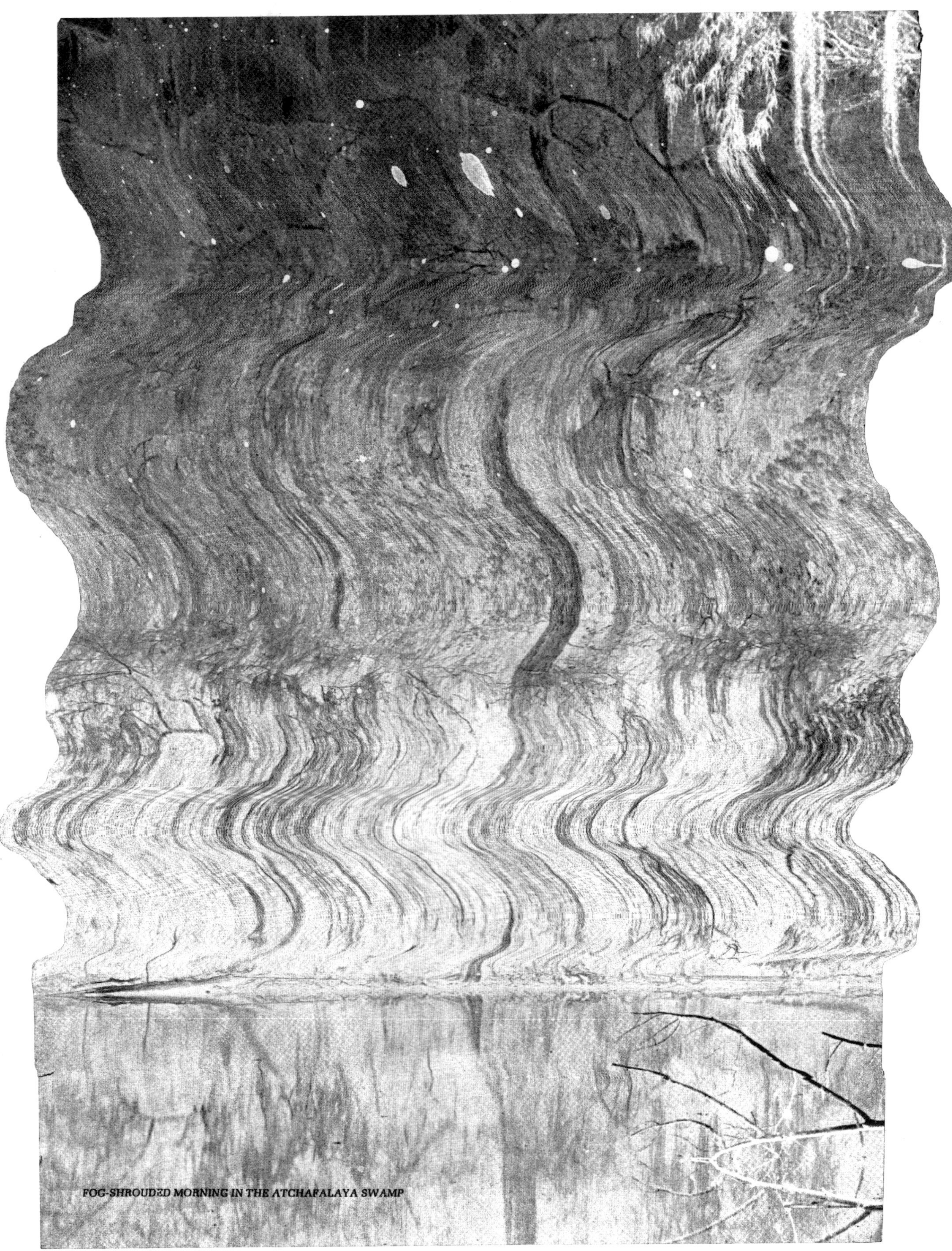

FOG-SHROUDED MORNING IN THE ATCHAFALAYA SWAMP

DA
DA

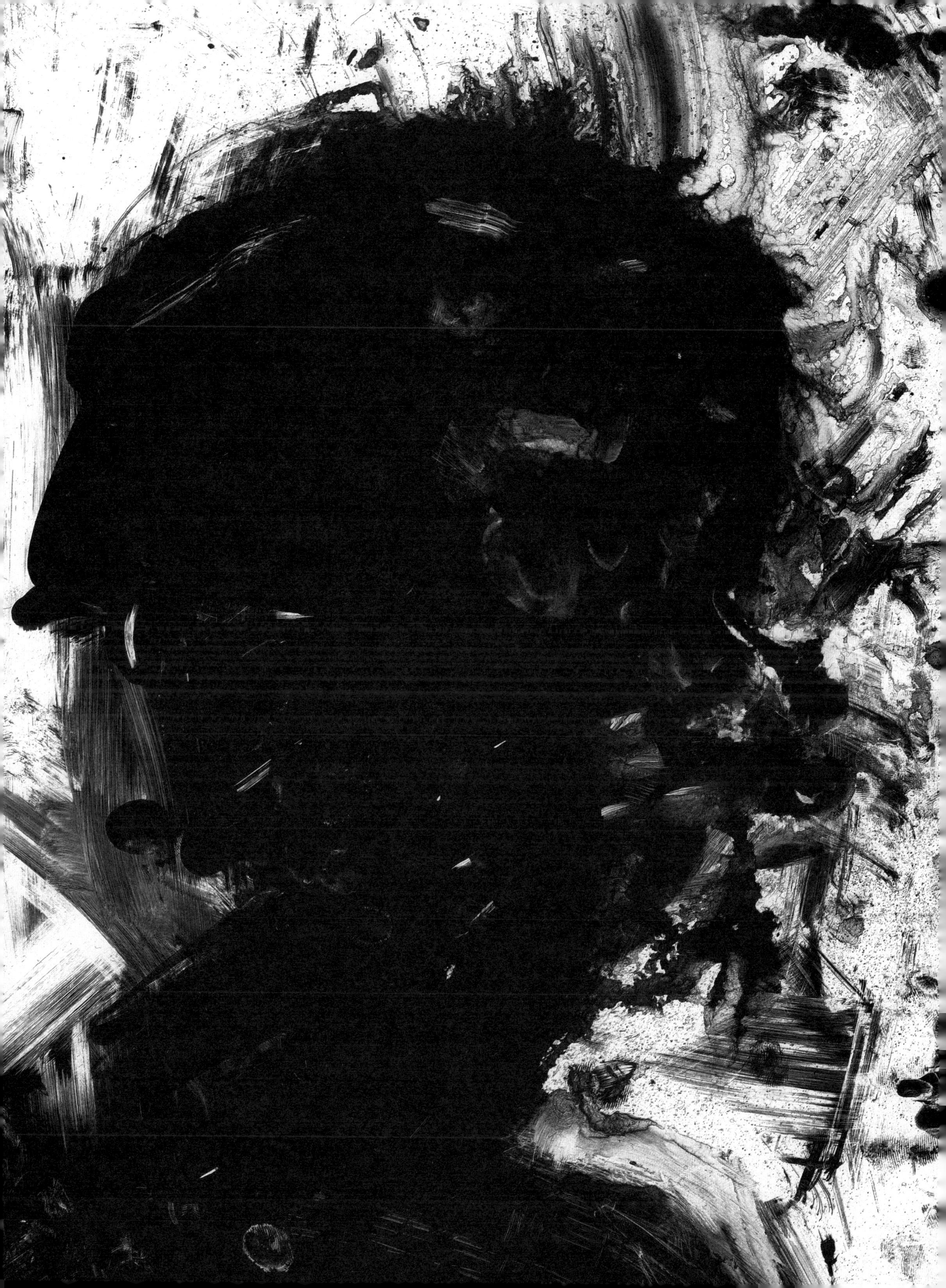

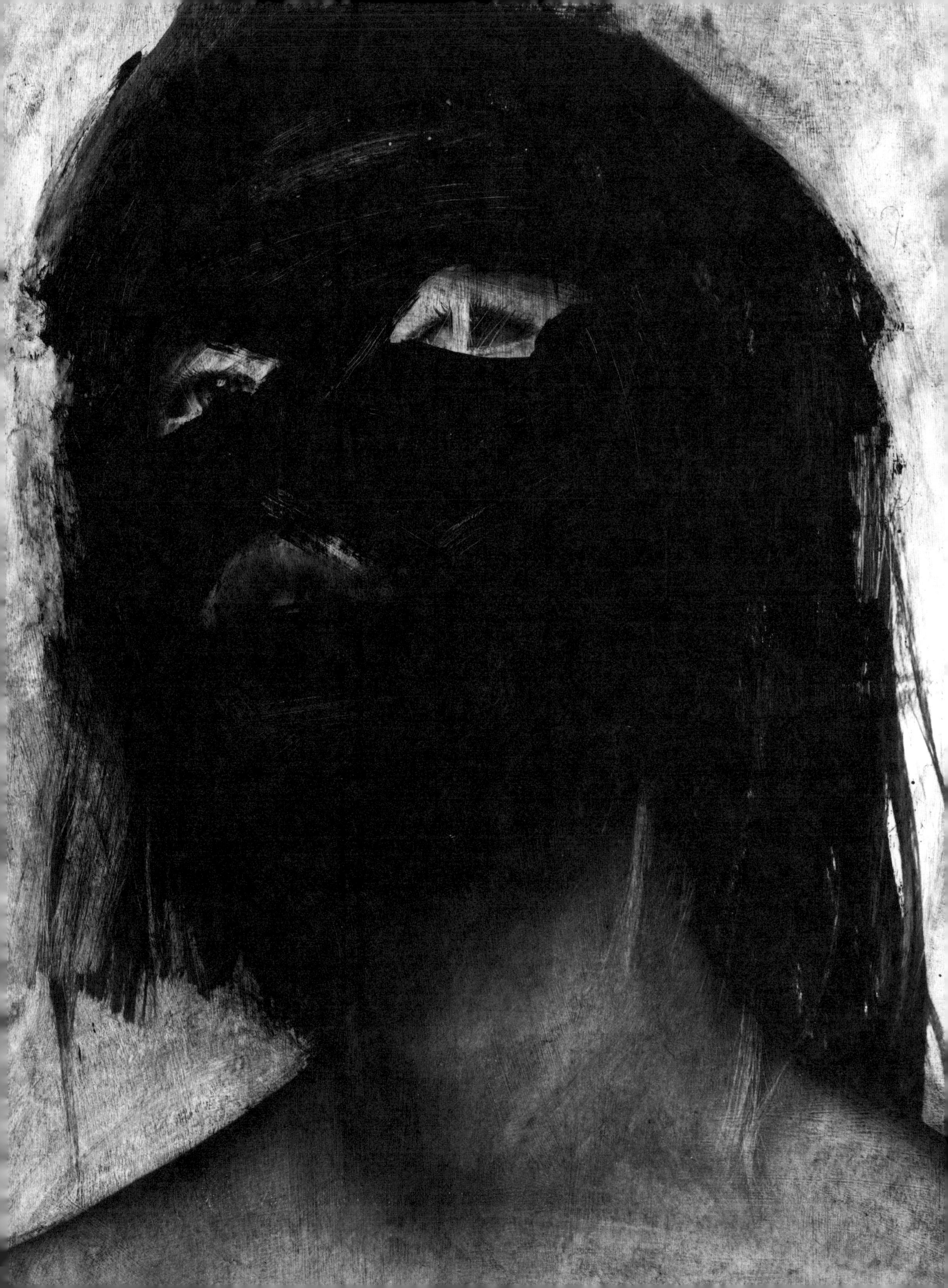

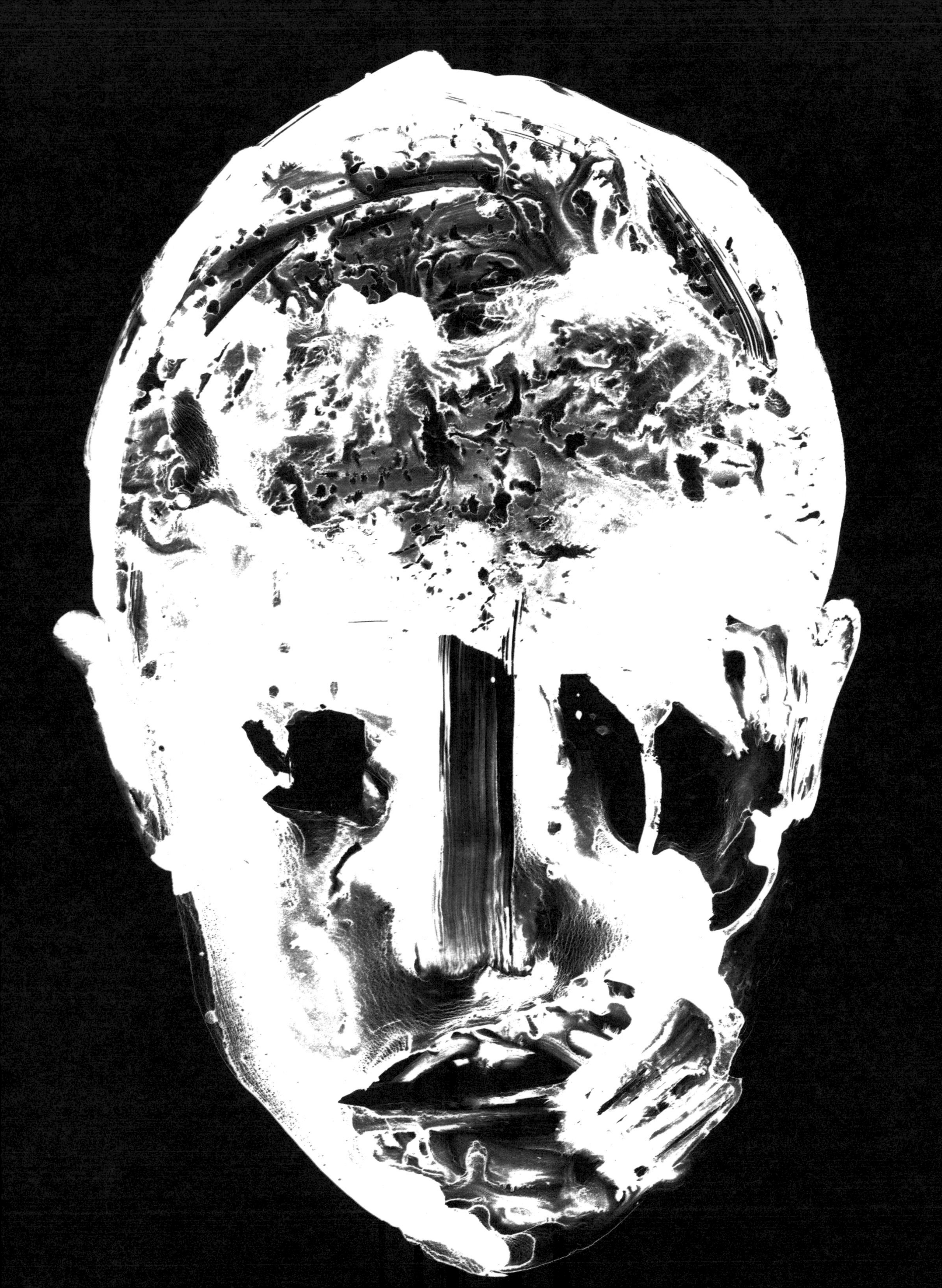

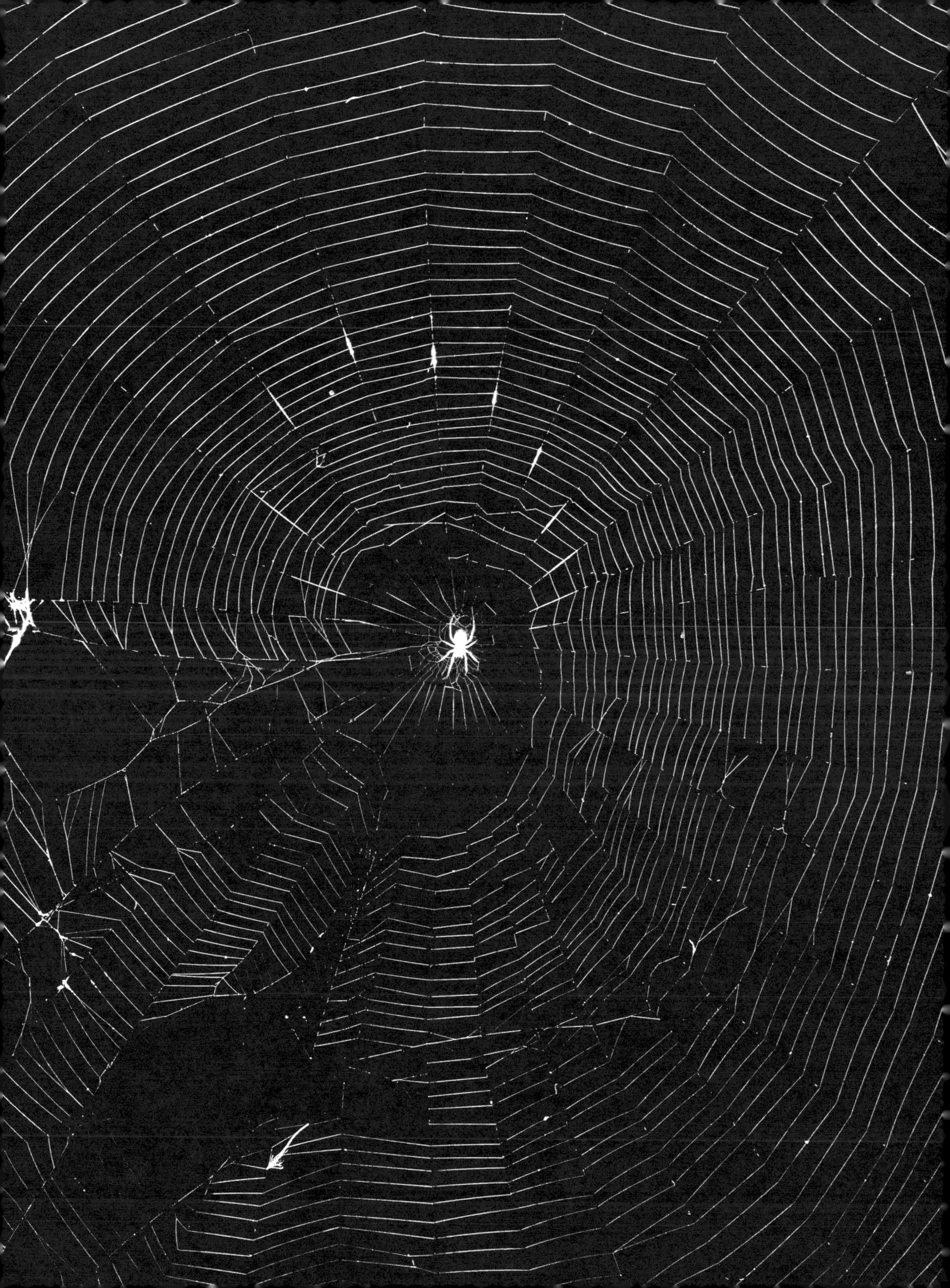

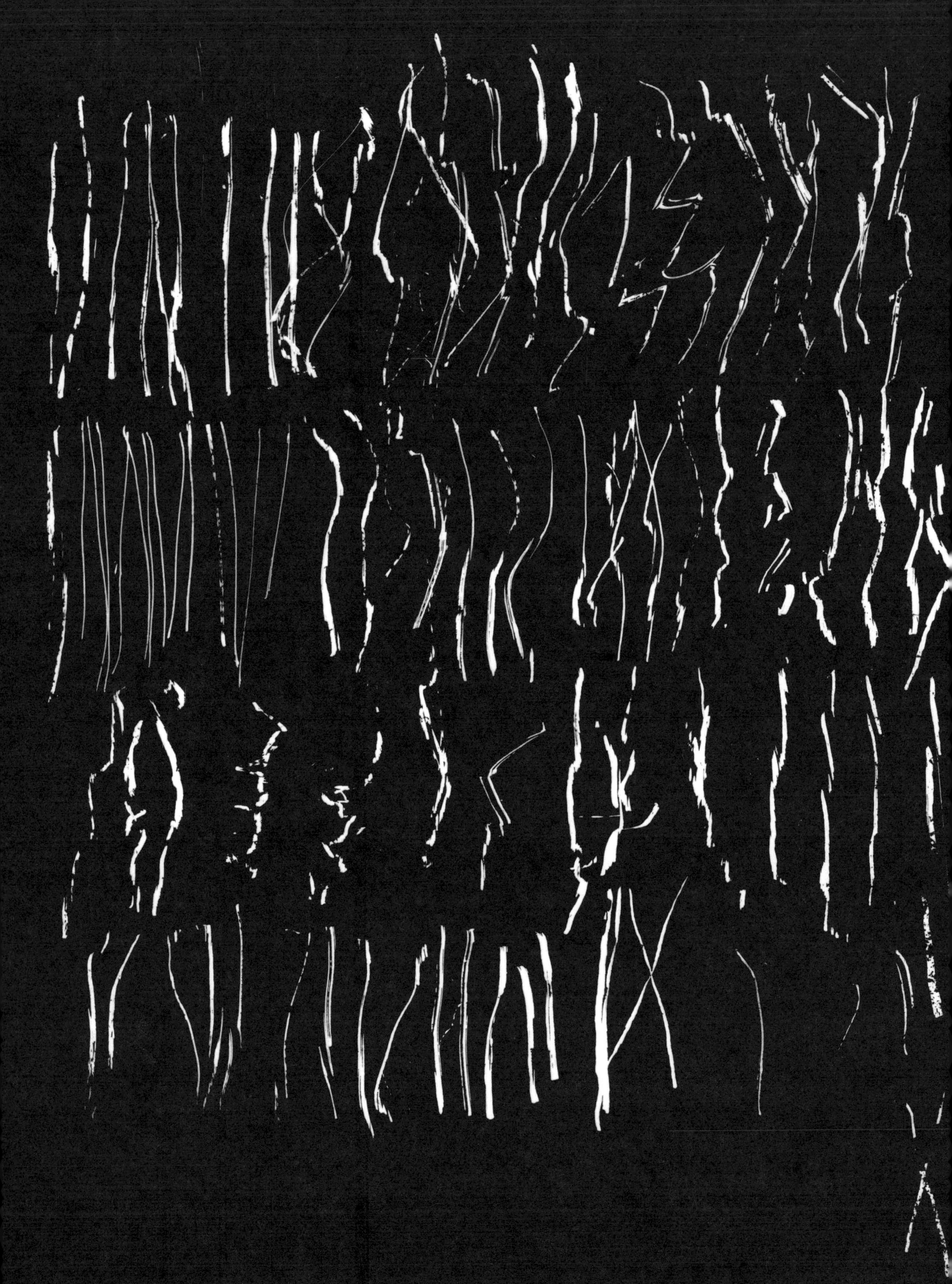

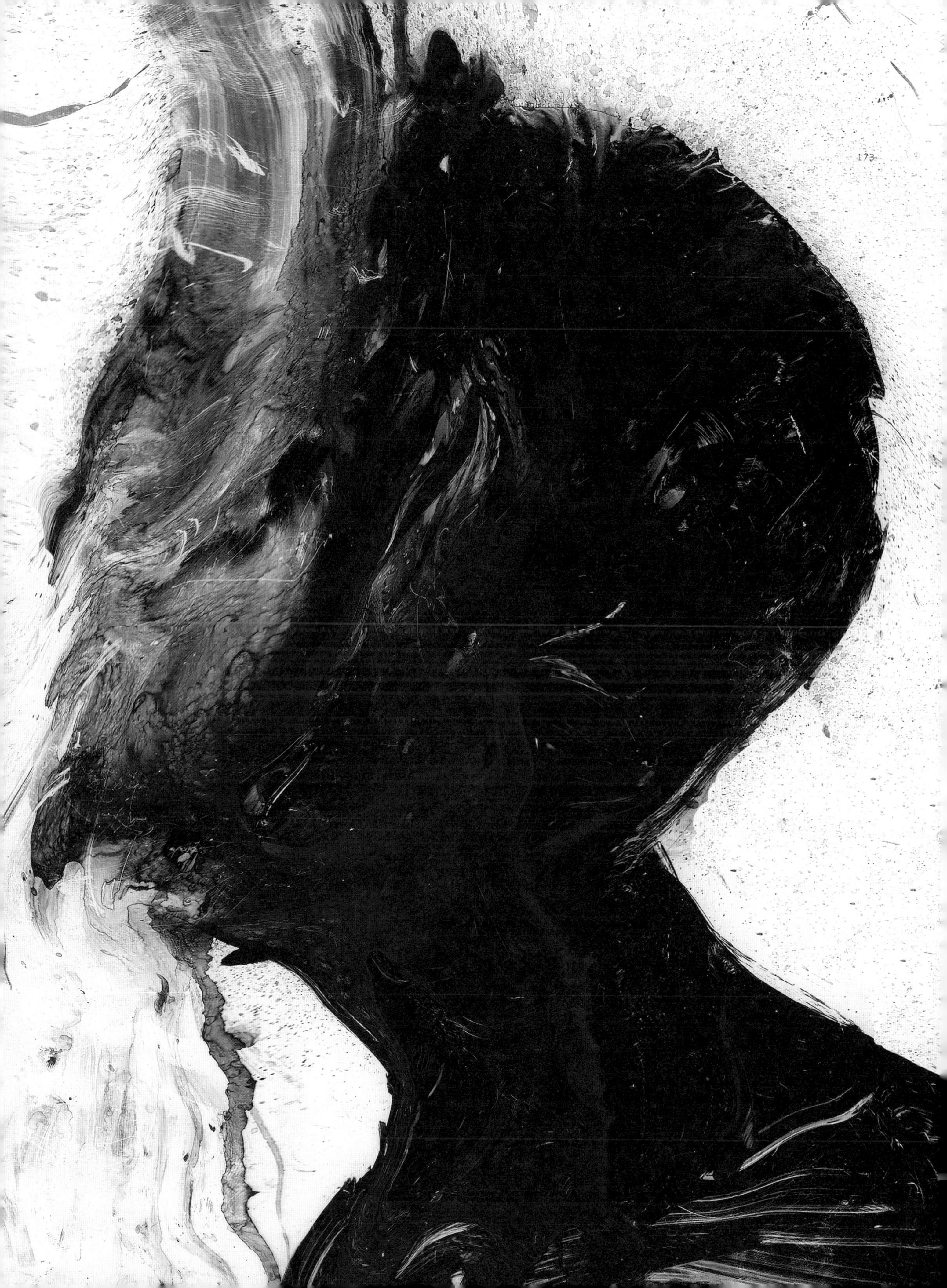

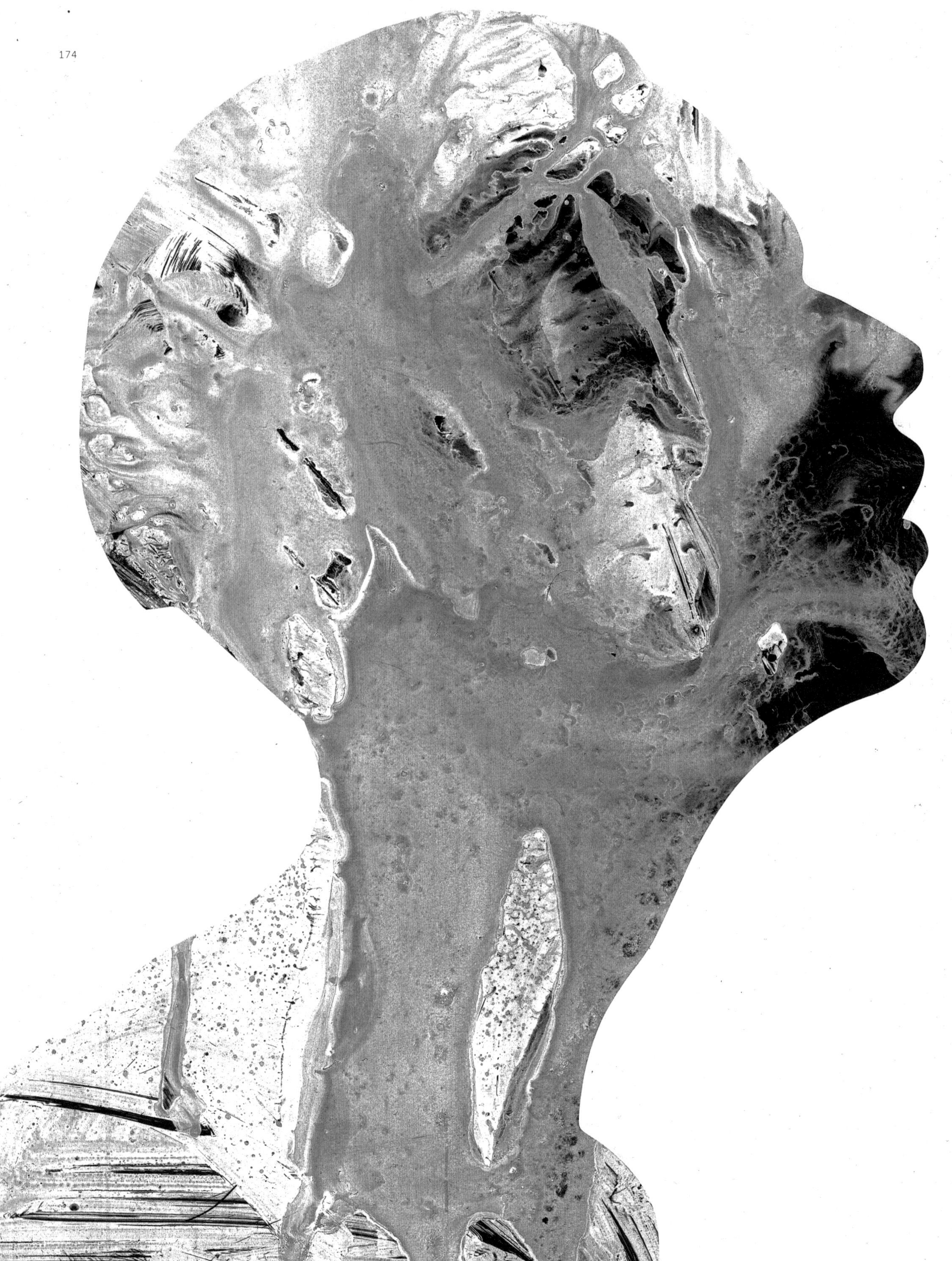

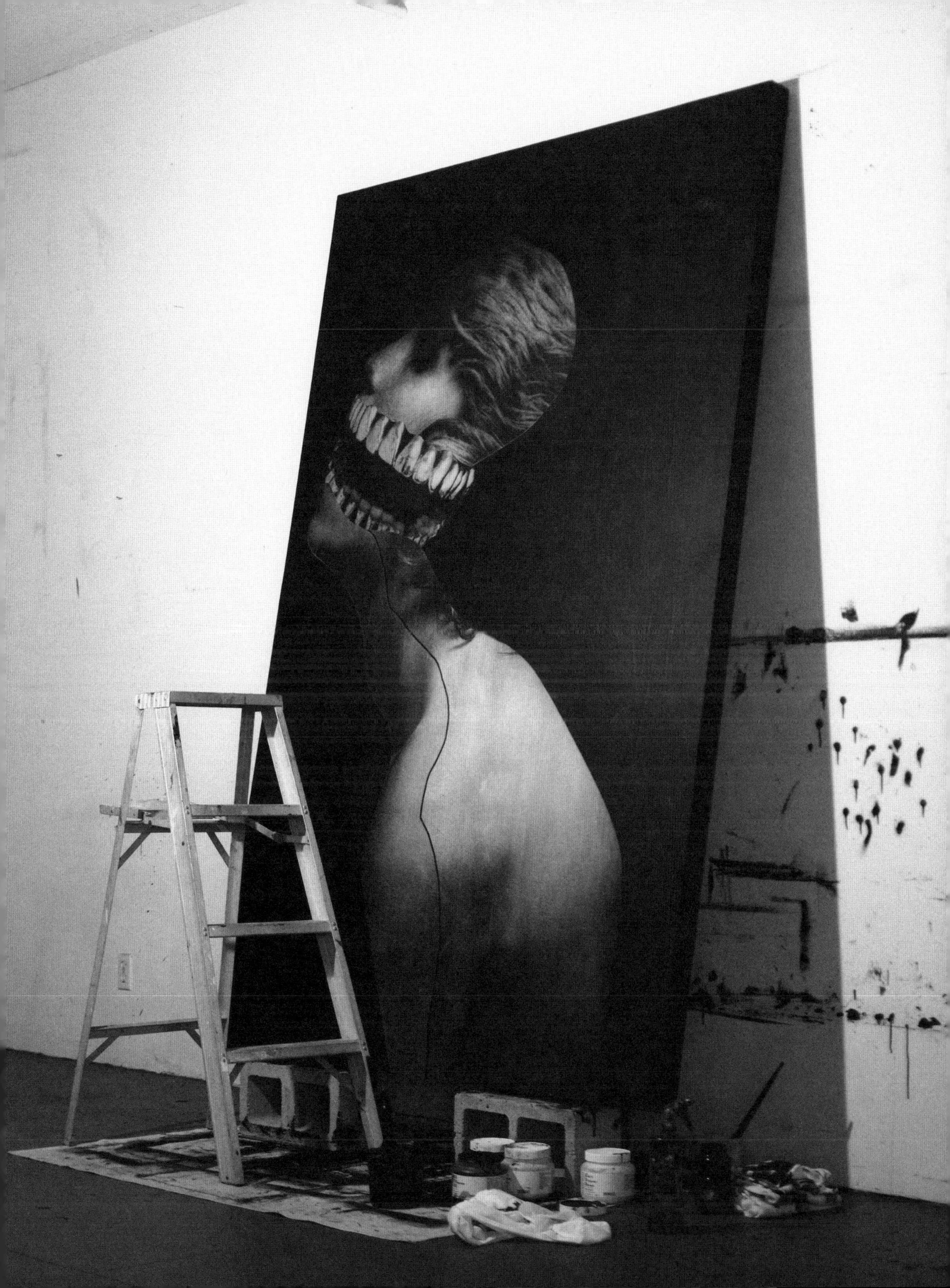

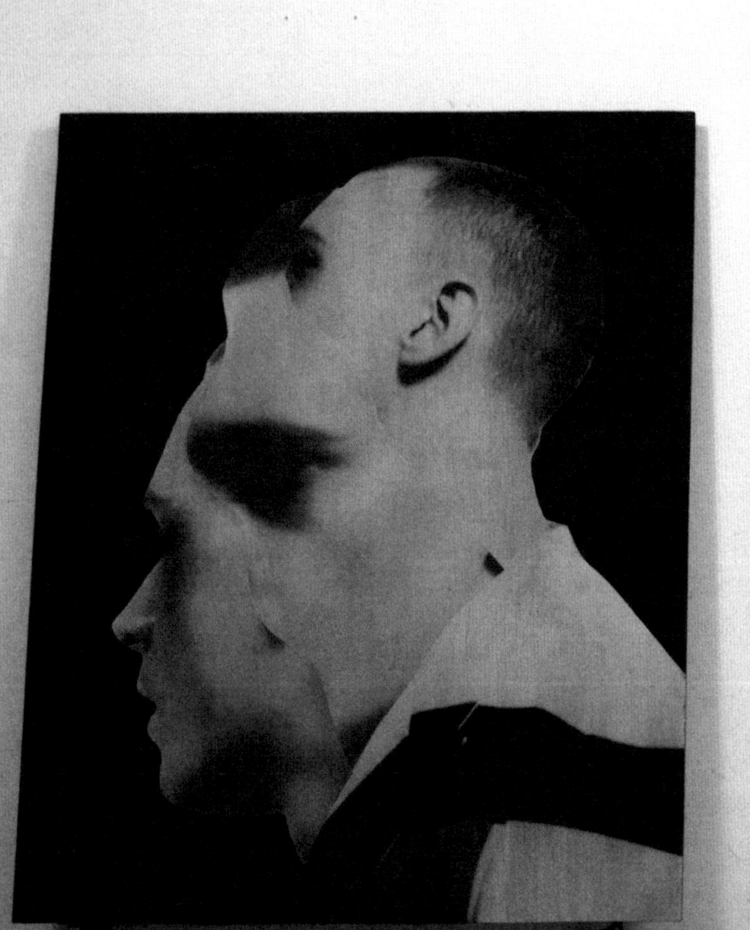
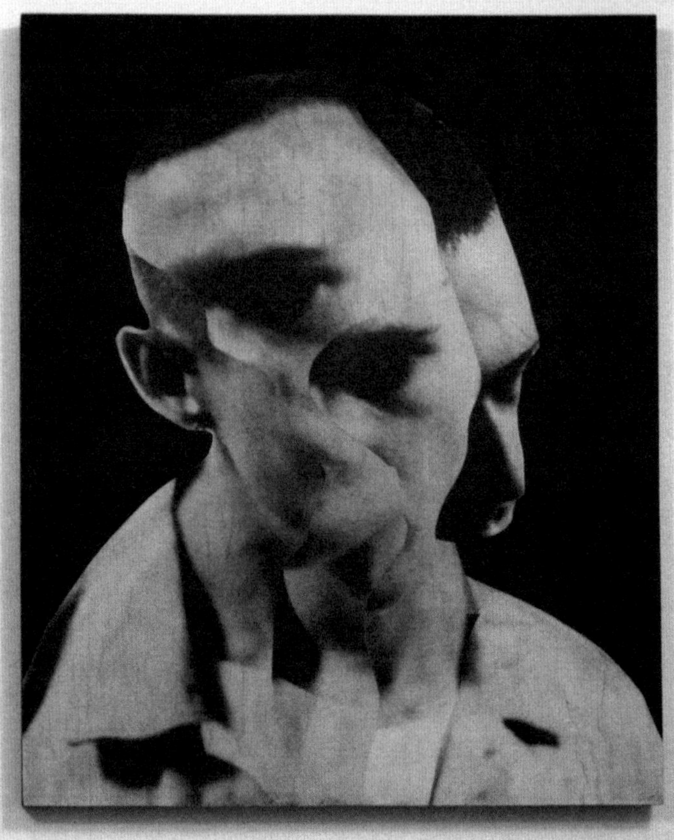

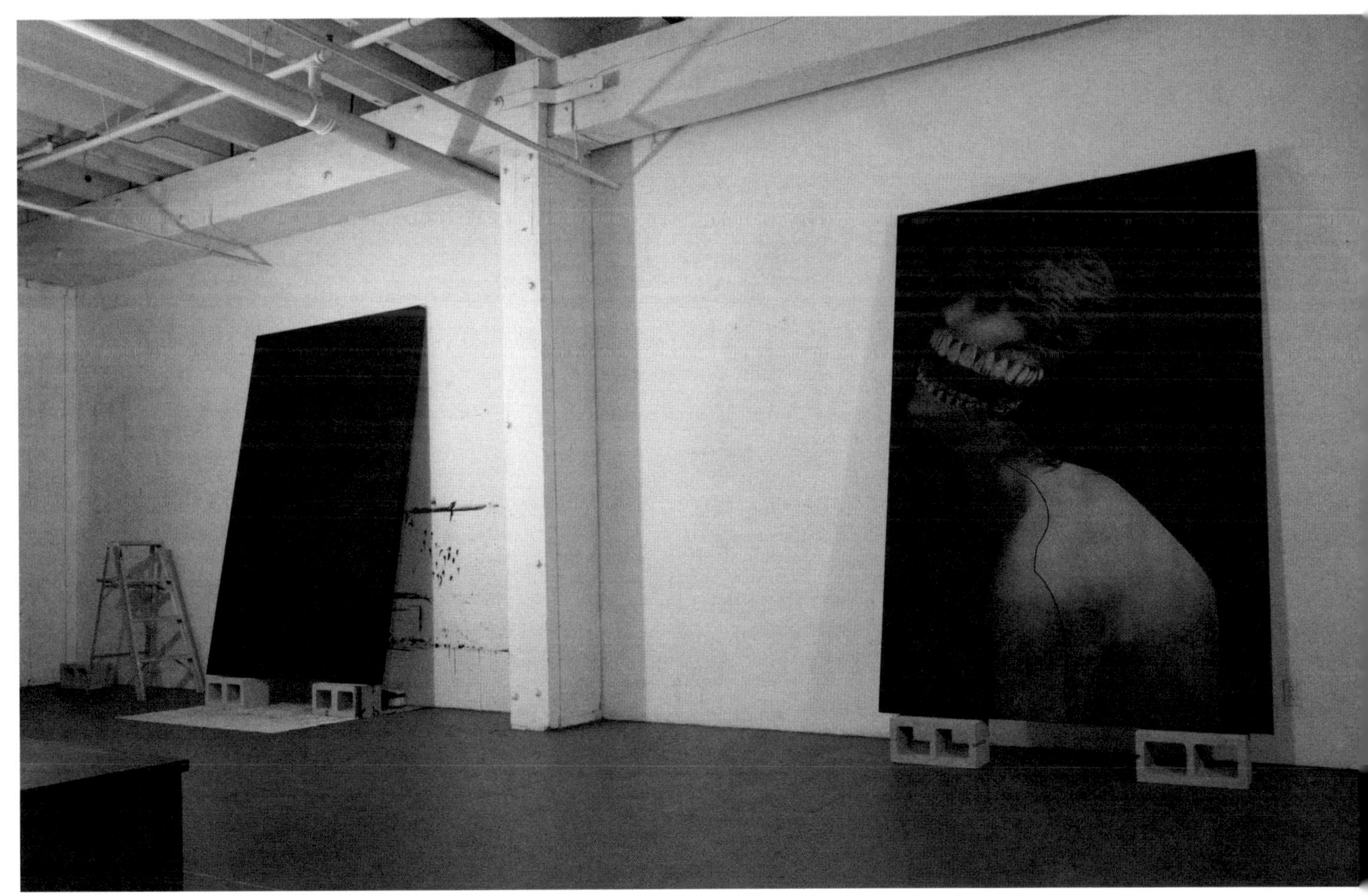

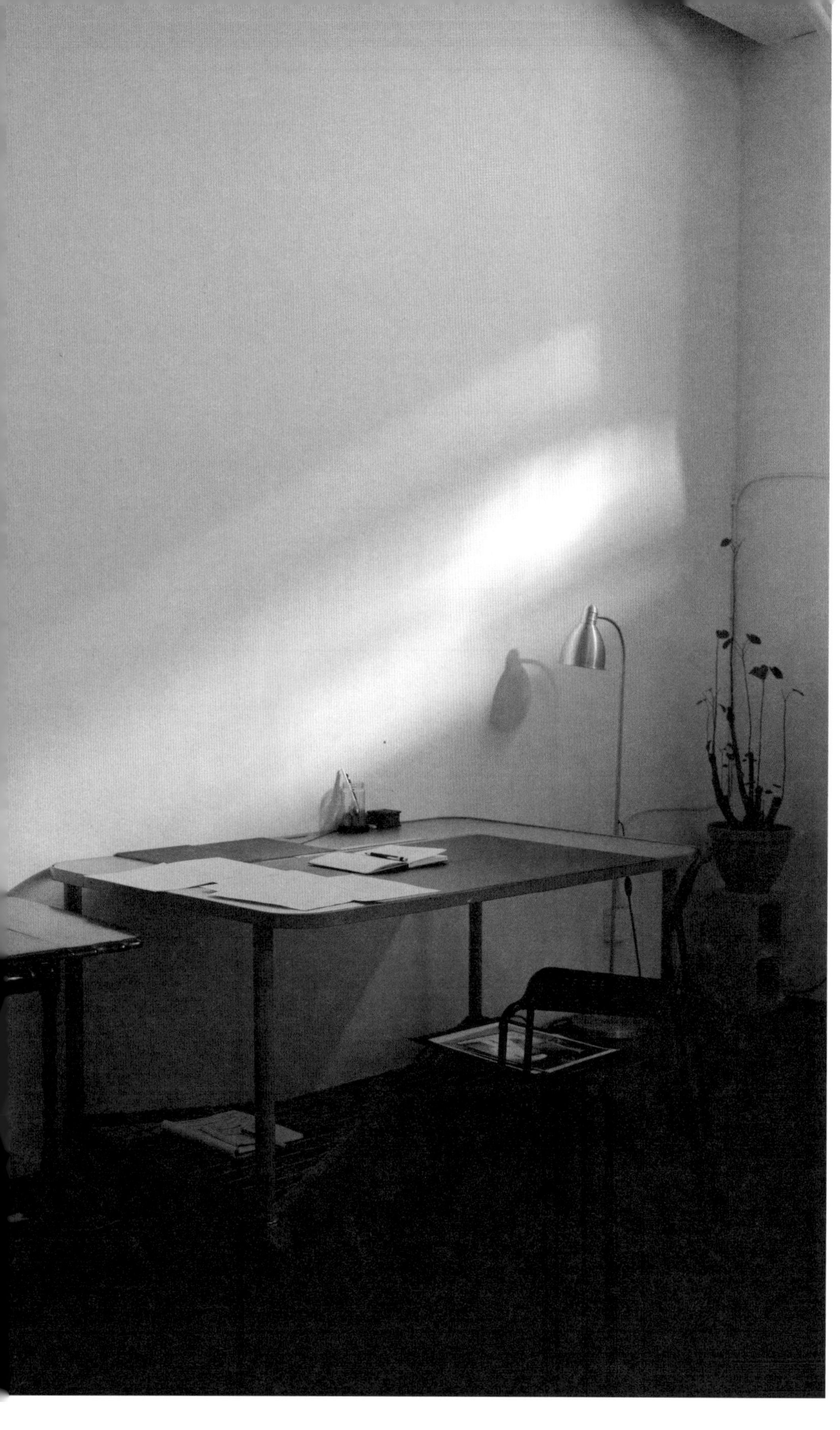

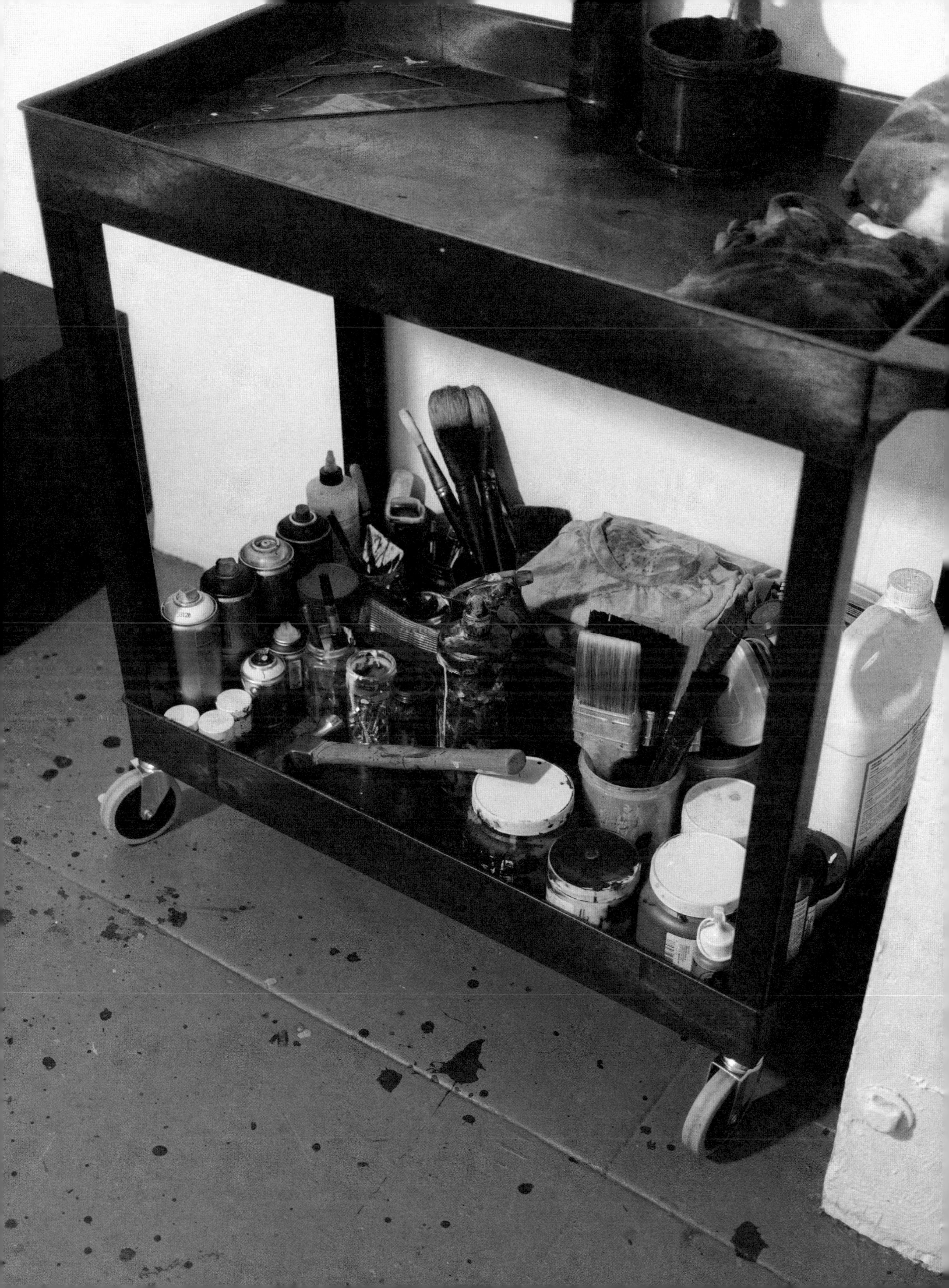

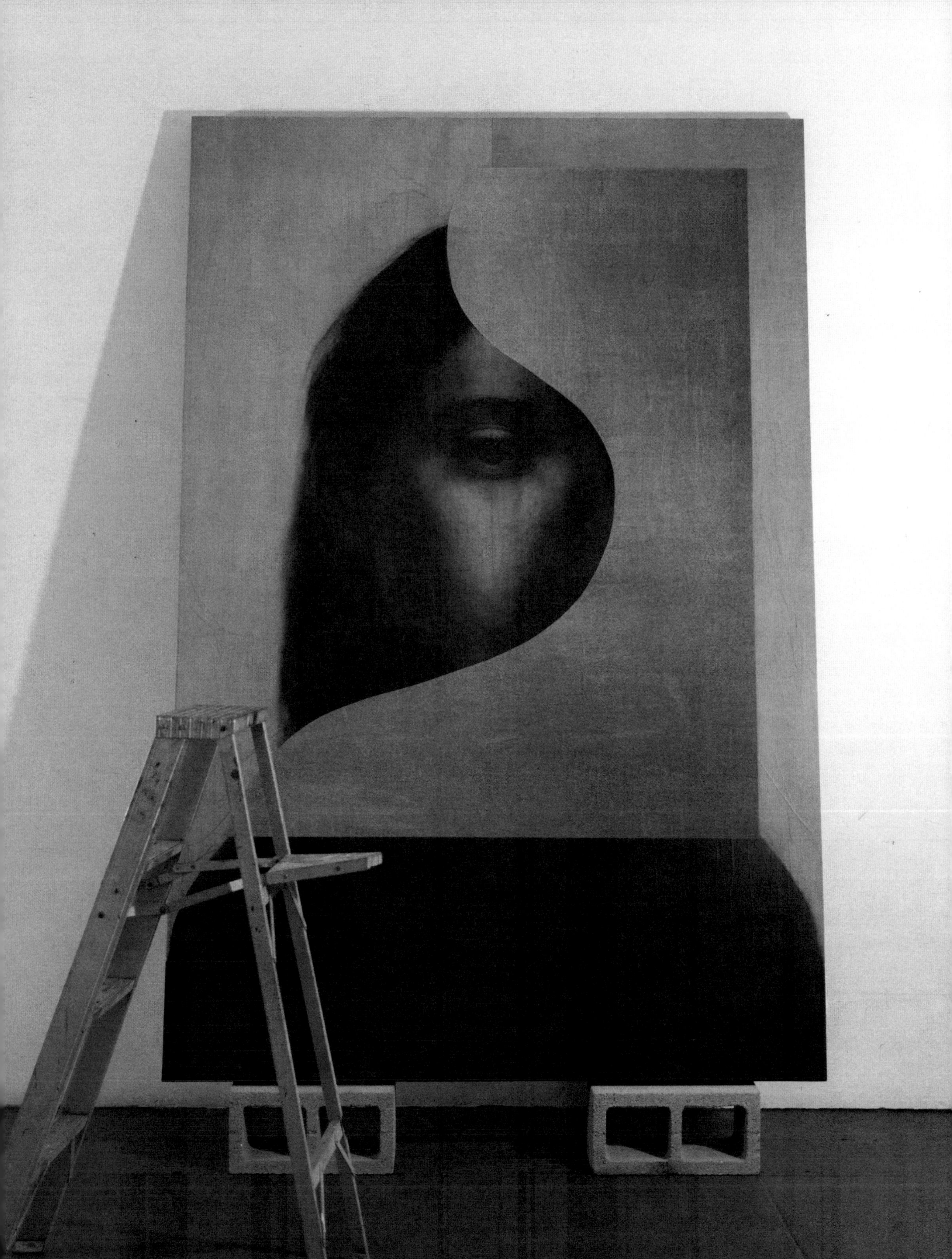